THE HILARITY OF COMMUNITY

The Hilarity of Community

Romans 12 and
How to Be the Church

Marva J. Dawn

WILLIAM B. EERDMANS PUBLISHING COMPANY
GRAND RAPIDS, MICHIGAN

Copyright © 1992 by Wm. B. Eerdmans Publishing Co.
255 Jefferson Ave. S.E., Grand Rapids, Michigan 49503

Printed in the United States of America

Library of Congress Cataloging-in-Publication Data

Dawn, Marva J.
   The hilarity of community: Romans 12 and how to be the Church /
Marva J. Dawn.
      p.   cm.
   ISBN 0-8028-0657-0 (pbk.)
   1. Bible. N.T. Romans XII — Criticism, interpretation, etc.
2. Church — Biblical teaching. I. Title.
BS2665.2.D39 1992
227'.106 — dc20   92-24698
                                     CIP

This book is dedicated —

to all who long for the Church to be the Church;
to all who understand that wholeness is found
in togetherness;
to all who rest in the profound Hilarity of God's grace;
to all who appreciate the glad Hilarity of community;
to all who suffer and need the community's care;
to all who need to learn to be caring;
to all whose care has enfolded me in community;
to Catherine, Betty, Hazel, Joanne, Yvonne, Julia,
and Marcia, who proofread the final version of this
book in the crisis of my sudden loss of vision;
and, especially, to the dearest member
of my Christian community
who brings the most Hilarity to my life,
my treasured husband, Myron.

Contents

•

Preface

MY WORK is so much easier today! Most days when I start doing revisions I have to prod myself to get going, and I find myself working only to get the job of polishing done. This morning Hilarity spurs my labors; I am eager to work because the subject matter of this book has become more real for me.

After my husband left to teach his third-grade class, a participant in my Sunday evening course on Sabbath keeping stopped by to thank me for how this week's description of the loss of intimacy in a technological society had helped her to understand what was going on at her job. Then she hugged me and left — with both of us strengthened for our work by the Hilarity of sharing.

To choose the title *The Hilarity of Community* for this book is risky. We must be careful not to make into an anachronism the Greek word *hilarotēs*, which Paul uses in Romans 12:8 to invite those who have the gift of showing mercy to use that gift with "cheerfulness." It would be wrong for us to bring the contemporary understanding of hilarity — merely a superficial "noisy merriment" or "boisterous gaiety" — to the text of Romans 12.

Rather, the gladness Paul intends with this choice of word arises from a deep sense of well-being founded in trusting the Grace-Giver to work through his[1] gifts to us.[2] I use the word *Hilarity* to describe the spirit of the Christian community, to summarize all the aspects to be explicated in this book, to name the glad hope that could characterize God's people.

The basis of our hope-full Hilarity encompasses all the dimensions of time. We experience glad Hilarity in the sure knowledge that we are loved by God, as manifested in the past by God's creation of us and in the life, death, resurrection, and ascension of Jesus Christ. Our present Hilarity is made possible by the empowering indwelling of the Holy Spirit in our lives. Our Hilarity is heightened when we look forward confidently to the wild ecstasy that will be ours at the end of time when all suffering is finished and we experience the eternal, incredible Joy of face-to-face communion with God.

I choose the word *Hilarity* deliberately because from the entire semantic field of terms to signify various sorts of gladness Paul does not pick one for Romans 12:8 that implies a dependence upon circumstances, nor does he select one that is necessarily expressed with physical movement (like "jumping for joy"). The word *hilarotēs* carries the connotations of "cheerfulness," which in some languages "may be expressed idiomatically as 'one's heart is laughing' or 'one's eyes are dancing.' "[3] So that we will always be cautioned not

---

1. Out of my concern to reach the widest audience possible, I have chosen to refer to God with the masculine pronouns *he, his,* and *him.* I recognize that these pronouns are inadequate, for God is neither masculine nor feminine, but more than all our words can ever connote. I apologize to anyone who might be offended by my word choices and pray that you will accept my decision to use our inadequate language as carefully as possible for many kinds of people.

2. See the comparable concept of Joy, described in chapter 12 of my book *I'm Lonely, LORD — How Long? The Psalms for Today* (San Francisco: Harper & Row, 1983).

3. Johannes P. Louw and Eugene A. Nida, eds., *Greek-English Lexicon of the New Testament Based on Semantic Domains* (New York: United Bible

to bring our modern connotations to the word, *Hilarity* will be capitalized when it is used throughout this book to signify its profound biblical definition.

It is necessary to use such a word in writing about the Christian community because I intend to present an ideal that is not being realized very well in contemporary Christianity. As I travel around the country to teach, I am deeply saddened by our failure to be what God designed the Church to be. People who have been Christians for a while are not very often characterized by the profound gladness that marked the earliest followers of Jesus and that frequently bubbles forth in present-day new believers.

One of the most powerful reasons for our lack of gladness is that ours is a culture of solo efforts. We live our Christian faith independently — not inextricably linked with other members of the Body of believers. Consequently, we do not experience the Hilarity of being enfolded in a moment-by-moment awareness of the good news of our hope and life in Jesus Christ. We don't experience the support that true community engenders. We aren't set free to be truly ourselves in the stewardship of our Spirit-given grace-gifts.

So I use the word *Hilarity* to describe the ideal Christian community, and my intention is to make us stop and think: what would it be like if the Christian Church were truly a community that thoroughly enjoyed being itself? It seems to me it could change the world!

What is happening in our culture? Intimacy and neighborliness are on the wane; violence and crime are escalating. No longer is ferocity confined to the bigger cities; our small

---

Societies, 1988), vol. 1, p. 301, 25.116. References to Greek definitions in this book are taken from this lexicon because its approach and methodology make use of the insights of modern linguistics, and because its definitions are based upon the distinctive features of meaning of a particular term in comparison with, and in contrast to, other related words in the same semantic domain.

city is presently haunted by the recent, sex-related murder of two elementary school children in a park not far from our home. Many of my husband's third graders who suffer great abuse and/or neglect in their homes cannot sit still, do not pay attention, pick fights with each other, and respond rudely to anyone who crosses them. Individuals and nations do not know how to relate to one another.

The Church stands at a critical juncture in history. More and more persons are becoming dissatisfied with the experience of liberal culture,[4] and the Christian community could offer an alternative society.[5] We must, however, understand the nature of the technological milieu in which we live in order to grasp more fully the kind of alternative that is necessary.[6]

4. See, for example, Robert Booth Fowler's *Unconventional Partners: Religion and Liberal Culture in the United States* (Grand Rapids: William B. Eerdmans, 1989).

5. For example, in a *U.S. News and World Report* feature on "How to Beat Drugs," the section on "Community Action" included under its third point, "Forge Strong Alliances," these comments: "Other institutions, *particularly churches,* make powerful allies. In New Orleans, the Third Shiloh Baptist Church bought two crack houses to close them down. Four black churches in Atlanta have 'adopted' 11 families, largely ones that have had trouble with drugs" (*U.S. News and World Report* 107, 10 [Sept. 1989]: 82, emphasis mine).

See also sociological research emphasizing the need for community in our society; for example, George Barna's *The Frog in the Kettle* (Ventura, CA: Gospel Light, 1990) or the well-known *Habits of the Heart* by Robert Bellah et al. (Berkeley: University of California Press, 1985).

6. Most of the basis for the next several paragraphs was gathered over the course of several years of dissertation research on the work of Jacques Ellul. Though specific references will not be cited because of the enormity of the material, see especially the following works: *The Ethics of Freedom; The Humiliation of the Word; Jesus and Marx; The Meaning of the City; The New Demons; Propaganda; Reason for Being; The Subversion of Christianity; The Technological Bluff; The Technological Society; The Technological System;* and *Violence* (full references given in the bibliography). See also my overview article about his concept of the Principalities and Powers in "An Introduction to the Work of Jacques Ellul," *Word and World* 9, 4 (Fall 1989): 386-93.

As modern Western culture has moved beyond the Industrial Revolution into the Technological Revolution, a myriad of factors have caused persons to become more and more isolated from one another. The original splitting of the family into different occupations (destroying its cohesiveness as an economic unit running the family farm or business) aggravated the tensions as each family member brought frustrations and confusions home from his or her separate daily sphere. Once home, family members now no longer do chores together; instead of preparing meals and cleaning up afterward together, for example, one person pops things into the microwave or dishwasher. Furthermore, the television replaced playing games together or singing around the piano, and soon multiple sets enticed us each into different rooms. Stereo headphones connected to personal radios or tape recorders separated us further. Computer games negated the need for a partner even in chess. And at the office, computer mail services replaced the opportunity to talk with anyone else in the company.

As persons have lost skills of interpersonal relations, the poles of technology and intimacy have become reversed. We recognize that intimacy is missing from our lives, so we advertise our technological toys with sexy models and try to make our technology more intimate with personal names. On the other hand, we do not know how to express intimacy, so we have to find technological assistance to do it. Sexual union formerly expressed the culmination of many growing intimacies — intellectual, spiritual, financial, recreational, creative, social, spiritual — and marked a committed covenant relationship. Now persons turn to sexual intercourse as a way to begin to know one another, and technical manuals are written so that it can be done as effectively as possible. The whole act of union carries an entirely different meaning.

This tragic misunderstanding became apparent to me

when I was leading a workshop on "Godly Sexuality" at a Christian college. Newly engaged to my best friend of seven years, I advocated waiting for sexual union until marriage and was surprised when the first question in the discussion period was "But what if you wait until you are married, and then the sex isn't good?"

I asked the student what makes sex "good." Is it its efficiency — that is the chief criterion in our technological milieu — or its extreme, albeit momentary, physical pleasure? Now that I am married, I am all the more distressed that our contemporary culture would reduce the beauty of an expression of lifelong fidelity to one's spouse to a mere experiment in sensual gratification. There are other ways to express affection for one's friends, to experience tenderness and intimacy, to enfold others haunted by their cosmic loneliness.

The Church has a wonderful message to proclaim — the hope of eternal meaning, the love of persons in deep relationship because God loved us first, the faith that we are accepted on the basis of the merits of Someone perfect and not because we have successfully managed to be the most efficient. Everyone in the world is longing for the Hilarity of that kind of hope, that fulfillment of being loved, that content of faith that will not change.

The superficiality of many parish fellowships belies the biblical possibilities. Why do Christians have such difficulty in truly loving one another, in being glad to belong to one another, in experiencing the empowering Hilarity that the grace of God and true community confer?

The apostle Paul wrote a careful letter to encourage the various house churches in Rome to build unity among the Christians there. The letter presents a theology of caring and glad Hilarity much needed in this twentieth century of indifference and technological non-intimacy and injustice.

The whole book of Romans emphasizes the doctrine that by faith persons can live in a right relationship with

God and, consequently, with each other. Because God's love for us depends entirely upon his character and not ours, everyone stands before him equally. No human being can do the slightest thing to earn God's attention. The fact that we keep choosing to make ourselves our own gods and masters separates us from him.

Yet God freely chooses to love each one of us. We respond to the wonder and Hilarity of that by loving him, but also by seeking to become more loving toward others. Relationships that float around on the surface deny the reality of God's gutsy love, a love so full that it compelled Christ to suffer depths of degradation and cruel crucifixion to demonstrate it to us.

Therefore, as we learn what that love means, we will want to respond with a Hilarious love that is also genuine, from the depths of our beings, holy. We will want to be like Jesus, demonstrating the Father's love and filled with the Spirit's power in the ways we deal with others, manifesting to everyone a reality that cannot be found anywhere else, creating a community of caring that frees us for Hilarity.

The twelfth chapter of Romans tells us how to do that. It teaches us what our age desperately needs to learn about caring for each other. We all long to find deeper love in our relationship with each other, especially in the Church. We all yearn for the Hilarity of deeper fulfillment and purpose.

Therefore I trust that, as we work through Romans 12, its message will change us, and, through us, God will change his Church and the world. When we faithfully study the Scriptures, more and more we will become what God intends for us to be. I dare you, therefore, to enter with me into a search for deeper meaning and Hilarity in our faith lives. Paul's letter will grip us; let us struggle together with its implications for our times.

This book is a very personal one. It has to be. We cannot talk about Christian community antiseptically — or at least we shouldn't. And yet we often relegate our Christianity to the cerebral dimension of our lives — speaking off the top of our heads and not getting the meat of the Scriptures down into our guts (or bowels, as the Greeks would say; or kidneys, as the Hebrews would put it). Those ancient cultures understood much better than modern-day Westerners that faith is a matter of one's personal depths, which should be talked about in a very personal way.

On the other hand, this book will not be superficially subjective, for it intends to offer a model of serious (but Hilarious!) in-depth Bible study. We cannot understand a text appropriately unless we look deeply into its meaning and application, and such interpretive *work* requires hard work.

Too many Christian books these days don't touch both the head and the heart. Serious commentaries on a text are often dry and impersonal. Personal devotional books are often quite flaky — lacking in substance other than nice Christian jargon. I want to invite you into some wrestling with the text and some personal stories about community — a combination of objective and subjective perspectives that can bring new insights into God's living Word. I want to build bridges — between your head and your heart, between the quiet of your daily devotional life and the bustle of your everyday existence, between your world and that of those who do not know the Hilarity of community, between you as an individual Christian and the community of God's people. Please let me know where these bridges are weak — and please walk across them if they are strong.[7]

---

7. I certainly would be very grateful for your critical responses to this book. Your contributions to such upbuilding of the global Christian community and strengthening of its Hilarity can be sent to me at 304 Fredericksburg Way, Vancouver, WA 98664-2147; or call me at (206) 693-5436.

1. Getting the Connections

Therefore, I urge you, brothers and sisters, *because of the mercies of God,* to offer your bodies as a sacrifice, living and holy and pleasing to God — which is your spiritual worship.

— ROMANS 12:1[1]

THE CAKE was a big surprise. I had been teaching all week at Faith Lutheran Church in Juneau, Alaska, and was greatly encouraged by all the fun of working with such wonderful people. On Thursday night the women's group spoiled me further with a big box of Christmas presents (in February!) and a cake bedecked in symbols.

Beside a frosting guitar and a colored-sugar picture of my first book, *To Walk and Not Faint,* the third sweet symbol

---

1. Unless otherwise noted, the translations of Scripture at the beginning of each chapter are my own. Translations in the body of the text follow the New American Standard Version (NASV) unless otherwise noted. Other abbreviations used are as follows: J. B. Phillips' paraphrase (JBP), Jerusalem Bible (JB), King James Version (KJV), Living Bible paraphrase (LB), New English Bible (NEB), New International Version (NIV), Revised Standard Version (RSV), and Today's English Version (TEV).

1

was an open Bible containing the word *therefore*. The cake decorator had listened well to our study of 1 Thessalonians the previous morning, when we had stressed the importance of the connecting words in Paul's letters.

Similarly, in this book we will learn much more from Romans 12 about the Hilarity of genuine community if we look closely at the word *therefore*. In the Bible the little connecting words are often the key to understanding the structure of a paragraph or an entire discourse. In our biblical interpretation we want not only to focus on particular words but also to grasp the movement of a larger section and of an entire epistle. We miss basic theological principles if we skip over significant connecting words too quickly.

The word *therefore* at the beginning of Romans 12 invites us to connect what Paul is about to say with what he has already said. This question challenges our search: how much of the book of Romans does Paul want to connect?

At first glance we might suppose that Paul wants us to connect the ideas of 12:1 with the magnificent doxology (i.e., hymn of praise) that closes chapter 11. For three chapters (9–11) he has been wrestling with the difficult problem of the place of the Jews in the plan of God. After much hard searching, Paul seems to throw his hands in the air and exclaim, "I just can't figure it out. God's ways are too magnificent for me to understand." He quotes Isaiah 40:13[2] and Job 41:11 in this ecstatic flight of Hilarity:

> Oh, the depth of the riches of the wisdom and
> knowledge of God!
> How unsearchable his judgments,
> and his paths beyond tracing out!
> "Who has known the mind of the Lord?

---

2. See my comments on that verse in chapter 13 of *To Walk and Not Faint* (Chappaqua, NY: Christian Herald Books, 1980).

Or who has been his counselor?"
"Who has ever given to God,
     that God should repay him?"
For from him and through him and to him
     are all things.
To him be the glory forever! Amen.

(Rom. 11:33-36, NIV)

Surely it is in response to this awed awareness of the infinite greatness of God that Paul now urges us to offer our bodies as a sacrifice. Nevertheless, if we know something about the style of this letter and about Paul's purposes in writing to the Romans, we will recognize that this *therefore* connects even more. In fact, this one word is the hinge between all of Paul's comments about God's love in Romans 1–11 (the doctrinal formulations) and about the Christian community's love for one another in Romans 12–16 (the ethical exhortations).

As we seek to apply the Scriptures accurately to our lives, we will want to know both the *cotext* (the rest of the particular discourse in which a passage is set) and the *context* (the historical situation of the writers and readers) of any section of the Bible that we study. Heresies arise when readers don't interpret passages adequately within the framework of the purposes and situation of the entire piece of literature. Because the Hilarity of the Christian community will be made more clear to us by a minute study of Romans 12, we will be careful to see the larger picture first and always in between. Therefore (there's that word again!), we begin with a broad sweep of the book of Romans in which to place all the details of our careful study.

Scholars argue extensively over the purposes of this unusual letter from the apostle Paul. Their disagreements revolve mainly around the significance of chapters 9 to 11, which deal with the place of the Jews in God's plan of salva-

3

tion, and the question of the authorship of chapter 16, which contains an unusually long list of greetings to individual believers and various house churches in Rome. Our understanding of the Hilarity of the Christian community will help us to resolve these questions and will enable us more thoroughly to interpret the *therefore* that begins chapter 12.

Paul's letter to the Christians at Rome is unusual because he was not the founder of Christianity there, nor had he ever even been there. However, he wanted to visit Rome and envisioned it as the base point from which he could travel on to preach in Spain (see Rom. 15:23-24). The church in Rome had been established by Christians who had moved to the imperial city from a diversity of places where belief in Christ had been introduced by Paul and others. Consequently, he knew quite a few particular members of the Roman congregations. This historical picture convinces me that Paul wrote Romans 16, though many biblical scholars believe that the chapter is a later addition to the text. In keeping with the subject matter of the rest of the book, Paul wanted to encourage his friends, to deepen the glad Hilarity of their Christian fellowship, and to establish his own credibility among the other Christians in the city so that his plan for further ministry might be facilitated.

We can also see from the list of persons in chapter 16 that the church in Rome was composed of numerous small house churches, under the leadership of both men and women. Some of the Christians there were converted Jews, and some were Gentiles. As Paul discusses (more thoroughly than in any of his other letters) the tremendous theme of one's right standing with God through faith, he encourages the Christians in Rome to recognize that under God's love and grace all persons stand equally before God. Therefore, no difference dare separate Jews and Gentiles or any members of different house churches. Love among God's people must be *thoroughly* inclusive. How much the Hilarity of the

4

contemporary Church would increase if we learned that important lesson!

Paul's emphasis on the inclusivity of the Christian community is focused in chapters 9 to 11, which do not simply insert a sidetrack but instead serve as the climax of the letter's doctrinal content and as a prelude to the ethical exhortations. The central core of Paul's formulations about God's plan for salvation by grace and not by legalism must include an understanding of how the Jews and Gentiles fit together. We must wrestle with the difficult issue of God's sovereignty in chapters 9 to 11 and come with Paul to this final conclusion: the wisdom of God is infinitely beyond our understanding and eminently worthy of our Hilarious praise.

When Paul begins chapter 12 with *therefore,* then, we must see the connection between learning to be a Hilarious community and the difficult questions of chapters 9 to 11. Questions about God's right to judge call for a response of humility; questions about the place of the Jews call for an unusual presenting of our bodies in the Church (see Chapter 2, "Two Kinds of Body Offerings").

Finally, the progression of the entire discourse of this letter from Paul gives us further insight into the importance of the word *therefore.* The first eleven chapters of Romans clarify doctrinal foundations and the basis for Christian Hilarity, and the last five chapters describe the results in our life-style of Hilarity. As you scan the following overview of the contents of Romans, you will see that the word *therefore* in Romans 12:1 is the hinge which connects these two major divisions of the letter:

> 1:1-17 — a summary of the Hilarity of the gospel: "The righteous will live by faith";
> 1:18-32 — the necessity for God to "give humankind over" to its mistakes;
> 2 — God's wrath and judgment against all those who

reject the truth, including the Jews who think that
they are saved by their obedience;

3:1-20 — God's faithfulness and humankind's total re-
bellion;

3:21-31 — God's gift of righteousness to all who
believe;

4 — the example of Abraham who was justified by
faith;

5:1-11 — a proper kind of boasting/Hilarity — in our
hope, in our suffering, in our God;

5:12-21 — a comparison of Adam and Christ, through
whom we possess death and life, respectively;

6 — the significance of baptism as death to our rebel-
lion and resurrection to the Hilarity of right standing
with God;

7 — death to the threat of law, but continuing struggle
against failures;

8 — freedom and life and Hilarity through the Spirit
and the immensity of God's love;

9 — God's sovereignty and the unbelief of the Jews;

10 — faith through the preaching of the Word and
Israel's rejection;

11 — the remnant of Israel, the engraftedness of the
Gentiles, the hope of salvation for the Jews, and an
exultant doxology;

12:1 — THEREFORE

12 — how to be a Hilarious community thoroughly
loving one another;

13 — the importance of submitting to authority and the
urgency of love;

14 — how love cares for both the weak and the strong;

15 — receiving the gifts of God's character, such as
hope and Hilarity, and Paul's desire to preach to the
Gentiles, especially in Spain;

16 — encouragement and greetings for Paul's friends

and exhortations to strive for unity among the house churches.

Notice the dominant theme of the chapters following the significant *therefore* of 12:1. Paul proclaims with a pervasive intensity the necessity for, and the vital characteristics of, love in the Christian community. This *therefore*, then, introduces specific and valuable directions for us and for our churches in this efficient, alienated, and lonely twentieth century.

We live in an age desperately in need of the kind of love that this letter describes — that is, a love founded in, and expressive of, glad Hilarity. However, such love cannot be created out of our own resources. We must be connected to life-changing experiences of God's love, of the power available when faith frees us from legalism, and of God's immense faithfulness toward his people. You might want to quit reading this book at this point and skim through the first two-thirds of Paul's letter to the Romans. Then, having been imbued with grateful Hilarity because of the thoroughness of God's love for you, you will be ready to connect grace and life with this *therefore*.

So many wonderful passages in those first eleven chapters invite our closer attention. Assurances empower us, exhortations stimulate us, compassion becalms us, ideas enthrall us, facts overwhelm us, hopes sustain us, love sets us free. We cannot read those chapters without feeling the Hilarity of being enfolded in the unutterable love of God. *Therefore*, we want to respond. We eagerly accept God's invitation to be changed into a community of caring.

In a radio lecture on Romans 12, Charles Swindoll noted that three special *therefore*s outline the major themes of the book of Romans. The first verse of chapter 5 offers the *therefore* of a good relationship with God; *therefore* in 8:1 introduces the theme of security. Now in 12:1, it presents the subject of life-style — which we will discover to be the Hilarity of love.

All of the great truths of the previous chapters to which Paul connects us are the basic elements of Hilarity, which motivate us to choose commitment. Then, as if that weren't enough, verse 1 of chapter 12 also adds the phrase, "because of the mercies [or pities] of God." This phrase further stimulates our desire to offer our bodies (an act to be considered in the next chapter).

The word translated "mercies" or "pities" is rarely found in the New Testament. It is almost always used in the plural, which implies that the abstract concept is manifested in all sorts of tangible forms. God does not merely sit around and think merciful thoughts toward us. Rather, his compassions can be experienced — and the experience of them fills us with Hilarity.

I experienced such a tangible manifestation of God's loving pities one evening when I was first working on this book almost ten years ago. Discouraged by some unjust criticism and saddened by the troubles of several friends, I prayed that God would help me somehow to get past the grief and frustration and confusion so that I could work decently. Soon the telephone rang; it was a call from my older brother in New York City, whose gentle care eased my homesickness for the security of family love.

Two hours later the telephone rang again. This time a Seattle friend was calling to offer transportation for an upcoming speaking engagement. Besides assuring me of necessary rides (because my visual handicaps prevent me from driving), he stayed on the line to let me cry out my confusion and pain.

One call would have been sufficient, but God's mercies came in double measure that night — special answers to prayer, revealing God's tenderness and restoring my Hilarity. Oftentimes we miss God's compassions because we are focused too much on our own struggles. J. B. Phillips' paraphrase of Romans 12:1 invites us instead to have "eyes wide open to the mercies of God."

Many things can block our vision. Our various bad attitudes — of pride or self-centeredness or greed — can prevent us from seeing the mercies of God. That is one of the reasons why we so desperately need the Christian community — to restore our Hilarity by reminding us to view God's mercies more carefully and by helping us to respond to them more faithfully.

The corporate study and worship practices of the Christian community and our daily personal devotional times develop in us the habit of looking at the compassions of God. Meditation on the Scriptures will open our eyes to see the wideness of God's mercies. That is why this book is structured so that you can study Romans 12 personally each day for a month or corporately for several weeks in a group. Whenever we catch sight of God's mercies again, we are ready for the connecting *therefore,* to experience the Hilarity of linking our life's responses to the facts of God's love, to connect all the motivation that the grace of God gives us (as expounded in Romans 1–11) with our participation (Romans 12–16) in the Hilarious community.

Questions for Further Meditation:

The intensive Bible study of this book will be mere words if we do not practically apply the ideas of each chapter to our individual and corporate lives. Since I cannot know the particulars of your situation or of the Christian community in which you participate, I will conclude each chapter with a set of questions for further reflection. Please make practical use of these questions — to meditate on the ideas of each chapter as you work through the day, to prepare for future discussions together with your community, to link what God is teaching you through the Scriptures with how you respond to him and how you reach out to others around you.

In other words, these questions can provide connecting *therefores* between God's principles and your personal and community life-style. (In most places these questions are asked in the plural, in the hope that you are studying this book together with other members of your Christian community, but the questions can certainly be used by individuals to empower you for strengthening your communities.)

Therefore:

1. What sections did we note as we skimmed through Romans that teach us more thoroughly about the basis for our Hilarity in the Christian community?

2. What other places in the Scriptures offer hymns of praise like the doxology at the end of Romans 11 and how do they increase our Hilarity?

3. Does this chapter cause us to recall other connecting words that Paul uses frequently in his writings?

4. How could we describe the connection between doctrine (formulations about the character of God) and ethics (our practical response)?

5. How have we seen the mercies of God lately — in our own personal lives and in the life of our Christian community?

6. What are our goals for our study of Romans 12? (For example, what kinds of changes in us as individuals and as a community do we anticipate?) How can we make our study more effective so that God's purposes in the Scriptures can be accomplished in our personal meditation and prayer and in our corporate study and discussions?

7. What is the primary Christian community for each of us? (A congregation, a Bible study group, a prayer circle?) Let us pray daily for our particular community and for the Christian community at large so that as we study Romans 12 we might be among those who serve to strengthen the Hilarity of the Church.

2. Two Kinds of Body Offerings

I appeal to you, therefore, *brothers and sisters*, because of the mercies of God, *to offer your bodies as a sacrifice, living* and holy and acceptable to God — which is your spiritual worship.

— ROMANS 12:1

THE NUN MOVED exquisitely. In my first exposure to liturgical dance, I was overwhelmed by its silent beauty. We needed no words or music as our sister danced the Lord's Prayer. The symbols flowing from her hands and body, the angelic smile on her face, and the radiance of her whole being spoke volumes — in fact, spoke prayers inexpressible.

Since watching that dance, I have learned many songs with sign language. We deepen our prayers by giving them melodies, for, in the words of Augustine, "those who sing pray twice." Signing a song, I feel like I pray thrice. I am more thoroughly involved when the words and music are underscored by the lifting of my hands and body into the message.

When Paul urges the Romans to "offer" their "bodies as a living sacrifice," he is prodding them toward a deeper presentation, a dancing of their prayers beyond the words and music. The word *bodies* can be interpreted to signify both individuals and the various house churches of the Roman congregation. As we consider both, we shall learn some important lessons for the sacrifice of our lives. The result of such sacrifice, we shall see, is a holy Hilarity, the true Joy for which we most deeply yearn.

First, the Greek word *sōma* is usually interpreted to signify our physical bodies. In that sense, Paul's plea is for each of us to put our whole selves into our relationship with God and, consequently, with each other. This fits in well with many other statements from Paul which urge us to give up our members as instruments of righteousness (Rom. 6:13) or which remind us that our bodies are the dwelling place of the Holy Spirit and are to be treated as such (1 Cor. 6:19-20).

Offering our bodies has all sorts of practical implications. The idea calls us, for example, to worship not just with our mouths, but with our whole beings — to *worship*, not to be a passive audience for the pastor and organist. We cannot be Christians merely intellectually; rather, we must respond to God's love by loving him with our words and attitudes, our emotions and actions.

To offer the Lord our bodies might mean doing physical work in his service. When I was first writing this book, I enjoyed immensely the opportunity to participate in a ten-mile CROP walk to raise money for the hungry, to put my feet into a concern that is often on my mind and in my mouth. Offering our bodies might mean mowing the lawn for our parents, going to the hospital to visit someone who is ill, or mopping the floor for someone disabled.

Too often we superficially love the world with our words. Paul's exhortation asks us to put legs on our prayers, to put social action into our pious proclamations. (We will see many practical consequences of that in future chapters of this book.)

Moreover, offering our bodies necessitates taking care of them. That challenge indicts many of us too-busy Christians (especially professional church workers!). Growing up in the midst of Lutheran school teachers who were so busy with their classes and music and administration and families and other responsibilities that they weren't very good to themselves, I did not develop good habits for physical disciplines.

When I began working for a congregation in Olympia, Washington, fifteen years ago, a colleague who is an avid jogger kept urging me to run. Later I discovered that swimming a mile every day was a better discipline for me. Now I have been in leg casts and on crutches for many months, so my exercise has changed to lifting weights and using a rowing machine. Through all these years, those workouts have kept me in better health, given me more energy, reduced my need for sleep and thus increased my time for work, given me calmness in tense times, offered me longer periods for meditation and prayer, provided an outlet for anxiety, and increased my endurance for hard tasks.

People in our culture are much more aware now about the need for physical fitness, but sometimes Christians struggle to justify time spent in exercise when that time "should" be spent caring for others. However, we can more effectively offer our bodies to God when they are in better shape. Furthermore, our whole beings are affected by the physical disciplines of adequate rest, careful nutrition, and robust activity. Our minds work better when the blood is circulating more thoroughly; our spirits are lifted when we dump our struggles into the pool.

One of the most important things that we can do as a Christian community is to encourage each other in such care for our bodies. Especially we need each other to practice Sabbath keeping — to set aside a whole day for worship, rest, and growth in community.[1] To be a people not caught

---

1. See my book *Keeping the Sabbath Wholly: Ceasing, Resting, Embracing, Feasting* (Grand Rapids: William B. Eerdmans, 1989).

up in the frenzy and pressured productivity of our culture would give the Church a tremendous opportunity to offer a splendid alternative to the non-intimacy and meaningless-ness of a technological society!

When we offer our bodies, we want to give God the best that we can, to put our whole beings into the offering. Our motivation for doing that, of course, is the Hilarity created by the revelation of his immense love and grace expounded in the first eleven chapters of Romans.

This emphasis on the response of our lives to God's love is underscored by our English verb *offer*. That word connotes freedom. We are not coerced. Instead, an offering is the gift of our choice. God's love for us is so rich and inviting that we want with our whole beings to offer up our whole beings.

When we are filled with gratitude for God's love, Paul says, we eagerly respond by offering our bodies as a "sacri-fice, living and holy and acceptable to God." The first at-tribute of that threefold phrase, "living," presents a paradox since the Greek word for "sacrifice" implies a burnt offering, the kind of sacrifice that demands a death. The mystery of the Christian life is that we can truly offer ourselves to God only if we are willing to give up ourselves. Yet in that death to our limited human concerns, God uses us in ways that demonstrate powerful life at work within us. Paul makes this same point in Galatians 2:20: "I have been crucified with Christ; and it is no longer I who live, but Christ lives in me; and the life which I now live in the flesh I live by faith in the Son of God, who loved me, and delivered Himself up for me."

Have you experienced the freedom and Hilarity of "a living sacrifice"? Think carefully of some times when you have abandoned yourself into whatever service you were rendering at the moment. Remember the fullness of life that you experienced in that offering. When our own needs or

14

fears are put to death, then we discover a source of life in God that is unexplainable.

This is the challenge of Paul's invitation for us: to remember those moments and thereby to be willing more and more to make such a complete offering. Always when we give ourselves up thoroughly in our loving, we experience a deeper reality of life and greater Hilarity in our caring.

A second possible interpretation of *sōma*, besides that of our individual bodies, is that since Paul uses the word *body* in Romans 12:5 to signify the Church as the corporate Body of Christ we should apply this larger sphere of reference also to his use of the word in verse 1. Then the term in the plural would refer to the various house churches into which the Christians in Rome were divided. If the purpose of Paul's letter is to unify those segments into a stronger whole, as suggested in the first chapter of this book, then such an interpretation of the word *bodies* would be more appropriate.

Another factor supporting this interpretation is that Paul urges the Romans to present their "bodies" as "*a* sacrifice, living, holy, and pleasing to God." He thereby exhorts them to deepen their unity by offering their various small bodies, or parts of the Church, as one whole, living, and holy sacrifice to God. In giving to God all of their respective groups, they would be drawn together by their service and worship into a more cohesive whole.

That interpretation offers exciting, practical applications to the churches of today. In a more complete offering of ourselves we will find deeper unity. Notice, for example, the transdenominational efforts of such groups as World Vision International, Bread for the World, or Habitat for Humanity. Christians from many different "house churches" work together to battle world hunger, the problems of refugees, government policies, the housing shortage, and the need for economic development in the poorer countries of the world.

Similarly, my lecture series on Romans many years ago in Olympia, Washington, brought together persons from a dozen different denominations. We were drawn together by our common desire to know the Scriptures more thoroughly and to live out the implications of our study more practically. In the offering of our bodies as a living and holy sacrifice, the barriers between denominations crumbled.

Two other elements in the first verse of Romans 12 increase our conviction that Paul intended the word *bodies* to signify Christian groups. Paul chose a verb to express his own purposes that carries closeness in itself. The verb is *parakaleō,* which is usually translated "to urge" or "to encourage." In contrast to other verbs meaning "to ask" for something, Paul chose this verb — probably because its field of meaning includes the sense of a personal invitation or a more earnest appeal.

We must remember that in Paul's time this word had a much more communal sense than "urging" or "exhorting" does in the twentieth century. To encourage someone in our times might involve sending a memo over the modem into her computer. In the age when Paul wrote, a much greater intimacy of personal encounters pertained, and urging or exhorting was done face-to-face or by personal letter (the writing of which seems to be a lost art form these days). The readers of Paul's letters were aware of the way the apostle worked and the care he invested in the people whom he served. Paul did not stand at a distance from the Romans and tell them condescendingly how to offer their house groups to God. Rather, he joined them as a fellow member of the Christian community to urge them to participate together in a wholehearted offering of the Body.

The second highlighting of the communal sense that Paul intended in Romans 12:1 is his use of the term of affection *brothers* [*and sisters*]. In contrast to other letters whose recipients Paul knew well, the longer book of Romans uses this expression to address his readers only seven times. In each instance Paul is stressing a particular concern (see, e.g., 1:13; 7:1; or 10:1). Here in 12:1 he calls them by a special term of endearment in order to underscore the relationships they might have with each other in their different groups. All together the members of each house church — whether Jew or Gentile, slave or free — are brothers and sisters together with Paul, who does not lord his apostleship over them. Instead, he stands beside them to encourage them to present themselves (their individual bodies) and the house churches (their worshiping, corporate bodies) as a united, living, and holy sacrifice to God.

Paul models the unity he envisions by being affectionate and on an equal level with those whom he is encouraging and thereby shows us the way in which we can best encourage each other. We cannot effectively tell one another from the outside or from above that the Christian life should be lived in such and such a way. The Christian community has no hierarchy. We struggle together, as brothers and sisters, to apply the challenges of the Scriptures to our lives.

Together in this book we are learning how to offer ourselves as a living and holy sacrifice; moreover, I pray that each of us is learning these things with other members of our local Christian communities. When your congregation offers itself and so does mine, we will have pulled the whole "Roman" church into a closer unity.

Especially I want to avoid the superficial use of "brothers and sisters" that I hear too often in Christian circles. "I love you, sister" is often an empty phrase tossed out without much thought or care. We will consider this more thoroughly in connection with verse 10 of Romans 12 (see Chapter 18, "Tenderly Affectionate Devotion"), but now we are invited to the Hilarity of a thorough commitment to each other as brothers and sisters, in the deepest sense of those names.

Therefore:

1. In what ways recently has my offering of myself or our offering of our community been superficial?

2. How have we experienced the Hilarious "living-ness" of true sacrifice?

3. How well am I taking care of the body I have to offer? How can we offer more encouragement to other members of our Christian community in the care of their bodies?

4. How might our congregation offer itself more as a living sacrifice?

5. How have we experienced the glad Hilarity of various bodies coming together in the unity of the whole Church?

6. What can we do to overcome the sterility of modern methods of communication in order to urge or encourage others in a more intimate way?

7. How can we deepen our relationships with our brothers and sisters in the Church? (This question anticipates future chapters about the practical meaning of love in Christian relationships.)

3. Set Apart and Acceptable

> Therefore, I appeal to you, brothers and sisters, because of the mercies of God, to present your bodies as a sacrifice, *living and holy and acceptable to God — which is your spiritual worship.*
>
> — ROMANS 12:1

WHEN I DIE there is going to be a great celebration! Besides my perfect Hilarity in finally knowing God intimately, as well as all the rejoicing of the angels and saints when they welcome me home, some people on earth will also be rejoicing — those who will receive some parts of me by transplant. I'm grateful that the donation of our bodies to medical science enables us to make our deaths a living gift.

This illustration first came to my mind because many of my parts already malfunction and will not be acceptable for others' use. In the same way, the sacrifices of ourselves to God are terribly marred by impurities that prevent them from being alive, holy, and pleasing to God. This is the paradox of our sacrifice: only when we offer ourselves wholly to God can we thoroughly live, set apart and acceptable as a sacrifice. Earlier in Romans Paul has stressed that we can be set free for a new life that is godly and powerful only when in Christ we become dead to disobedience against God. Only then will we really learn how to love unselfishly, creatively, Hilariously.

That is why Paul urges the presentation of our bodies with a once-for-all verb that implies a decisive action and then follows up his exhortation with this threefold description of what our offerings are to be: "living," "holy," and "pleasing to God." Such a sacrifice will be our "spiritual worship." In this chapter we will consider how all these characteristics depend upon God's love and issue in the Hilarity of our love for others.

In order to strengthen our Christian communities as an alternative society, we must keep in mind the reality of our loveless, hopeless, Joyless world. The principalities and powers of evil work overtime to mess up the offering of our bodies. Many temptations to selfishness and power destroy our gladness and the effectiveness of our outreach to others. Thus, they rob us of the Hilarity that could characterize our relationships.

In my travels as a free-lance speaker I often get involved in counseling relationships and intensive teaching situations that require of me more love than I possess. As long as I remain dependent upon God to produce his love and care through me, he faithfully gives all that is needed for ministry. When I rely on my own abilities, however, my compassion quickly burns out. Similarly, burnout or power plays or corruption in churches spoils the offering of congregational bodies.

Keep in mind both of the interpretations of the word *bodies* that we discussed in the previous chapter. Pause for a moment and assess the ways in which obstructions from without and self-centeredness from within are working against you as an individual and in your Christian community to hinder the offering of your body as a living and holy and acceptable sacrifice.

I am sure that your reflections caused you to grieve over our failures to be the persons and the churches God intends for us to be. Martin Luther's trilogy of "the devil, the world, and our flesh" is a terribly strong combination of adversaries, eager to destroy the credibility of our claims concerning the power of God at work in our lives. You have undoubtedly failed at times to withstand the temptations from Satan, the culture around you, and your own desires. Of course you have; you are a sinful human being just as I am.

Earlier sections of Romans prepared us for the terrible realization at this point that our sacrifices are not perfect. In the seventh chapter, Paul illustrates vividly this very real battle in the Christian life: the constant war between our distorted desires and the godly life imbued with the Holy Spirit's power. Many contemporary scholars contend that the seventh chapter describes only the life of the person who has not yet come to believe in God's forgiving love. However, Romans 7 seems to me to present an immediate daily struggle, which Martin Luther helpfully defined in terms of our being both saints and sinners at the same time.

We are saints because God has declared us to be, though we don't always act like the saints that we are. Our human tendencies to make ourselves gods still exist and will continue to plague us until we become entirely perfect beings and new incorruptible bodies at the end of time. Meanwhile, as Paul says in 2 Corinthians 5, we still groan in our human fallibility and limitations. Contrary to puritanical beliefs, our bodies do not make us sinful. *Sōma* (body) is not the same idea as *sarx* in biblical Greek. The latter is the "flesh," human desires contrary to the will of God.

Because of *sarx* we must constantly battle temptations that draw us into disobedient behavior which mars the perfection of our offerings. Nevertheless, Romans 7 is followed by the hope and grace of Romans 8. The last verse of Romans 7 begins the transition. When Paul throws his hands up in despair over the struggle and cries, "Wretched man that I am! Who will set me free from the body of this death?" he answers immediately with Hilarity: "Thanks be to God through Jesus Christ our Lord!" (7:24-25).

Then Paul continues with these words: "Therefore, there is now no condemnation for those who are in Christ Jesus" (8:1, NIV). Because Christ has made forgiveness possible for us (and thus created our "sainthood" in God's perspective), we do not stand under condemnation for our sinful character and for those frequent times when we have given in to selfish lovelessness.

Though we have blown it, we need not despair. Forgiveness gives us new hope. Though from a human perspective our offerings are anything but pleasing as a sacrifice and far from holy in the way we live, yet God receives them as such when we respond to his love in our worship. All kinds of things spoil our offering — nasty words, cruel actions, judgmental thoughts, selfish failures, manipulative insensitivities, proud stubbornnesses. What a great Hilarity it creates in our lives when, for all these errors, Christ offers forgiveness and removes the condemnation!

In chapters 9 through 11 Paul has shown the primary disruption that marred the offering of the house church *bodies* in his time — namely, the conflict between Jews and Gentiles in the Christian community. Similarly in our time the conflicts between denominations and between factions within church bodies prevent us from offering ourselves as a sacrifice, living and holy and acceptable to God. How greatly the Christian witness to the world loses its credibility because of our lack of unity!

The same words about forgiveness to which we desperately need to cling as individuals are also essential for our life together in community. How much we need God's forgiveness for our inability to be genuinely a Body. And how great the mercies of God are! Because of infinite divine compassion, we can indeed start with a clean slate to sacrifice our communal bodies, and we can graciously offer God's forgiveness to each other to purify our offering. Only by grace is our sacrifice living, holy, and acceptable to God.

The previous chapter already discussed the paradox of a sacrifice that is living. At this point we need only recognize the problem, as Charles Swindoll stressed in a radio lecture, that *living* sacrifices like to crawl off the altar. Both as individuals and as corporate communities, we frequently need Paul's exhortation to offer our bodies decisively. In our congregations and Bible study/prayer groups, we want to renew continually our commitment to God and to each other.

One reason to stress the corporate use of the word *bodies* in Romans 12 is to recognize that our various communities have unique identities to offer. To remain a *living* sacrifice, the Church won't destroy the different characteristics of denominations but will offer them all in Hilarious service.

Second, the sacrifice of our bodies is also *holy*. Though that adjective has lost its power in twentieth-century thought, the word carries rich connotations throughout the Hebrew Scriptures and the New Testament. The Hebrew Scriptures record the setting aside of vessels for use in the tabernacle and later in the temple. Those vessels were thus consecrated into holy service.

In the same way, we who are God's people are set apart as special vessels for his purposes. That does not mean, of course, that we are better than anyone else. Pride has no place when we realize how often we lose our love and the Hilarity that motivates it. However, we do understand what distinguishes us from those who do not believe — not our success at acting more holy, but God's loving forgiveness which sets us apart as holy.

That concept frees us from defensiveness over our failures. When our faith is criticized because it is not expressed in a perfect life-style, we can readily acknowledge that we don't act like the saints that we are. Yet the Hilarity of our faith is this hope: in his perfect love Christ forgives us. He makes our communities holy in God's sight.

When Jesus says, "Be perfect, therefore, as your heavenly Father is perfect" (Matt. 5:48, NIV), the Greek might also be translated, "You shall be perfect" (as JBP recognizes). The simple future indicative verb, in that case, announces the state that results when we depend upon the Father's perfection. We don't work at trying to crank up perfection. Rather, God is creating that perfection in us as he continues to change and empower us with his perfect love.

I am certainly not denying the value of spiritual disciplines, but I am stressing that we destroy the hope and empowerment of a verse like Romans 12:1 when we create false guilt. Paul does not call us to offer a holy sacrifice in order to drive us to despair, but to invite us to the Hilarity of the fact that by his grace God perceives our offerings as holy. When we offer our bodies as a living sacrifice, we receive his love, which sets us apart as holy, and we express our desire for his holy action through our lives.

Finally, our sacrifice is *pleasing to God.* That phrase comforts me immensely. For a few years long ago I worked in a situation in which I knew that my colleague was basically dissatisfied with who I was. His mind was closed against me, with the result that nothing I ever did could please him. The more I tried, the worse everything seemed to be. A deep tension began to pervade my life because I knew that I had failed even before I began.

Now for more than twelve years I have worked under the Board of Christians Equipped for Ministry (CEM), and I feel an exhilarating freedom in their strong support. Basically, who I am is pleasing to them. Therefore, I can enjoy doing what I do best because I know they will be glad for it. Furthermore, I can gratefully receive their criticisms of my work because I know those constructive rebukes come within the framework of general approval.

Multiply that many times over, and we can begin to understand the freedom that God wants us to have in our relationship with him. Having begun with his love and keeping our eyes wide open to the implications of his mercy, we know with great Hilarity that we are pleasing to God. Nothing depends on an ability to be pleasing — very much the opposite, in fact. We are set free to *do* pleasing things because we already know that we *are* pleasing. How much more effective God's love is as our motivation. When we know we are already acceptable, we don't have to waste a lot of time and effort trying to prove ourselves.

That is why it is so important for the Christian community to enfold its members in this sense of acceptance, this "therefore" of "eyes wide open to the mercies of God." Work ceases to be drudgery and becomes a Hilarious adventure when we know that others, especially God, will like what we do.

Paradoxically, the phrase *pleasing to God* also calls us to discipline, for as we choose to please God and God's people we might not necessarily please the world. At times we will consciously reject human methods in favor of God's holy ways as we seek to offer ourselves, or we will face human hostility because our living sacrifice has been faithful to God's commands.

Paul summarizes these qualities by calling our sacrifice our "spiritual worship." The Greek noun that is used here, which can also be translated "service," carries connotations of both rites and duties; Paul also used it in Romans 9:4 to designate rituals in the temple. The ambiguity is very nice here because it reminds us that our worship rites and Christian service are inextricably related. All of life is of a piece as we respond to God's love in the Hilarity of both praise and action.

The adjective that is used here is usually translated "spiritual" in our English versions (primarily because its only other use in 1 Peter 2:2 is more figurative), but it actually carries a much larger field of meaning. The Greek word *logikos* (from which we get the English word *logical*) is related to the verb *to think* and the noun *word* and actually means being genuine, in the sense of being true to the real and essential nature of something. Thus, the idea of spiritual worship emphasizes that which is rational. The NEB captures the ambiguity of Paul's adjective well in its translation: "the worship offered by mind and heart." Worship begins in one's attitudes and results in actions that are well-reasoned offerings of service. The concept has numerous implications for both of the interpretations of *bodies* suggested in the previous chapter.

As we interpret *bodies* to signify our individual persons, then the phrase "spiritual worship" involves our attitudes in sacrificing every dimension of our lives. That eliminates all differences between sacred and secular. Our jobs — as waiters, mechanics, businesswomen, or artists — are a living, holy, and acceptable service. Our workplaces are places of worship, and all the activities of our days are part of our worship. I worship as I brush my teeth, exercise, take a nap, care for someone, kiss my husband, scrub the kitchen floor, or start a cozy fire and listen to a symphony.

Moreover, such a wholistic concept of worship pervading our congregations will lead to a better balance of true spirituality in the Church. We will recognize that sharing our faith (evangelism) is not something we do, but that a witness is something we are. We will be more open to whatever opportunities God gives us to reach out to others with simple gestures of love and Hilarity.

These realities will be discussed more thoroughly in later chapters of this book, but at this point we might anticipate the Hilarity we will experience when our churches become more aware of all the dimensions of spiritual worship. Then we will care more profoundly about one another's ministries in whatever places God has called us to serve. Then, also, our time in our churches will be spent more profitably to become equipped for those ministries.

One final implication of all the qualities of our sacrifice carries us back to the temptation and disobedience, the repentance and forgiveness with which we began this chapter. A most encouraging fact for me is the realization that, when I offer myself or we offer our community wholly to God as an act of spiritual worship, he provides the power to transform situations of temptation into moments of holiness and acceptability.

For example, when first working on this book I was single and often quite lonely. One evening I was working with a non-Christian who did not understand my commitment to Scriptural principles of sexual morality. Because at that time I struggled with sexual temptations in my need to be loved, to work with him could have been terribly difficult. But God used my thinking about this chapter and my prayers in anticipation of the evening's work to prepare in me a greater strength than I'd even realized. Instead of temptation, I experienced the Hilarity of God's complete control of the situation. The conversation was an act of worship that set me free to care about my colleague without selfish needs obstructing God's love through me.

Similarly, in the times when our Christians Equipped for Ministry Board has wrestled with difficult issues, it would have been easy for us to become divided by petty personal interests or by my need to defend myself against the Board's criticism. However, our desire to offer CEM completely to God has kept us in the grace that enables our sacrifice to be holy and pleasing.

God's love sets us free to be holy and pleasing. To give our bodies — individually and corporately — in response to

27

God's love enables our worship to be spiritual, our service to be genuine, and our communities to be Hilarious.

Therefore:

> 1. What does being holy mean?
> 2. How do we behave when we don't feel holy?
> 3. How can we learn not to rely on our feelings of holiness, but to believe and act on God's declaration that he sees us as such?
> 4. How can the fact that we are saints help us to act more like saints?
> 5. How have we experienced the Hilarity of knowing that we are already acceptable to God?
> 6. How can we affirm others and encourage them to live out of the awareness that they are already acceptable and do not have to justify their existence? How can our Christian communities grow to be more characterized by such inclusive acceptance?
> 7. How will our daily lives be affected by the Hilarity of knowing that every part of them can be spiritual worship and reasonable service?

4. Not Squeezed into a Mold

And do not be conforming to this age, but be [in the process of] being transformed by the renewing of your mind.

— ROMANS 12:2a-b

O NCE A LITTLE BOY was trying to open a flower bud. Under his persistent efforts the blossom fell apart in his hands. In exasperation he looked up at his mother and asked, "Why does the bud fall apart when I try to open it, but when God opens it the flower is beautiful?"

Shocked at his profundity, his mother was speechless.

Soon, however, the child exclaimed eagerly, "Oh, I know! When God opens the flower, he opens it up from the inside."

That story is a charming illustration of the difference between being conformed and being transformed. The former forces someone's personhood or a group's identity from the outside. The latter opens up the individual or the community from the inside. The difference in results is dramatic.

When God opens persons from the inside, they can truly be themselves, the uniquely gifted individuals they were created to be. Unfortunately, however, all sorts of influences obstruct God's opening processes. Oftentimes our society, our families, even our churches force us to conform. The technicization of our culture multiplies the requirement to conform because of the need for efficiency, the potency of propaganda, and the manipulation of human beings by political illusions.

The Greek verb in this first phrase of Romans 12:2 urges us not "to form or mold [our] behavior in accordance with a particular pattern or set of standards" — in this case, the standards of this aeon. Furthermore, the verb is a present imperative. That verb tense and mood stress the continuing action necessary to avoid conformity. All the time we must be on our guard against those influences that would force their patterns upon us. We will consider here what some of those might be in order to guard more effectively against their destructive effects in our lives. God's people — both individually and corporately — continually must resist the pressures to conform to our culture's materialism, sense of time, immorality, mind-set, and methods.

One extremely disturbing evidence of conformity is the way in which the culture around us has drawn Christians into its values. Our model Jesus taught us to sell our possessions and give to the poor, to be generous in our hospitality. But our society urges us to compete for possessions and to hoard them for ourselves. We struggle to choose intentionally a simpler life-style and to resist cultural pressures to crave, to buy, to own.

Strong appeals and pressures to conform are so pervasive. Television, radio, and magazines bombard us with ads urging us to join the materialistic craze. We are warned that we are socially deficient if we don't drive the most luxurious car, own the latest technological toys, or wear the right designer clothes. Stock company advertisements claim that "the quality of life depends on the quality of our investments." Subtle pressures persuade us that the best churches are those with the biggest buildings, the largest staffs, the most modern communications equipment.

As a result we get inferiority complexes, or become envious, or lose our sense of priorities. We would be as good as the next guy if only we could possess things properly. So our spirit of Hilarity is lost because we are dissatisfied with what we have and who we are.

Even more subtly, we become easily enculturated into a technological society's need to be efficient, its sense of time, its pressure to advance. We sacrifice thereby the Hilarity of deep relationships, of keeping the Sabbath, of doing our work with care and love.

"Do not be conforming," Paul urges. We do not have to buy the values of this age. J. B. Phillips paraphrases the clause, "Don't let the world around you squeeze you into its mold." Here in wet Washington state, we make a wordplay out of his noun *mold* and find it quite abhorrent to think that sometimes we let the world shove us into its smelly green fungi!

The spirit of Hilarity in the Christian community enables us to work together to resist the strong pressures that surround us. We need each other to support our desires for a simpler life-style. One of the delights of being newly married is that my husband's shared concern makes it far easier to observe the Sabbath wholly, to eat and exercise carefully, to concentrate on conserving resources, to refrain from accumulating possessions.

Similarly, when I was first writing this book, a friend in Seattle wrote:

Thank you for the gift of your friendship. Sometimes I get discouraged when people come down on me for not thinking, saying, and doing the conventional things. Even when I know I am right, I still start questioning my stance, wondering if it is really worth the effort. At times like this, it is knowing that you are fighting the same kinds of thinking and criticism that helps me to carry on.

Part of the Hilarity so needed in a hopeless world is a mutual commitment that encourages us to keep on holding to biblical values. We are not alone, but we share a common struggle to live as Jesus taught us to live.

A particular area of conformity that deeply worries me is the realm of sexual relationships. Why has the Church not taken a more vigorous stand against the immorality of our world? I do not mean that we practice Christian love in a loveless world by denouncing those who choose our culture's patterns for sexual behavior. Rather, I want the Church positively to build a strong case for deep sexual commitment within marriage and to set up the ideal of strong friendships that involve pure affection and non-manipulative love.[1]

For years I have been teaching that we who are God's people have a lot to offer the world as an alternative to its understanding of human sexuality. Two years ago I had a chance to test out my own theories. I was invited to address seven "Family Living" classes at a public high school in Omaha. I was not overt about my Christian orientation in my presentations, but simply told the students about our human (God-created) design for committed relationships, about the need for love to be built on many intimacies besides the sexual, and about the security that comes when genital sexuality is enjoyed only within the framework of a permanent, covenant, faithful marriage relationship. I was astonished by how eagerly the students listened to my words; I was even more astonished by their thank-you notes the next day. Numerous cards said such things as "I will *never, never, never* forget what you said!" "I talked about your

---

1. I am presently working on a book on this topic, tentatively entitled *Sexual Character: An Ethics of Intimacy in a Technological Society.*

presentation with my parents [or boyfriend or classmates]." "I'm going to save sex for marriage — thanks for the encouragement." "Nobody has ever told me about this better way to understand relationships. Thank you for coming to our class." (And two months later when I had surgery to rebuild my foot, those same classes sent get-well cards, signed by all the students!)

Indeed, the Christian community can offer to the world such positive alternatives out of our understanding of the goodness of God's created design for marriage and sexuality. Instead, however, many leaders in the Church are conforming to the sexual mores of our society.

I have a friend whose pastor (!) encouraged her sexual involvement with a young man as a healthy antidote to her low sense of self-esteem. Her affair resulted in a pregnancy (which, thank God, she did not terminate by abortion, another critical issue that calls for a much more thorough offering of additional positive alternatives). However, her psychological and spiritual life has been scarred by that pastor's unbiblical advice. She knows that she is forgiven, but that original conformity continues to haunt her relationships with men and to prevent wholesome discovery of her own sexuality.

Similarly, why have we allowed divorce to become so common in churches when Jesus declared that marriage is not to be cut apart (Matt. 5:31-32 and 19:3-12)? Certainly the Church must learn better to bring healing love to those who are broken by the ravages of divorce, but we also could more thoroughly offer preventative medicine, urging the young to take seriously the permanence of marriage before they enter into it, exhorting those struggling with marital problems not to give up so easily, and standing by them with assistance for their practical needs. Those who want to keep trying in the face of a trying marriage need the support of the community to enable them to resist the pressure to conform to our society's pattern of easy divorce. Indeed, God's love is sufficient for the needs of those who must endure severe heartbreak and turmoil, but it needs to be incarnated in a caring community.

Teenagers especially are subject to the attacks of the conforming principle. Peer pressure to drink, to experiment with drugs and sex, even to engage in violence is almost intolerable. All of us in the Christian community — not just parents of teenagers — can be standing by our sons and daughters in faith to enfold them in graced Hilarity to help them find worth in themselves rather than in the degree of their conformity to the standards of their peers.

In the midst of troubled times, some teenagers find impressive security and Hilarity in their faith. Rather than scrambling for power or popularity, they are set free to care about each other — relying not on their conformity to surrounding values but on their Lord to give them wholeness.

Perhaps the toughest kind of conformity to fight is that which we force on ourselves. Because of pressures from our own fears and misconceptions we sometimes establish for ourselves or our communities a mold into which we try to cram ourselves. Robin Scroggs calls any kind of conformity a "performance principle" under which we labor.[2] The term aptly describes the inappropriate expectations that stir up most of the dissatisfaction in our lives.

Because I had participated vigorously in sports before the onset of debilitating disease and physical handicaps, I keep putting myself under the performance principle of my former athletic abilities. Consequently, I struggle not only with the pain of the physical problems themselves but also with a self-imposed pressure to keep up somehow.

Paul urges me not to be squeezed into any molds of what I *should* be able to expect from myself physically. I want to learn to rest in the knowledge that I am doing all I can to take care of my body. There are no requirements.

2. Robin Scroggs, *Paul for a New Day* (Philadelphia: Fortress Press, 1977).

What about you? What kinds of pressures are you under because you have let yourself, society, your family, or others around you put you there? How has that pressure caused you to function even less effectively because of the guilt and frustration associated with the failure to meet the performance principle? Notice how such conformity destroys our Hilarity as Christians.

Particularly, we allow personal expectations raised by cultural values to squeeze us into conformity with our society's assessment of success in our work. When church leaders especially conform to false standards of what constitutes a successful ministry, we fall into the numbers game and think that if we are drawing large crowds we must be good preachers.

Nowhere in the Bible does Jesus call us to be successful. Greatly to the contrary, he calls us to be faithful — and faithfulness in ministry might result in failure according to society's standards. Much more important than numbers should be the depth of love and Hilarity and commitment engendered by our work. Much more valuable than crowds are persons who are being changed by the good news of God's love and the principles of the kingdom of God.

Corporately, our churches fall into the traps of conforming to our culture's methods for many dimensions of their work. Certainly we can make use of whatever available technology can be helpful tools in our stewardship of time and money. On the other hand, we want to withstand the pressures of societal systems for raising money, for building ostentatiously, for elevating the rich and neglecting the poor, for choosing programs over spending time with persons, for preaching humanitarian gunkety-gunk rather than the Scriptures, which decisively confront us with our failure to be the Church.

This is especially noticeable in many church youth groups that are trying to attract kids by means of a great investment in "fun and games." Social activities are indeed

35

a valuable part of a congregational youth program, but, unless learning the meaning of the Scriptures and how to apply them to daily life is the focus of the youth's gathering together, the program is off base. The Church's unique gift to youth is to help them to become followers of Christ; we must not let that gift get hidden in merely entertaining flim-flam.

The high school youth in Omaha demonstrated to me that teenagers today have an enormous hunger for deeper relationships and meaning and security. The Christian community can offer positive alternatives in its presentation of the Scriptures and in its commitment to true human values. Our churches do not need to conform to superficial fun and games to draw youth to the reality of Christian love. The Hilarity of true community is much more appealing. A high school Bible study group in Moscow, Idaho, that we began with just four persons hit a record attendance one night of seventy youth.

Finally, our churches themselves sometimes distress-ingly force conformity on their members. Some groups (are we all guilty?) seem to say that to be a good Christian one must do such and so and be like this or that. The problem is that when those qualities are so tightly defined none of us really fits the mold without a great deal of squeezing and destruction of what is true.

God wants each Christian and each community to be unique, opened up from the inside to reveal in a special way possible only for that person or group some of the dimen-sions of God's grace in a particular combination that no one else can reveal. When churches force conformity on mem-bers or denominations force conformity on congregations, those unique revelations of love — and the Hilarity of being truly ourselves — get lost in the fixed and rigid patterns.

No, NO, *NO!!!* God's desire is for us to be transformed from the inside out and to flee from the pressures that would force us into values imposed from the outside. His love enables us to stand firm against those pressures. And he changes us so powerfully and dramatically from the inside that those outside forces don't really have a chance at all against the Hilarity of such a transformation. To that work within us we will turn in the next chapter.

Therefore:

1. How have we let society's values squeeze us into their mold? How has such conformity destroyed our Hilarity?

2. How can we withstand our culture's emphasis on materialism and success?

3. What can we and our churches do to promote lovingly an alternative, more positive sexual ethics than our society offers?

4. How can our church maintain both a caring attitude toward those hurt by divorce and also a firm stance against conformity to the values that so greatly foster marital breakdowns?

5. How has our church fallen into society's methods in certain dimensions of our work as the people of God? How can we fight those conformist tendencies?

6. How has our church forced us as individuals into a mold that has stifled the transformation that God might want to work in our lives?

7. How have we hurt ourselves by forcing ourselves into a mold that pressures us into conformity against the true selves which would open from the inside? What performance principles do we lay upon ourselves?

5. Transformation to the Truth about Ourselves

... but be [in the process of] being transformed by the renewing of your mind.

— ROMANS 12:2b

THERE ARE TWO WAYS to make weird-shaped balloons.

One way is to take an ordinary balloon and tie it securely with strings that force it into the shape of a poodle or whatever one wants to make. The problem is that those strings put enormous pressure upon the fragile balloon; a slight prick will cause it to explode and be destroyed. Sometimes, too, the strings become displaced or broken so that the shape is lost. Obviously, to squeeze a balloon into such a mold from the outside is not the best way to create a poodle.

The other way is to fashion the rubber itself into the shape of a poodle. Then when the balloon is completely filled with air, it is transformed into its shape from the inside out.

Even so, we are transformed by the Holy Spirit's work within us. In his magnificent creativity, God the Designer has fashioned us each into a unique personality; moreover, he has given each of our communities a unique identity. Then, when the Spirit dwells in us and fills us with his power, we take the form that we were created to manifest. Now there is not the pressure of being squeezed into a mold from the outside, nor the risk of losing our shape when the outside forces change, but rather a tremendous potential for freedom and the glad Hilarity of being truly ourselves.

Everything begins with creation — a very good place to start, don't you think? God in his infinity seeks to reveal himself to our finite minds by the diversity of his creation. Notice how often the psalmists burst into praise because they have observed new dimensions of Yahweh's character by means of that which he has created. (See, for example, Psalm 8 or Psalm 104.)

Especially our sense of self-worth is strengthened when we know that we are each uniquely fashioned by God's infinite care. No two of us have the same combination of kinds of intelligence, skills, gifts, personalities, physical features, desires, and idiosyncrasies; no two churches have the same qualities of worship, skills of leadership, combinations of spiritual gifts. This fact alone is a strong motivation to resist conformity. Why spoil a good thing by twisting it into another shape with outside cords?

God has put just the right combination together to make us our special selves. As the Psalmist says,

> I will give thanks to Thee, for I am fearfully and
>   wonderfully made;
> Wonderful are Thy works,
> and my soul knows it very well.
>
> (Ps. 139:14)[1]

---

1. See my comments about that verse in chapter 22 of *I'm Lonely, LORD — How Long? The Psalms for Today* (San Francisco: Harper & Row, 1983).

We were wondrously shaped in our mothers' wombs from the magnificent plan of God designed before the beginning of time.

Now this second verse from Romans 12 invites us to be transformed into that special shape with which we were designed. The Greek imperative is in both the present tense and the passive voice to indicate *continuous* action *upon* us as we are constantly becoming transformed into the person or community God delights for us to be. How appropriate is the button that says "P B P; G I N F W M Y." Still in the process of being changed, we can request, "Please be patient; God is not finished with me yet." One reason why members of the Christian community can have glad Hilarity is that we can afford to be patient with one another — knowing that God is still changing each of us and the whole of us corporately. We need not have the world's expectations of perfection or productivity concerning brothers and sisters in the community.

As we grow in Christian faith and life, we are always becoming who we are meant to be. That continual process, however, gets aborted (a proper word choice since it is death to God's creation) when we allow ourselves to be crammed by our society, ourselves, or even our churches into a mold that violates his original design for us.

Specifically, people of God have a unique freedom to take the shape of their possibilities. Not under any "performance principles," we don't have to conform to society's values and become like everyone else, futilely chasing after false gods of success or prestige that produce nothing but emptiness. Nor do we have to prove our worth to one another; rather, we can be Hilariously free to explore our unique possibilities within the affirmation of the completely accepting love of God and the consequent love of the community.

Our technological society has to force us to conform — because it needs us to function in a certain way for the efficiency of the whole. Because the principalities and powers manifest themselves as they do through the economic and political structures of our times, they demand obedience to their laws. As people of God, on the contrary, we are privileged to stand against those powers, to live out the implications of the gospel, which sets us free instead to be transformed into an alternative life-style following the model of Jesus.

How many people can you find who are totally free to be themselves — not hiding behind any facades, not struggling against any performance principles? The "hippie generation" became amusing — asserting their right to be freely themselves and yet all wearing the same kinds of clothes and doing the same things. That didn't seem very creative at all.

Unfortunately, not very many Christians either are radically free to be themselves. Tragically, when we lose sight of our release in God's love, we no longer understand its transforming power as did the early Christians who blew the world apart with the exuberant Hilarity of their openness to the creative power of the gospel. How can our churches more thoroughly become communities engendering the freedom that fosters such transformation?

Arthur F. Miller and Ralph T. Mattson insist in *The Truth About You* that every person is uniquely created and finds deepest happiness and fulfillment when living in accordance with that design. In 100 percent of their case studies, their understanding has proved to be true. They teach a method of analyzing one's most fulfilling childhood experiences to discover patterns that reveal the individual's motivations and gifts and truest desires.[2]

Their study amazed me because it proved true for me, too. Happy memories from childhood — enjoying religion classes throughout Lutheran elementary school, singing

2. Arthur F. Miller and Ralph T. Mattson, *The Truth About You: Discovering What You Should Be Doing With Your Life* (Old Tappan, NJ: Fleming H. Revell, 1977).

special songs in Christmas programs, writing and directing a play in the fifth grade, and teaching second grade when I was in third — reveal patterns of my created personality that continue to be fulfilled in my life's work. No wonder being a free-lance theologian, musician, author, and teacher is such great delight; the tasks let me live more truly out of myself.

This is God's intention for the Hilarity of his people. Through the encouragement and support of the Christian community and because of the transformation that the Spirit is working in us, we are enabled to live freely and creatively and genuinely the truth about ourselves. Of course, this is an ideal, and none of us in this world can be totally free to be ourselves, but our goal in working on this subject together is to strengthen our communities so that they will be more supportive of such a Hilarious freedom.

A powerful implication from this living of truth is that it destroys all the nonsense about roles. As followers of Jesus, who said, "Blessed are the gentle, for they shall inherit the earth" (Matt. 5:5), we certainly don't want to be character-ized by pushiness or clamoring for our rights. On the other hand, the Christian community supports all liberation movements that seek to free persons from oppression and conformity to certain roles imposed upon them by their culture. However, the Scriptures and God's definitions of holiness are always our guide to moral freedom.

Many of the perversions and confusions about roles in our society are the result of cultural expectations that make persons fearful of being themselves. When our culture con-vinces us that how we were created must be somehow wrong, our very fears foster terrible corruptions of spirit. For example, sensitive heterosexual men are often criticized for their tenderness by our "macho" culture and then mis-takenly accept the sociological category of homosexuality for themselves rather than learning about genuine male friendship. Women often think that the only way to break the glass ceiling for advancement in the corporate world is to adopt the styles of their male counterparts.

We do not have to be conformed to the roles that might be assigned to us by our culture, ourselves, or our church. Please notice that my comments do not advocate a "do your own thing" mentality that has no care for others. By espousing a freedom from the legalism of conformity, the Christian community does not at all condone libertinism (liberty without responsibility) or antinomianism (liberty without any rules). The key to the perfect balance between the extremes of legalism and false liberty is the way in which the transformation of Romans 12:2 takes place. Paul urges us to be continually in the process of being transformed by the "renewing of our minds."

Other passages in the Pauline letters that describe renewal with the same Greek word or its related words lend us insight into the meaning of this powerful phrase. First, Colossians 3:10 reminds its readers (in the context of v. 11, another wonderful passage about the unity of the Christian community) that they "have put on the new self," which is "being renewed to a true knowledge according to the image of the One who created" them. The basic fact that we were made in God's image teaches us to find our truest self in accordance with his principles, in a spiritual renewal. Thus, we won't want to live with a "do your own thing" attitude that disregards biblical guidelines or the needs of others. God's character at work in us recoils at such a suggestion.

Second, the same noun from Romans 12:2 occurs in the reminder to Titus that God saved us "according to His mercy" (as in Rom. 12:1) by means of "the washing of regeneration and renewing by the Holy Spirit" (Titus 3:5). The justification wrought in baptism leads to the transformation of life in the continued sanctification of the Holy Spirit.

Third, Paul specifically uses a related verb in 2 Corinthians 4:16 to proclaim that the inner person is being renewed day by day. Thus, we cannot define once and for all what our role in life is; we never have to get stuck in the same mold. The person who I am today might not be the same tomorrow — which leads to incredible freedom and adventure. Yahweh continues to say, "See, I am doing a new thing!" It is already springing forth (Isa. 43:19).

That concept strikes me with its practicality. Between the first writing of this chapter and these new revisions several years later enormous changes have occurred in my personal life and in my free-lance ministry. God's love keeps coming in new and surprising — life-transforming — ways. A new friend whom I had just met when I was first working on this book is now my new husband after seven years of friendship. Some congregations that I have observed for ten years have become enormously transformed as the Holy Spirit has renewed their attitudes, raised new awarenesses, and deepened their Hilarity.

Finally, we must stress that God's transforming work is done by the renewing of our *minds*, the center of our conscious thought and understanding. This challenges us to recognize the value of daily personal devotional habits and corporate Bible study. When we use our minds together with our hearts to investigate God's goals and principles as outlined in the Scriptures, we find ourselves and our communities changed. When our minds engage in fervent prayer and profound meditation upon the messages of the Bible and our daily experiences, we grow to know God and, thereby, the truth about ourselves.

An enormous danger to the Church is an unthinking Christianity that slips into society's patterns of living without investigating their validity. We should fear bandwagons that draw in participants who haven't really thought through the significance and meaning of a particular movement for their lives.

We've got to use our minds! God's renewing process through the Scriptures should shatter our stagnation and complacency and pride. Sometimes Christians are rightfully branded as narrow-minded because we seem to fear that God or the Scriptures will be proved wrong if we plumb the depths of truth. Or do we fear thinking things through because we narrow-mindedly resist the radical changes of God's transforming processes?

We need, then, to recognize the idiocy of our fears. God is eminently reliable and infinitely loving. He will always prove to be true no matter how much we investigate. And his purposes for us will always be tender no matter how much they might change us. We don't ever have to be afraid of what might happen if we open our minds to learn the truth about ourselves. We might find ourselves dramatically — and Hilariously — transformed.

Therefore:

1. What are some of the uniquenesses in God's creation of each of us?

2. How have we seen God change us as individuals and as a community over the last few months?

3. In what ways have we been afraid to be truly ourselves and how has this stifled our Hilarity?

4. How can we know that who we truly are will never violate God's principles?

5. How can the Hilarity of God's love set us free from the rules that our culture or family or others might want to impose upon us?

6. What means do we want to use to make more possible the renewing of our minds? On the other hand, how can we open our minds to greater truth and still avoid the over-objectivized, rationalistic scientism of our culture?

7. In what dimensions of our life as the people of God have we not been thinking thoroughly enough? What do we want to do to change that sloppy thinking?

6. The Constant Adventure of Discovering God's Will

Then you will be able to test and approve what God's will is . . .

— ROMANS 12:2c, NIV

TO ALL observers, my buying a three-story, five-bedroom house seemed insane. Ten years ago, however, that home provided an excellent means for me to pursue God's will.

My belief that it was God's will to buy the house was not simplistic. As I agonized over the need in Olympia, Washington, for a home for women in crisis, the Board of Christians Equipped for Ministry, under which I work, wrestled with me to discover God's guidance. Though now the particulars of my professional and personal situation have totally changed since the making of that decision, I could certainly see throughout the time that I owned the big house that God had led us in making the decision.

Probably one of the most frequently asked questions in Christian circles is the plea, "How do I know the will of God?" The topic is much too large for us to pursue thoroughly here,[1] but the issue is relevant for our search for love and Hilarity in a loveless and dispirited world. We can at least begin to overview some of the questions and a few of the answers.

Though we are studying Romans 12 in very small segments to learn about finding glad Hilarity in the Christian community, we must not lose sight of the connections between concepts. The phrase we are considering here must be carefully linked to the focus of the previous chapter: we are "able to test and approve what God's will is" primarily because we are in the process of becoming transformed by the renewing of our minds.

We are totally dependent upon the Holy Spirit's inspiration to discover and act on God's will. Conforming to anyone else's system won't enable us to find his will (although one of the greatest blessings of the Christian community is that the corporate work of all who share in the process can give us helpful clarity). Rather, we learn God's desires and purposes when we let him transform us from the inside out. Furthermore, we recall that God does his transforming work through the renewing of our minds. He teaches us about himself and his will through objective means. We don't discover it only subjectively, with our emotions, but also rationally, with our minds.

This contradicts at the outset a terrible heresy that confuses many Christians who are earnestly searching for God's will. Some think that God reveals it by some sort of hocus-pocus from the sky, that we must uncover some mystical or dramatic way to know his will. Misunderstandings about

1. For a more complete discussion of finding God's will I heartily recommend the following: Garry Friesen's book (with J. Robin Maxson) *Decision Making and the Will of God: A Biblical Alternative to the Traditional View* (Portland, OR: Multnomah Press, 1980); M. Blaine Smith's *Knowing God's Will: Biblical Principles on Guidance* (Downers Grove, IL: InterVarsity Press, 1979); and Philip Yancey's *Guidance* (Portland, OR: Multnomah Press, 1983).

signs (to be discussed later in this chapter) often lead to such misconceptions. Let us not forget this vital connection: our ability to test and approve the will of God comes directly out of his work to transform us by renewing our minds.

The link is underscored by the Greek structure of this sentence. Paul uses a Greek idiom to indicate purpose and thereby stresses that an outcome of the Spirit's transforming renewal of our minds is the consequent constant checking of God's will. The present continuing tense of the infinitive in the idiom emphasizes that the action is a process. Paul urges us and our communities to be constantly approving the Lord's will, to be continually matching up our attitudes with the reality of God's purposes.

The image here in Romans 12:2 challenges us to engage in a thorough process of testing. The wide divergence of translations of the verb hint at the breadth of the concept of this verb. The standard definition of "prove" (KJV and NASV) is paraphrased to "prove in practice" (JBP) or to "learn from your own experience" (LB); sometimes the translations emphasize that our proving makes us "able to know" (TEV) or to "discover" (JB) or "to discern" (NEB) or "to test and approve" (NIV) what God's will is.

For Paul's readers the Greek verb, *dokimazō*, signified, first of all, "to try to learn the genuineness of something by examination and testing, often through actual use." Paul uses the verb in this way in 1 Corinthians 3:13 and 11:28; 2 Corinthians 8:8, 22 and 13:5; and 1 Thessalonians 2:4. From this first meaning, the word came to connote the results of the examination, even as gold is proven. This is how 1 Peter 1:7 (NIV) uses the verb: "These [trials] have come so that your faith — of greater worth than gold, which perishes even though refined by fire — may be *proved* genuine and may result in praise, glory and honor when Jesus Christ is revealed" (emphasis added).

Furthermore, the result of the examination might be

that the person doing the testing regards something as being "worthwhile" or "appropriate," "genuine" or "good." This seems to be the primary sense in which Paul uses the verb in other places in the letter to the Romans. We gain insight into Paul's use of the verb in chapter 12 and its implications for finding God's will when we see his progression of thought in the whole book.

Paul first uses the verb *dokimazō* in Romans 1:28 in an idiomatic expression describing the refusal of those with depraved minds to acknowledge God. In contrast, in 2:18 he repeats the verb in his criticism of those who know God's will and "approve" of what is superior because they have been instructed by God's laws, but who yet fail to keep the law perfectly and do not trust the gospel for salvation. Romans 12:2, then, offers a great contrast to the preceding two groups, for now Paul is writing about the Christian community — those who are testing and approving of God's will as they are transformed by the renewal of their minds. Finally, Paul uses the verb again in 14:22, where he proclaims the well-being of the one "who does not condemn himself in what he approves" — that is, one who has the proper understanding of the relationship between weak and strong Christians and of matters of conscience within the Christian community.

In Philippians 1:10 Paul uses this same verb to emphasize the process of finding out "the things that are excellent" so that his readers may "be sincere and blameless until the day of Christ." Thus, this word's whole field of meaning — to "test," to "regard as worthwhile," and "to judge as good" — seems to be implied when Paul chooses the verb for the process of Romans 12:2. He asserts that as we experience our transformation by the Holy Spirit's renewing of our minds, we will be enabled thereby to examine and accept for our own lives what the will of God is. The New International Version includes both of these options in its translation of the verb as "test and approve."

The two paraphrases noted above, the Living Bible and Phillips' Modern English, place a significant emphasis upon experience and practice, which are included in the meaning of this verb. To approve God's will implies living it out. When we test it thoroughly, we discover that to live in the center of God's gracious will is the only way to be truly satisfied. After all, because he created the shape into which we are being transformed, he must know what is best for us. We will experience the Hilarity of true freedom only when we live according to the shape of our design.

However, we cannot rely merely on experience without the prior renewing of our minds. The order must be kept straight. With grief I watched several friends make terrible mistakes because they "felt" that God was leading them to do certain things, and no persuasion could move them from those feelings. We must remember that feelings are not reliable sources for wisdom; they can be too easily deceived, especially if we are highly emotional persons or if we are coming from intense pain or struggles that affect our emotional judgment.

This is the major danger in misunderstanding "signs." Any outcome of a sign can be twisted to fit our own emotional needs. Surely our prior expectations affect the way we observe the evidences of signs.

Gideon's use of the fleece for signs to know Yahweh's will is often held up as a good model. However, we must read carefully the entire story of God's call to him in Judges 6. By means of the rational statements God had given, Gideon should have been able to accept Yahweh's will and to act upon it. However, he needed some further confirmation, and God, in his tender love, did what he asked regarding the fleece in order to help him become more sure that to go into battle against the Midianites was really his assignment.

In the same way, by intelligent processes, in which the

Holy Spirit is a powerful influence (but in which also our brains are actively at work and in which the whole community takes part), we discern what God would have us do in a particular situation. If signs are added, they provide excellent confirmations of what God is already teaching us. However, signs are too flimsy and too easily misconstrued for them to be the primary means by which we choose what to believe about the will of God.

In the example with which this chapter began, a rational process of Scripture study, prayer, and observation of the needs in the Olympia community led to the decision to purchase a big house in which we could minister to lonely and depressed women. After that decision had been reached, it was confirmed by many signs — the closing of the deal on the house, the truly miraculous gathering of the money that I needed for the down payment.[2] Eventually a Catholic Worker house, Bread and Roses, was founded to meet the needs we had observed. In the meanwhile our year-long crisis ministry helped me to understand those needs better and to discover my role, not as a house director meeting them directly, but as a teacher calling attention to them. God's guidance throughout the whole process was confirmed by the wonderful developments of the situation.

Furthermore, we must recognize that much of our difficulty in finding the Lord's will arises from the panic that engulfs us as we search for it. We get desperate, thinking that we are going to fail and mess up our lives forever.

Characteristically, this symptom of panic emerges because we put ourselves under such performance principles. We act as though our decisions will affect adversely the way

2. The whole story is told in my book *To Walk in the Kingdom: God's Call to Discipleship from Luke 12* (Chappaqua, NY: Christian Herald Books, 1981).

God feels about us and how he will treat us, as if the failure to find his will might cut us off from him forever.

We must go back again and again to the Hilarious truth of who God is. He has already recorded his approval of us, as Chapters 1 and 3 emphasized. We are never condemned because Christ Jesus has secured for us our relationship with God. His cross also secures for us his loving presence and empowerment in our constant struggle to live out the implications of that relationship.

What kind of God do we have? Does he sit up in heaven arbitrarily choosing to keep us in the dark? Does he hide his purposes from us to make us grope through a gigantic guessing game with cosmic implications? Hardly! That's not the kind of God the Scriptures show ours to be. Rather, he reveals himself to us as a God who really wants us to know him, who indeed created us for intimacy with himself. Certainly, then, he would make it possible for us to know the best way to maintain that relationship with him (see Chapter 7).

God wants us to know his will. If we start with that fact, we will be set free from the panic of trying to find it. We will trust that in his time he will make his will known to us by both objective and subjective means. Perhaps we will discover it only at the time that we must know, but we can believe him for his revelation. It will not come a moment too late.

The prophet Habakkuk in his search for answers to questions about the justice of God records this comforting assurance from Yahweh:

"For the vision is yet for the appointed time;
     It hastens toward the goal, and it will not fail.
Though it tarries, wait for it;
     For it will certainly come, it will not delay."

(Hab. 2:3)

The vision in Habakkuk's time concerned specifically the ending of injustice in Israel by means of the Babylonian captivity. We can be assured that not only that event but all things within the plan of God come in their appointed times — never too late or too early. Just at the right moment when we need to know, we will know — provided we are open to God's action in our lives and his renewing of our minds. Then we can approve it for our own lives and live it out with confidence and Hilarity.

The passage from Habakkuk has been especially comforting to me because of the vivid image it contains. The second line of the text says literally in the Hebrew that the vision "pants after its own fulfillment." Just as a dog pants in eager anticipation of a time of play, so the purposes of God are eager to be accomplished and will surely be culminated. We need not panic as we wait for God's timing, for his revelation, for the effecting of his will.

Finally, one terribly overlooked aspect of testing and approving the will of God is that we do that within the framework of the Christian community and not alone. I first learned about searching together with other Christians for the will of God from members of a Mennonite congregation to which I belonged while working on my doctoral program in South Bend, Indiana. Confronted with a difficult decision, I asked my pastor for counsel, and he called a "meeting to discern the Spirit." Having never experienced that before, I was overwhelmed by the graciousness of several congregational members who spent an evening asking me questions to help me think, sorting things out and praying with me. By the end of the evening, God's will had become much more clear.

Myron and I experienced a similar, lovely enfolding in the Christian community when we were deciding whether to marry. We asked many friends — even some that we thought would disagree with the idea — to pray for us and for God's will in the matter. We urged them to ask us questions to help us think things through more clearly and requested that they share with us any messages that the Spirit led them to give. We spent two weeks gathering their input and found ourselves immensely surrounded by love and caring, wisdom and profound searching. Every person responded favorably and supportively, so we knew that our future marriage would have immense prayer support. In the counsel of the Christian community, we believed that we knew more clearly what the will of God was for our friendship and future.

I will never again make a major decision alone. Certainly God's will can be more clearly perceived when many hearts are attuned to the Holy Spirit. One of my major goals in seeking to strengthen the Christian community is to bring back to other denominations this gift of mutual decision making and mutual searching for God's will — so that we may discover the Hilarity of testing and approving it together.

Moreover, as we discover God's will within the community, we find greater motivation to pursue it. Ultimately, we do have a choice. God doesn't cram his will down our throats. But you know as well as I do that his will always turns out to be the best for us. To that concept we will turn in the following chapter. Meanwhile, we can delight today in the strong assurance that God does indeed want us to know his will. Therefore, we can trust that in appropriate ways — especially within the framework of the Christian community — he will enable us to discover it and to be transformed to approve it.

Therefore:

1. Does our Christian community seek God's will together? How could we develop the practice?

2. How have we experienced God's guidance by the renewing of our minds?

3. What means does God use to renew our minds?

4. How have we as individuals or corporately misunderstood his will by depending on signs that were too much influenced by our own emotional perceptions — or, conversely, by being too rational and ignoring the Spirit?

5. What protection do we have against formulating misconceptions of God's will in our minds — or in our emotions?

6. How does it help us to know that God does want us to know his will?

7. How have we experienced the Hilarity of living out God's will in the sense of approving it?

7. The Goodness of God's Will

> . . . his good, pleasing and perfect will.
>
> — ROMANS 12:2d, NIV

LIVING IN OUR community house ten years ago was good for me. One night before going to sleep, my housemate Julie came down for awhile to talk and pray. As she was leaving my basement study she suddenly began to sing, "Abide with us, oh Lord, for it is now the evening. The day is past and over." I picked up the canon when she got to the second line. There we stood in the middle of the study — uplifted by a song of prayer.

Now I am newly married, and it's so good for me! My husband was busy all day today planting flower bulbs to make our home beautiful next spring. When I took a break from writing, for a few moments together we enjoyed laughing at a radio program, and he encouraged me in my work by the assurance of his love.

How do we know what is good for us? The answer is easy for such positive things as relationships with Julie and with my husband. However, many — if not most — of the aspects of our lives are not simply matters of clear-cut lines of demarcation. Learning to discern how God's will is good, pleasing, and perfect requires an entire chapter so that we might continue to pursue here a Hilarious communitarian life-style according to the pattern of those three characteristics.

By a careful building of biblical principles in this chapter, we will delineate concepts of good and evil and of God's will on several levels. Thereby, prayerfully, we will gain greater insight into how God reveals his will for our lives and how we can bear with the suffering that comes because we live in a marred world, cut apart from his good and perfect will.

On the simplest level, first of all, we recognize readily that certain things are good and other things are evil. Good things can be described by such adjectives as *fit, useful, beneficial, right, morally pure, appropriate,* or *kind.* We can easily think of all sorts of examples. Right now as I write I am listening to a beautiful symphony by Rachmaninoff. The musicians are good — they play their instruments right, in accordance with the music. My radio is good — it works properly to pick up the sound waves. My computer is good — it is beneficial for putting these words down on paper faster and with greater legibility than if I wrote in my scrawl, which is not good. Besides, if I wrote by hand, I would probably experience more pain because the skin of my fingers is cracked and will bleed. Bodily breakdown is not good.

Supper will soon be ready; my good husband is preparing it so that I can continue working. The homemade soup that he is warming will taste good and is good for us. Cake certainly would taste good, but just as certainly consuming extra sugar would not be good for us.

These are simple examples, but we must start with such a process of recognizing the basic good or evil of things, as well as the fact that some things not necessarily bad in themselves are not good for a particular individual. Criteria must be carefully chosen to help us assess what is good for us and what is not.

Second, we must remember that God is the Creator of all good. Things that are not good are not part of his design. This point is often misconstrued — with terrible heresies as the result. Pain, sickness, suffering, and death are not part of God's original plan for his creation. Those things were introduced when human beings tried to make themselves gods. The potential for evil is inherent in the possibility of choice for good — but God is not its perpetrator.

So, for example, eyes are inherently a good gift from God, but one of mine has become blind because of retinal hemorrhaging. This problem was not created by God; I do not thank him for its existence in my life. But I can thank him for all the good things he has brought out of the situations that arise because of my visual limitations.

That is the third point. Those who are believers know that God can take even those things that are not good, that are contrary to his perfect designs, and turn them into good things in the midst of his purposes. Paul emphasizes this earlier in Romans when he declares that "we know that God causes all things to work together for good to those who love God, to those who are called according to His purpose" (8:28). The emphasis that God *causes* all things to work together for good solidly battles against the heresy that all things *are* good for the Christian. Indeed, part of our Hilarity is knowing that God is able to take the things that are not good and work them together so that good might come out of them.

Now, fourth, we must consider our choices. Our freedom as persons (rather than instinctive creatures) enables us constantly to choose between that which is God's good will and that which is not. When we choose to follow God's will for us, we know that it will be good. He who made us knows what is good for us.

However, fifth, we sometimes mischoose. Others sometimes do, too, and their choices affect us adversely. We live in a selfish world, and the result of that sickness is frequent mischoice. We are not perfectly wise, and sometimes we make tragic mistakes. Usually the choices themselves are impossibly difficult, between various shades of gray rather than simple black-and-white decisions. When we choose what is contrary to God's plan, we pick what is not good, and the results are pain, unhappiness, grief, death. God's people can be greatly comforted by the assurance that his love is great enough to transform even those things into that which can become good.

These last several points have become very clear to me through the past three years because of a physical disability. When I originally injured my foot, its problems did not show up on X rays, so doctors had a difficult time diagnosing the malady. Because it seemed that expanded blood vessels were making my foot swell so abnormally, I was told to walk as much as possible to keep the blood circulating. Tragically, miles of walking pushed several foot bones 90 degrees sideways, and the result was several months in casts and then several more months in a cumbersome brace. Finally, more than a year after the original injury, a specialist in Seattle reconstructed my foot by totally eliminating the middle bones and screwing the metatarsals to my heel. In three months the foot healed miraculously — only to have my leg break as soon as I began putting weight on my left side!

Perhaps you have struggled, too, with the deep depression and sorrow that accompany our various human troubles. Sometimes I have struggled with great grief over the loss of easy walking, with fear because amputation remains a possibility, with despair at this continued breakdown of my body. Perhaps you have experienced other tragedies that have led to long, dark nights of sobbing grief, frantic groping toward some sort of hope, and a profound despair, accentuated by terrible fears that you will not be able to survive the pain. In our moments of great sorrow only the tender love of God as it comes to us through his people and the Scriptures can give us the courage to go on.

The greatness of God's love is that even when his best plans are spoiled, he can still bring much good. Though I grieve over the shattered state of my foot and leg, I can see now that God has used the times of discouragement to draw me closer to himself. Surely, he has also taught me many things about ministry to the physically challenged through my own frustration with the terrible things that people said to me when my situation looked hopeless.

That is why we can be sure, when we are God's, that even in the midst of turmoil we can experience good. Whatever is of God is good. Furthermore, whatever is good is pleasing to him. For example, when I am very deeply discouraged over the situation of my body, the good is to choose to trust God to care for me. His will is for me to depend on him, and when I choose the good of faith, he is pleased. I don't always trust him, however, and when I don't, I have chosen to experience my own hopelessness and fears about the future. If I could trust him, then I would experience his peace and hope and love even in the midst of pain.

On the other side, I had to learn that grieving can be good. Mourning over what should not be is right and beneficial; grief brings the goodness of God's healing. Our sorrow over various mischoices in our milieu pleases God, for we share in his pain. That is why Jesus said, "Blessed are those who mourn, for they shall be comforted" (Matt. 5:4). Anguish is not good in itself, of course, but its effects on our spiritual growth are.

That leads to the last point we must distinguish in order to bring together all three characteristics of this chapter. God's will is perfect. We are not. We will never be thoroughly

60

successful at choosing and approving his perfect will. We are not able to discern his perfect will in all the murky choices that confront us. Our actions and choices will never be totally pleasing to him because we can never live out what is good. Yet the fact of his perfect will determines our direction. As we live towards the goal of his desires, we experience his good things, what is pleasing to him, and the perfection that he designed — though to a limited extent. Someday when we are made completely whole, we will know the perfection of his will. Meanwhile, our proving it does not make God's will good. Rather, in our testing it, we discover its goodness. We want to choose it, and that pleases him. We long for the final perfection of his will in our lives.

We are, indeed, groaning for maturity. The Greek word translated "perfect" is an expansion of the root that means "to bring to the finish." The root verb is used to record Jesus' cry from the cross that his work of suffering was finished. Paul uses the expanded form to describe the maturity to which God is leading us in our faith. We can finish certain tasks in this world, but we who are sinners can never do them perfectly. God's will is that total perfection toward which we move, but at which we will never arrive in this life. However, his will always provides the goal, the direction in which to walk.

This understanding of God's good, pleasing, and perfect will must be applied very practically to the nitty-gritty situations of our daily lives, and this is especially the arena in which the Christian community is immensely important. Because our world is so marred by sin and so many things run contrary to God's perfect designs, we need each other for encouragement and hope. We can help one another to sort through options, to search for the ways in which God will bring good out of evil, to share the Hilarity of serving God even in the midst of trying circumstances.

For example, my housemate Julie came home from

work right in the middle of the first writing of this chapter and cried with me over her job situation, which was not good at that time. She had not been able to find permanent employment that used her artistic gifts, and so she was deeply frustrated that her life's work had been so disappointing.

I grieved with Julie that she hadn't been able to find a job in art. However, the fact that God is not the author of that which is not good gives us a different perspective with which to sort through such situations.

The fact that God's design for the world is spoiled is seen in the meaninglessness of many persons' jobs. As Julie and I prayed about her situation, we had to keep reminding each other that the difficulty of her situation was not God's plan for good, but that he could bring good out of it. We had to cling to hope that those difficult times, too, could be valuable in making Julie the beautiful person God has designed her to be. Furthermore, Julie could choose to do that which is pleasing to God, to accept her present not-good situation with a peace that would reveal God's love to those around her. She could find many ways to minister to others through her own pain and frustration. Thus, what is not good can be lived out in dependence upon God, which is pleasing to him. Furthermore, as she chose attitudes from him, such as hope and confidence in his best purposes, she would experience the good Hilarity that such trust could bring into her life.

Someday God's more perfect will might be available to Julie. We continue to pray for, and to seek, a job requiring her gifts. In the meanwhile, her pain can be assuaged only by the comfort of knowing that God can bring good even out of this time and by the support of a caring Christian community.

Certainly we realize that God's bringing good out of evil does not mean that we continue forever putting up with that which is evil. However, it does give us the courage to endure suffering until things can be changed into good. In the Christian community we search for ways both to change things and to support one another in the trials of the meanwhile. Glad Hilarity is actually possible because we never stand alone. We can laugh in the face of our afflictions because we are a people together seeking God's good and perfect will and knowing the delight of pleasing God even in adverse circumstances.

The very practical questions of good and evil in light of God's will are not easily answered. We do ourselves and those in pain a great disservice if we skip over them too lightly. The greatest help we can give to those struggling to find God's will is to stand beside them in the struggle, to offer them his words of hope and comfort, and to surround them with his love through ours. Only the hope of knowing a God whose will is ultimately perfect and good can free us from the despair of fighting seemingly insurmountable evil.

This all takes us back to where we began: the Hilarity of receiving God's love, which transforms us as the Holy Spirit renews our minds. This also leads us forward to the hope that we will find in the next verses of Romans 12.

Therefore:

1. What criteria do we use to distinguish between good and evil? How would we define what makes something good?

2. How have we seen God work good things out of evil circumstances?

3. In what battles against which not-good things or situations are we presently involved?

4. Who that we know might need to hear the comforting assurance that God can bring good out of that which is not good, and how can we share the Hilarity of that hope and comfort in tangible ways?

5. In what ways have we made wrong choices that God has nevertheless turned into good for us?

6. How have we experienced the Hilarity of knowing that we have been choosing that which is God's good, pleasing, and perfect will?

7. How might we learn in the Christian community to work together more in sorting out gray options in order to see more clearly God's perfect will?

8. Thinking into a Sane Assessment

> For by the grace which has been given to me, I say to each one who is among you not to be thinking more highly [of yourself] than it is necessary to think, but rather to be thinking for the purpose of sane thinking, as God has assigned to each one a measure of faith.
>
> — ROMANS 12:3

FOR ALL ITS EMPHASIS on thinking, our society is certainly not very good at it. For all its talk about processing information, our culture does not demonstrate much wisdom. Consider for a minute all our idiomatic expressions, such as these, that refer to thinking:

> Let me think a minute. He's a thinking man. The "think tank" . . . Why don't you think about it? I'm sorry; I just wasn't thinking. When will you learn to think? Go take a think! As a man thinketh, so he is. I'm having a hard time thinking. What do you think of her? I'm so tired I can't think. A penny for your thoughts.

How people think is the basis for who they become. The Christian community offers an alternative to our paradoxically over-objectivized and yet mindless society if we are able to think well about who we are and our purposes in life. The Christian community thinks well because it thinks corporately and wholistically with mind and heart and Spirit.

The value of good thinking is underscored in this third verse from Romans 12 by four occurrences in one sentence of various forms of the basic verb *to think*. The importance of the mind as it is renewed in the transforming process has already been stressed in the previous verse, but now Paul goes on to explain why one's basic thinking is so critical for self-discovery and for the unity and cooperation and Hilarity of the community of God's people.

The extreme importance of what Paul is about to say is anticipated by his introductory phrase, "by the grace given to me I say to every one of you." Two aspects of this formula increase its impact.

Notice, first, that Paul speaks by grace — God's overflowing, infinitely wise love, freely given, though undeserved and never repayable. Paul thus declares that his forthcoming message is not his own conviction, but comes from outside himself. The very fact that Paul humbly describes his message as created by grace indicates the forcefulness and authority he wants it to carry.

This phrase in Paul is comparable to the formula of the Hebrew prophets, who proclaimed, "Thus saith the LORD." In the three chapters before this twelfth chapter of Romans, Paul had been emphasizing the faithfulness of the covenant God of Israel; Yahweh continued to keep his promises to his people. That constant care for the Jews is but one dimension of the infinite love that has been a theme throughout the book of Romans. Grace has been the key to all the mysteries of the book, ever since the greeting of the letter (Rom. 1:1, 5, and 7) and especially since the announcement of the epistle's theme in 1:16-17, which describes grace's action. The great freedom of God's love, as opposed to the slavery and death of human attempts to create a relationship with God, has continuously undergirded the Hilarity of grace that Paul has been unfolding throughout the whole discourse of Romans.

Now he applies that grace specifically to his own ministry and stresses that the exhortation he is about to deliver derives from the same source. With grace he gives it; with grace the Romans are to receive it.

Second, Paul specifies that he is proclaiming the following message to every one of the Roman Christians. The accent on the individual in connection with the message that follows might imply that there were certain problems among the Roman Christians — petty jealousies, feelings of inferiority, or the false elevation of certain more prominent individuals. We do know from the fourteenth chapter of the epistle that there was a conflict specifically between "the weak" and "the strong." Consequently, Paul firmly insists that each Roman believer must hear and apply this word of truth. Each person will contribute to the community of faith by learning to think appropriately.

Paul's message certainly must be a critical one since he took such great care to introduce it. Basically, the message is composed of these three parts: (1) that Christians should not be too proud, (2) that Christians need to have a healthy assessment of themselves, and (3) that the criterion by which such thinking can be accurately done is one's measure of faith.

First, each one of us needs at various times the admonition not to think of ourselves more highly than we ought, not to have an "unwarranted" or "exaggerated opinion of [our] importance." Constantly we are tempted to make ourselves gods, to place ourselves at the center of everything, to give ourselves more credit than we deserve (since actually everything exists by the *grace* of God). Probably we have already been adequately (or perhaps overly!) warned against pride, so we simply need here a brief reminder not to get a swollen head about things.

However, a phrase in the original sentence, which usually isn't rendered well in our English translations, modifies the statement somewhat. The Greek phrase says literally, "not to be thinking more highly than *it is necessary* [or 'proper' or 'binding'] to think." In light of what we will read in the next phrase, this one hints at the fact that *to some degree* it *is* proper and necessary to think highly of oneself. One must be careful, however, lest those thoughts get out of perspective, over and above what it is appropriate to think.

Then the second phrase offers this strong contrast: "but [greatly to the contrary] to be thinking toward a sane thinking." The word I translated "sane thinking" involves "good sense, sound judgment," "understanding about practical matters," the ability to "be sensible." We might paraphrase this exhortation, "but don't think more lowly of yourself than you ought to, either." In this technological age when the necessity for efficiency and the deficiency of intimacy cause a great proportion of people to suffer from a low sense of self-esteem, perhaps this side of Paul's admonition needs to be more carefully heeded. In fact, counselors discover that most cases of seeming pride in persons actually derive from great insecurities and lack of self-esteem.

A friend of mine once outlined the structure of Romans 12:1-8 according to the recipients of the gift of ourselves. He had noticed that the first two verses of Romans 12 speak of giving ourselves to God; verses 4 and 5 describe giving ourselves to the people of God; and verses 6 to 8 summarize giving ourselves to our ministries. Verse 3, however, is a necessary prerequisite to those last two sections, for it emphasizes giving ourselves to ourselves. We are encouraged to "try to have a sane estimate" of our "capabilities" (JBP) that acknowledges our worth as valuable persons in God's plan for the whole community. This verse gives us the Hilarity to give ourselves to others.

The balance defined by this third verse is determined by the grace in which we stand and the grace out of which Paul speaks. God's undeserved love reminds us that we are nothing except for what God does in and through and for us. Consequently, we dare not think of ourselves more highly than we ought, than we are compelled to think by what the facts warrant. On the other hand, that same grace also chose us, each of us uniquely, for special ministries within the community. Therefore, we dare not think of ourselves more lowly than we ought or our service will not be as effective as it could be.

"Think for the purpose of thinking sanely," Paul says literally. The Jerusalem Bible captures this emphasis with its rendering, "Think your way to a sober estimate." We are challenged to undertake a process of critical analysis to know appropriately our capabilities and how God might use them.

Unfortunately, the idea of a "sober estimate" might connote to us a straight-faced, tight-lipped, puritanical judgment of who we are. The phrase seems to imply that if we are going to assess ourselves realistically we will be stern with ourselves and not let our pride get out of hand. Such an attitude in our church circles has resulted in a loss of the Hilarity that could come when, with sane judgment, we discover the uniqueness of our special creation. I know very few Christians who are delighted with who they are.

Of course, not one of us is satisfied with our spiritual progress. I'm not advocating a smug complacency without repentance. Truly, as our spiritual sensitivities get more and more refined, we know all too precisely how much we fail to be the people God designed us to be.

However, our times seem to need a greater emphasis on the other side of the picture. Our society is desperately searching for people with a sense of adventure and Hilarity, those who feel good about themselves and delight in their own capabilities and visions and gifts. Truly, we who are God's people are the only ones that have the potential to be so delightfully free. With sane judgment we discover that we are specially created, which should fill us with Hilarity, rather than overwhelm us with a weighty burden.

This is especially important to me because my husband so richly affirms who I am, in spite of my failures and memories of rejection. Not only does his encouragement uplift me personally, but his appreciation brings more power and creativity and Hilarity to my teaching and studying. Life is more FUN.

Is that an inappropriate word for the people of God? Why isn't the Christian community more characterized by the FUN that could be ours as we delight in the exquisite creation of God? Why are we so afraid to go full tilt into life? Where is the Hilarity of sane thinking?

Of course, the Christian life is not without strain and suffering and hard work and difficulties. Nevertheless, when we learn to have a healthy appreciation of who we are, life will certainly never be boring. God will constantly be unfolding to us new dimensions of the mysteries of ourselves.

Perhaps we don't delight in ourselves because we assess our own worth by comparing ourselves to others. If we pick out people who are inferior to us in certain ways, we will think more highly of ourselves than we ought to think. If we look at all the people who surpass us, we will think more lowly of ourselves than we ought to think. I used to teach that the proper balance could be sought by individually thinking of *ourselves;* I emphasized that the criterion for sane thinking is not the measure of others, but an honest assessment of our unique creation (therefore think highly) as children of God, whose love has made our specialness (therefore don't think too highly).

However, the emphasis on community throughout Romans 12 changed my mind. We usually read these sentences with minds afflicted with the crass individualism that pervades our society. Verse 3 is thus translated and interpreted that way — without adequate attention to the cotext or context.

If we read verse 3 within the cotext of the whole discourse about offering our Christian communities as a sacrifice to God and within the context of the society at the time when Paul wrote — which was not characterized by the heavy emphasis on the individual that predominates in our culture — then we will discover that the solution to false thinking about ourselves is to think about the entire "ourselves," the community as a whole. Before we try to figure out who we are as individuals, we need to think sanely about what it means to be the people of God (which is exactly what we are doing in this book!).

Furthermore, the community as a whole helps each one of us as individuals to think into a sane estimate. Understanding ourselves according to our particular place as a part of the whole Body, none of us would have any basis for pride. On the other hand, each would recognize his or her absolute necessity in the Body. Unless you are there, your particular function is missing. I need you; you are the only one who can fill your place in our community.

Thus, we could all help each other find a better balance between the extremes of pride and low self-esteem. Sanely estimating our gifts and potentials together would increase our eagerness to contribute our own unique functions to the wholeness of the Body — and the whole community would experience greater Hilarity in celebrating together who we are as the people of God.

These results (and the many others considered in this book) are certainly worth the strain involved in working together. Of course, community involves a lot of struggle, but the model of Romans 12 offers us hope and vision for what could happen if the people of God really took these verses seriously.

In the Church we explore our sense of self together. We are who we are as individuals because of our place in the whole. Such a sense of place and identity *because of the community* does not characterize the world around us — but it gives us, as Christians together, the glad Hilarity that we offer to those dissatisfied by our culture's frenzy of having to prove oneself.

The Christian community sets us free from comparing ourselves with others and having to prove our own importance. Instead, the basic criterion for assessing our worth is "the measure of faith God has given." Paul uses the Greek word *metron* here to signify a measuring instrument or standard, not a measured quantity.[1] We don't compare our different kinds of faith to see whose is greater or smaller; instead, the certain measure of faith that we each have is the standard by which we think about our unique participation in the Body. The fact that all of us have our own particular measure of faith to offer connects us vitally to each other — with equal importance.

Jesus stresses this in Luke 17 when the disciples respond to his words about forgiveness with the plea, "Lord, increase our faith." Jesus answers that with faith the size of a mustard seed one could command a mulberry tree to be uprooted and moved (17:1-10). The discourse proceeds to talk about obedience and demonstrates that the question is not how much faith we have, but whether or not we are being obedient with what we have.

Similarly, Paul's exhortation to the Roman Christians urges us to assess realistically our individual standard of

---

1. Leon Morris, *The Epistle to the Romans* (Grand Rapids: William B. Eerdmans, 1988), p. 438 n. 31.

faith, appropriate to our place in the community. Thinking sanely together encourages each of us to live fully in accordance with our own measure, in the Hilarity of being truly ourselves.

My friendship with Tim illustrates this principle well. My perspectives on the Scriptures come primarily from study and translation while his come more from long hours of meditation. I don't have nearly the depth of trust that he has, but a sane assessment of our unique measures enables us each to offer the other gifts of insights without jealousy or inferiority.

Finally, the declaration that God assigns our particular measure of faith sets us free from another heresy that we must continually combat. Several years ago I was told that my eyes had not been healed because my faith was not strong enough. I spent several months thereafter begging God to give me more faith and agonizing to crank it up. None of the miracles of Jesus demonstrates that he healed according to the size of people's faith. Furthermore, we limit God too much if we seek only physical healing. How God answers our prayers for healing does not depend on our being able to crank up enough faith to convince him to change our physical situation. Such a reductionistic notion of healing misses many of the lessons that God wants to teach us about his wholistic healing, his sovereignty, and our need to grow in faith and hope.

We must never forget who assigns our particular measure. Who are we to question God's decisions? Jesus said, "From everyone who has been given much shall much be required, and to whom they entrusted much, of him they will ask all the more" (Luke 12:48). We are silly to be jealous of someone who seems to have been given more without realizing that of that person more is asked. God knows how much we can handle and has, therefore, given us each the appropriate measure of faith to serve him most fully.

How delightful to know the wisdom with which God assigns our measure of faith. God is not arbitrary or malicious. Everywhere in the Scriptures he is revealed as a God who knows what is best for us. In accordance with his good and pleasing and perfect will (see the previous chapter), he has given us the right measure of faith and calls us to be Hilariously realistic about it — together with other members of the Body of faith.

What a freedom not ever to have to be like anybody else! We can honestly pour ourselves into being who we are within the whole of the community because we know that no one else can do the particular ministry to which God has individually called us. Yet we cannot do that unless the whole community takes care to think sanely about how we can offer ourselves together. And we cannot offer ourselves except for God's grace. Once again we have come full circle.

With grace Paul began, speaking out of his own call and faith from God. Now his exhortation reaches out to touch us with a proper sense of realism, a sane thinking that sees with Hilarity the particularly grace-full appropriateness of our unique measure of faith within the Christian community as a whole.

Therefore:

1. Why does Paul use such an elaborate introductory formula for the message of this verse?

2. Which do we need to hear more today — a warning against pride or an invitation to a better sense of self-worth? Why?

3. What things cause us to be too proud about who we are?

4. In what dimensions of our existence do we think too lowly of ourselves?

5. How can we find a good balance in our assessment of ourselves and our capabilities? How would this increase our Hilarity?

6. How would we describe the unique measure of faith that God has given us as individuals? What are some of its qualities?

7. How does our unique individual measure of faith fit in with the whole of the community? How could we as a community work together more to assess sanely the way in which our individual measures of faith support and undergird each other?

9. The Benefits of Genuine Community

> For just as we have many members in one body, and
> all the members do not have the same function, so we,
> who are many, are one body in Christ . . .
>
> — ROMANS 12:4-5a, NASV

PEOPLE IN THE LOCKER ROOM would shake their heads in disbelief.

While she and I discussed orders for teaching tapes or transportation arrangements, my secretary Sandy would take care of my feet after our daily swimming workouts. Because of my visual handicap and susceptibility to infections, she would check for wounds and cut my nails. We were rather a strange ministry team; sometimes Sandy even packed my suitcase or cleaned my house so that I could study longer before she took me to the bus station for speaking trips.

Similarly, when we were using my house for the CEM crisis ministry, a visitor to our home thought that it was unfair for Julie to have the whole top floor to herself. Whereas others had only a bedroom for their own space, Julie also had an art studio. "She should pay more rent," the visitor exclaimed. She didn't understand that in our Christian community Julie had extra space because she needed it to use her gifts freely. We wanted to provide her with plenty of room for her painting.

How rarely it is truly understood in the Church that we are really all together one Body in Christ, and each member has a different function! To our great loss, the idea of unity in diversity in the Christian community is often talked about as a nice theory, but rarely put into practice. We all can see how wonderful the pictures of the Scriptures are, but the friction comes when we try to put them into tangible relationships and structures. Seldom do we actually manifest true unity/diversity in the Body, and, therefore, rarely do we set one another free for functioning in our own unique ways.

For example, how are Sunday school teachers recruited in your congregation? Your parish might be a bright exception, but frequently Christian education committees panic whenever there aren't enough. "We've got to get more Sunday school teachers," they exclaim, and then they corner people with the force of "You've got to teach; we need you." Distressingly, the result is that many teach under duress, out of obligation, without Hilarity. Or what about officers for your women's group or congregation? Is it tough to get them? Does gathering enough names to fill the ballot cause a major hassle?

Perhaps in some parishes superintendents should cancel Sunday school rather than utilize persons not eager to teach. Maybe the women's group should disband. Should the congregation dispense with officers and committee members? The pressure to fill all the "necessary" positions sometimes tears down the Body and prohibits any true sense of community or any Hilarity in serving out of one's truest self.

Another manifestation of the lack in understanding of

true community is the fact that some functions are thought to be more important than others. Why do the noticeable, up-front positions usually receive the affirmation and thanks? Those who do the tasks behind the scenes are often not appreciated for their immense contribution to the functioning of the whole Body.

This chapter is tremendously important to me because in many ways for the last twelve years in Christians Equipped for Ministry we have been experiencing "body-ness" as Paul pictures it. The results in CEM make us realize how much more Hilarious the Church could be if it were a true community.

In the first place, let's return to the *therefore* that began this book. It is only "with our eyes wide open to the mercies of God" that we can begin to learn to be a community together. Romans 12:4-5a stresses that we are "one body *in* Christ*.*" Because of our vital union with him, we find our places in the Body. Because each member of the CEM Board lives in relationship to the same Christ, we can corporately work at developing our Christian community. A basic principle of CEM has always been that we exist to serve Christ; his Lordship determines how we are brought together and made into a whole.

Another of the founding goals of CEM was that all decisions should be made by total consensus, and our various presidents throughout the years have superbly in-sisted on gathering everyone's opinion so that we have the best possibility of hearing the Holy Spirit's guidance. We turn matters over to prayer when we do not unanimously agree on a decision.

One of the longest-serving board members has been especially good at rebuking me. One new member of the board has a much-needed skill in analyzing problems and applying his business savvy. Our first vice-president was an outstanding woman of prayer, and now another member of the board especially loves to give that vitally necessary intercessory support. Another board member very quietly adds wise perspectives at critical times, and still another wrote an excellent letter to our prayer supporters when we hit a financial crisis.

We have been especially delighted by the way in which God has provided gifts for the working of our community as the ministry has expanded. For the first three years our secretary Sandy handled all the finances on a volunteer basis. She also recorded all my lectures, duplicated the tapes, mailed out books, ran errands, prayed with me, drove me places, and even mowed my lawn so I could study and write. Now I live in another city, so we work together from a distance, and another person takes care of the expanded tape ministry, but still Sandy uses her gifts of administration to set me free to teach and write.

Imagine what would happen if our congregations truly functioned by means of each person offering his or her gifts to the working together of the whole, if we all understood ourselves not so much as individual Christians but as members within the framework of the unity of the Body. For example, envision how much more our pastors could concentrate on the Word and prayer (see Acts 6:2-4) if we could set them free from all the "administrivia" that bogs them down. Or perhaps congregational members who have gifts for compassion and mercy could focus on some of the pastoral calling so that a professional worker could be free to use his or her gifts more effectively in other areas. Each person contributing his or her special gifts to the whole in the Christian community would create so much Hilarity — like the glad exuberance I saw last night when a chamber music ensemble so much enjoyed performing their unique individual parts together in a Brahms' string sextet that they burst into grins as they played.

This is a visionary chapter. Dream with me about the

tremendous vitality and Hilarity the Church would have if those capable of particular functions eagerly volunteered to offer their gifts so that the whole community could be strengthened. We would never have to scramble to find secretaries, janitors, banner makers, singers, preachers, kitchen organizers, Sunday school teachers, youth counselors, officers, ushers, baby-sitters, or anything else.

Furthermore, apply the principle of "Body-ness" to our personal living situations so that we can reach out from them more effectively to the world. What would happen if Christians learned to live more closely together and to share more deeply in all the aspects of life? When we first established our EPHESUS Community for the crisis ministry, many brothers and sisters contributed their gifts to help us take care of our big house. One good friend chopped down a huge tree for us and spent all day making firewood. Others remodeled the woodstove, cleaned and painted walls, redid our wiring systems, rehung the lights in my study, built new bookcases, rebuilt a lawn mower for our use, and baked food for our singles' fellowships. As I look back on those years, I am overwhelmed by the amount of work that was contributed to the EPHESUS Community by people willing to give of themselves to strengthen our ministry.

Most especially, the "body-ness" of our household came out when I was working on my book on the Psalms. For several weeks as I pounded away at the typewriter, other members of the household took over all of my chores so that I could be set free to finish the final draft. When each person contributes his or her functions to the whole, we find great freedom from a false guilt that others bear extra dimensions of the workload for a time.

Now imagine with me what could happen if more Christians began really to live as a community with each other. The good gardeners could help those who have black thumbs. Those who like to fix things could offer their services to those needing such assistance. Those who like to dance and sing could bring gaiety to everyone else in the community. (Sometimes, I'm afraid, we think that only the practical gifts are those that count in the strength of the Body. Yet those who teach us about color or texture, those who inspire us to greater sensitivity through their gentleness, those who uplift us with their music, those who understand story and drama and poetry and clowning enable the rest of us to find more Hilarity in our work. My husband is a great example.)

To work and share together more closely as a community is beneficial not merely for its own sake — although that certainly is sufficient reason to advocate it. Beyond that, the results of such sharing would increase the credibility of our message of Christianity. Diversities of gifts offer more possibilities for manifesting the presence of Christ in our midst and for being more open to all kinds of people. As Ernst Käsemann writes, "Christ takes possession of every status, every present capacity and weakness of his members. He uses the most divergent forms of discipleship symbolically to penetrate the world instead of withdrawing from it."[1]

Because the style of community in which all individual members contribute uniquely is so different from the conformity of our culture, the surprise it causes would lead to questions. Consequently, we would have new opportunities to tell others how the love of God draws all our diversities into unity.

In addition, our evangelistic opportunities would be coupled with greater social concern because of the economic interdependence that comes from genuine sharing of potential. We could save and redirect great amounts of money,

1. Ernst Käsemann, *Commentary on Romans,* trans. and ed. Geoffrey W. Bromiley (Grand Rapids: William B. Eerdmans, 1980), p. 339.

energy, and time by joining together in such ventures as gardening and maintaining whatever property is necessary for our lives and ministries.

We must all ask the question of how much is enough. How many things that we think we have to own could be shared in the Christian community — things like lawn mowers or ladders and other tools, food processors and preservers, even cars, laundry facilities, sports equipment, and so forth? Several friends in Seattle who have built their homes together as a community on a farm all share one big workshop and its tools. To learn to share in such ways would free up much more for the poor. The Church could reach out of its own functioning more effectively to create for others the means for survival as well as opportunities to use their gifts more freely.

So now what about you? The extent to which each of us can live with others as members in community will vary, but the challenge of being the Body of Christ to extend his presence in the world is a vital one for all of us in these times. Especially in this chapter I plead with you not to close this book with a mere "that was interesting." Let us take this chapter into our prayer times so that God can direct us into specific applications of its message in our personal lives and in the life of our churches. Studying the following questions by ourselves and with others will enable us to catch new visions for the meaning of the Body/community and for the Hilarity of being members one of another.

Therefore:

1. How have we experienced the glad Hilarity of the unity of the Body in our family or living situation?

2. How have we experienced the Hilarity of unity in our Christian congregation?

3. In what ways does our congregation fail to utilize the functions of its members?

4. How can we encourage our Christian community to take more seriously the importance of each member?

5. How can we share our particular functions with the Body of Christ more thoroughly?

6. How can we contribute our particular functions to upbuild the persons with whom we are closest (i.e., families or housemates or work colleagues)?

7. What economic resources for dealing with the hunger and poverty of the world could deeper "body-ness" in our communities free up?

10. Each Belonging to All

. . . and each member belongs to all the others.

— ROMANS 12:5b, NIV

WHEN I WAS a sophomore in high school, an epidemic of measles swept through our small-town school, and I chuckled a bit at being one of the victims since I had escaped them in childhood. After my bout with measles, however, my failure to recover was no laughing matter. I began to lose weight and strength. Once an active basketball player, I couldn't even get the ball up to the hoop. I became so thin and weak that my back bones cracked painfully on the gym floor when I fell down after sit-ups. Something was terribly wrong.

My thirst grew insane, and I ate like crazy. Still I kept getting weaker. My skin was dry; my color, nonexistent. I became an ugly shadow of myself with no flesh on my bones. Though 5'6" tall, I weighed only 84 pounds. Something was dreadfully wrong.

When we discovered that the measles virus had incapacitated my pancreas, all the symptoms suddenly made sense, and as soon as I was put on daily insulin injections all my other bodily functions began to serve me properly again. I had learned profoundly that each member in a body belongs to all the others. If one function is not being performed, the rest of the body suffers.

How little the Church truly understands that we actually belong to one another! How much power is short-circuited, how much Hilarity is lost because we have not learned, or are not free, or do not want to belong to each other?

The remaining chapters of this book will explore various manifestations of belonging to one another, so at this point we will concentrate on what blocks belongingness. If we recognize the forces that hinder our community, we can fight those obstructions more effectively. We can face the difficulties of choosing to be members one of another because we anticipate the great Hilarity our communities will experience as more and more belongingness happens to us and in us and because of us!

We can basically summarize our fears of community or our lack of desire to work at it under three main categories: our attitudes about God, our attitudes about ourselves, and our attitudes about other members of the community of God's people. Of course, these three problems summarize human alienation since the Fall — for that story demonstrates how Adam was alienated from his God, from himself, and from Eve. How do these effects of human sinfulness hinder the corporateness of the Christian community?

Certainly, our separation from God is the root cause of our separation from ourselves and from each other. Our analysis dare not be superficial and merely blame our troubles on "sin," but, on the other hand, our culture tends to downplay sin and to excuse it or rationalize it. The more deliberately we penetrate the problem of sin, the more thoroughly we can cut its effects away.

Radically the manifestations of our sinfulness are due

to unbelief. We get greedy because we do not believe that God truly will provide for all our material needs. We become anxious because we do not trust God for the future. We resort to violence because we think that we have to create our own way. We are selfish and possessive because we fear that we will not be able to satisfy our emotional desires. When our devotional and worship lives suffer, we lack the relationship with God that enables us to find harmony with others and with ourselves. Lacking peace with God, we cannot be at peace with anybody else. The root of our failures to share in community, then, lies in our unbelief.

Fundamentally, part of what it means to be made in God's image is that we are all created with an intense longing for God. If we cannot meet that need, we desperately try to fill the gap with all sorts of other gods. We try to satisfy our yearning with possessions, successes, relationships. If we focus on the first two of that triad, we tend to destroy the third. If we focus on the third, we often hinder genuine relationship by our manipulations.

As long as we look for our needs to be met by persons, we will always be disappointed. This is especially true in marriage relationships, because such an expectation imposes a terrible burden upon one's partner. No person is perfect; no one can take the place of God in our lives. Rather, in Christian marriage and in true community we learn together that we will find our needs thoroughly met only in our relationship with God. Our alienation from him prevents us from discerning ways in which other persons can minister to our needs.

This became very practical for me several years ago. A friend having difficulty in both work and marriage could not find affirmation anywhere and clung to our friendship as one source of hope. In such a dependence, he could never be satisfied and always demanded more time from me. I am not god. I cared about him, believed that he has tremendous gifts to offer, and valued his friendship over the years — but I could not meet his deepest needs.

Our nature as human beings is always to crave more, never to be finally satisfied. Our surface problems of tight schedules and distance from each other are not truly the source of human restlessness. Its cause is the longing for eternity in the very depths of our beings.[1] Ultimately, our needs can only be met by an infinite God; he alone can satisfy the longing for himself that he created.

When we truly grasp that, then we will rejoice in the persons that God gives us to meet our needs without having to cling to them possessively. If we try to get rid of our longings by belonging to the community, the longings will continue to grow. If we want the Church to erase our loneliness, it will become a deeper ache. On the other hand, when we realize that God is the Source of all satisfaction, then our attitudes can change to rejoicing in the moments and the persons that he gives to bring us comfort and care. Moreover, in the times when no one is there to be with us, we can remember those moments when God has provided persons in order to strengthen us for the lonely times.

How we belong to one another in the Christian community is a sign of God's enfolding love, which is sufficient for all the times of loneliness or fatigue or pain or grief that we might have to bear. In all sorts of tangible ways the love of God can be conveyed to those who don't feel that their needs will be met in the belonging. Above all, we must continually recognize that the only source of ultimate contentment is God. All other gifts just point to his adequacy. Only his grace carries the promise of sufficiency for all our needs (2 Cor. 12:9).

If our relationship with God is sound, then we are set

1. See my comments on this issue in chapter 6 of *To Walk and Not Faint* (Chappaqua, NY: Christian Herald Books, 1980).

free to work to dismantle the barriers that alienate us from one another. Oftentimes, however, the barrier lies in ourselves.

Some members cannot take the risk of belonging to a community because they feel that they have nothing to offer. Certainly we all suffer at times from such a lack of self-esteem. One young man who came to me for counseling had been verbally abused extensively in childhood. As a result, he was really afraid to give himself in a belonging relationship with most people. He covered up his deep hatred of himself with a super-boastful ego. So many times when I heard his conceit, I wanted to hug him and somehow help him to know that he was really loved — first by God and then by the rest of us.

Probably most of us suffer from some sense of inadequacy and a consequent fear of belonging. Take a moment to think about yourself and the persons around you. How do you see in them signs that they are afraid of rejection, that they are not willing to get too close to others or to let others get too close to them? Do we have any insights into why they might feel that way? What kinds of signals can we learn to pick up in others so that we can recognize when those who are with us are not feeling good about themselves? What means can we use to affirm others and help them to recognize their own worth?

When we use skills of constructive listening and positive affirmation, we learn to express our care for others more effectively. As a result, we gain from our listening new appreciation for them and the gifts they bring to the community. Most of all, we want to enfold others in the grace of God — and we need to find that grace around ourselves so that we can be set free to enjoy the unity and to deepen the Hilarity of the community.

Another aspect of alienation from ourselves lies in a failure to believe that somehow our needs can really be met. Sometimes we run away from the community by trying to meet our needs in other pleasures, but often we simply don't believe that our lonely aches can be dispelled. Consequently, we reject whatever the community might offer us to indulge in our own pity parties.

Finally, we must look at the source of our alienations from one another. Besides the effects of the technological milieu that are discussed in the preface to this book, there are certain barriers within the Christian community itself. Tragically, many persons don't believe in the effectiveness of the community because they have been too deeply hurt by it. They have suffered from rejection or lack of affirmation in their churches, so they have difficulty trusting enough to risk again. One shouldn't expect too much of the Christian Body, they feel, if it has failed them in the past.

You and I can begin to do something practical about this problem. If our churches are not affirming, supportive, loving places to be, then we can start to make them so, beginning with ourselves. Most of the rest of this book will deal with the meaning and practice of our love for each other and in outreach beyond our community. As we learn more and more what love entails, we will more deeply belong to each other, not in the sense of a tight possessiveness that grasps at others to control them, but in the sense of giving ourselves freely to minister to one another and to upbuild the community as a whole.

When persons think more lowly of themselves than they ought, we can affirm them by listening to them, by encouraging their contributions to the community, by seeking practical resources to meet their material needs, by listening to their sorrows (see especially Chapter 25, " 'Withness' in Human Emotions"). Moreover, we can serve those around us who experience these alienations by stirring up in ourselves and in others visions for how the Church can create a more effective, thorough sense of belonging for her people.

Even more important is the use that we can make of the Scriptures. In small groups in our churches we can discuss the Bible together and allow participants to find forgiveness for their failures and to feel valuable as graced individuals who belong. Probably a major factor in spoiling the sense of belonging in the Church is the numbers game which causes us to believe that larger is necessarily better. The early Christians rejoiced in being together with each other frequently, meeting not only in the large assemblies but also (and, it seems, more often) in one another's homes. Small groups are more effective for helping persons to know more surely that they have much to contribute. The atmosphere is safe, they know they are loved, and they are more personally affirmed for the unique individuals that they are.

One of the congregations for which I have led retreats is organized into numerous "CASA" or "Caring and Sharing" groups (*casa* is Spanish for *house*). One particular CASA group has been meeting together for at least five years. Its members know that in any need at any time they can call another member of the group. One woman described to me her tears of gratitude as she sat on a hospital bed just before surgery and knew that all the members of her CASA group were praying for her. Her sense of self-worth and belonging were enormously boosted by their great care for her; her ability to trust God was undergirded by the support of their love.

Many who go to worship every Sunday feel lost and unimportant in large groups. In their small living-room gatherings, that CASA group lives out the truth of God's love for persons. They demonstrate vividly that belonging in the Christian community overcomes one's alienation from self and others.

My goal in this chapter is for each of us to discover some very practical steps in the process of tearing down the alienations that separate us from each other so that God's intention for us truly to belong to each other can be realized. We must face the fears, insecurities, mistrusts, and grievances that obstruct belongingness in our families and churches, in our neighborhoods and places of work. Once again, I want to encourage you to study diligently the questions that follow so that eminently practical application can be made of this text in each of our lives. What might be the insulin that we could inject to enable all the parts of the body to which we belong to function together again more effectively — and thereby more Hilariously?

Therefore:

1. How do we observe that all fear of belonging is rooted in unbelief?

2. How does our fear that we don't have anything to offer keep us from more thoroughly belonging?

3. How does our fear that our needs won't be met keep us from experiencing how they could be?

4. How do our experiences of past rejection make us unwilling to risk belonging now?

5. How can we help others to discover the Hilarity of feeling better about themselves and the gifts they have to offer?

6. How can we help others and ourselves more to see that needs can only be met by God, but that he has given us to each other to work together to find our answers in him?

7. How can we start now to create in our congregation a warmer spirit, a deeper love, and a more thorough sense of belonging to each other?

11. Gifts from the Fullness of Grace

But having grace-gifts according to the grace which has
been given us — different . . .
                                                    — ROMANS 12:6a

THE FIELD LOOKED LIKE a lavender lake. The lovely lacy
flowers profusely covered the whole side of the farmyard
with a graceful carpet. I lay down in them to get a bee's-eye
view of their splendor. There were skillions of them.

The grassland didn't force itself to have them. In many
meadows beautiful flowers spring up to cover the grass with
their delicate hue. "God's extravagant hobby," somebody
once called the wildflowers. Just for fun he creates all those
exquisite blossoms and then doesn't just lightly sprinkle
them; he pours down a whole lake-full of lupines right into
the pasture.

Against the blue sky, red rocks, green trees, and frosted
gray sagebrush of eastern Washington, the flowers offer a
dramatic symbol for the grace-gifts of God. Abundantly
given, precisely unique each in itself, they brilliantly set off
everything around them. But the most important fact is that
they were there. Simply there.

92

Most of the English translations of Romans 12:6 miss the utter simplicity of the text as it describes God's grace-gifts. They are not worked for, cannot be created by us, and could never be bought or sold or acquired in any way by human effort. They simply are there. Given.

The Greek text begins literally, "But having . . ." In fact, the English additions of such phrases as "we have different gifts" and "let us use them" all add extra pronouns and verbs that are not in the original letter. Paul's very cryptic style accentuates the bare fact. "Having" them, we are able to respond, do, be, use.

The apostle puts "having" in a continuing present participle form and thereby proclaims that we are characterized by the constant state of having. We simply continue to have the grace-gifts that have been given to us. They are an immense power inherently there, waiting to be used and exercised for the benefit of the whole Body of Christ. Since we are members one of another, we are called to a great responsibility in that having.

Now what exactly do we have? The Greek word is *charismata*. The term derives from the Greek word for grace, *charis*, and thereby signifies gifts that come from, and reveal, God's grace, God's unlimited and undeserved love. The noun is plural, which seems to suggest not only that the community as a whole has many gifts, but also that individuals probably have more than one.

We err gravely if we limit the grace-gifts. The pushiness in some churches to "find your gift" is not biblical. Nowhere in the Scriptures is there an injunction to find the one specific gift that is our particular manifestation of God's power and character.

Rather, the biblical texts indicate that we each have unique combinations of gifts, very much in the plural. As will be considered in the final point of this chapter, our gifts are different according to times and circumstances and personalities and tasks. Therefore, we begin to understand grace-gifts by refusing to limit how God wants to manifest his magnificent love.

The very idea of grace implies lavishness. My marriage two years ago brought the term *overgraced* to my vocabulary because I have been so often overwhelmed by the superabundance of God's love-signs through my husband. In the midst of some very sad moments and trying struggles because of my shattered foot and increasing blindness, Myron has brought me music and beautiful flowers, prayers and gentle words, surprises and tender care, and many other reminders that nothing can ever separate me from God's love.

How has God's grace been poured out upon you today? With barely any effort we could list hundreds of graces. We breathe, our hearts pump, our blood flows, our digestive processes work, our cells burn energy, our minds contemplate, and our faith is being strengthened by the Hilarity of thinking together about the immensity of grace.

Grace. The very word is amazing. How could God be stingy about his gifts which distribute grace? Certainly he gives an abundance of them.

We mistake the fullness of God's grace to his people, furthermore, if we limit the kinds of gifts that God would give. Because the four lists of gifts in the Scriptures have different elements in different combinations and with different inclusions and exclusions, they are evidently intended to be sample lists. The eighteen or so gifts that are listed in Romans 12, 1 Corinthians 12, Ephesians 4, and 1 Peter 4 by no means exhaust the various manifestations of God's power at work through individuals. For this additional reason we must avoid the practice of urging a person to "find" his or her gift. We don't even know what they all are. If we are looking to see if we qualify for one of the eighteen of somebody's system, we might miss the very best gift that God has for pouring his grace through us to others.

For example, many years ago I went every Monday to visit and sing at a convalescent center with a five-year-old named Michael. That lad had an uncanny sense about when certain residents needed to hold somebody's hand. He would simply walk to the person's wheelchair and extend his own hand. A grinning lady would take his little one in her arthritis-gnarled hand and crush it with affection. Now what could we call that gift? We might have a difficult time trying to categorize it, and yet there could be no doubt that Michael's grace-gift of holding hands brought Hilarity to the community in that convalescent center. His gentle gesture of care brought more grace to many of those residents than any of my songs or theological words.

Paul gives us a list of gifts in the following verses, and we will consider them each carefully so that we can watch for manifestations of gifts in ourselves and in others. That way we can foster the use of gifts and encourage freedom in others. We dare not, however, limit ourselves to the seven that are given here in Romans 12.

The very fact that seven are itemized here confirms that the list offers samples. Throughout the Scriptures the number seven is used symbolically to indicate perfection. Genesis begins with the seven-day outline that shows the perfection of creation. You are probably familiar with the extensive significance of sevens in the book of Revelation and in the Gospel of John. Paul uses sevens in a similar way simply to offer a symbolic representation of all of the grace-gifts.

Just at this point in revising this chapter I'm hearing from the radio a concerto for two flutes played by Jean-Pierre Rampal and Ransom Wilson. Those men have such outstanding abilities that they make the extraordinarily difficult music sound astonishingly easy and incredibly fun to play. I laugh with the Hilarity of God's wonderful gifting as I listen to the good time they're having — a tremendous picture of this definition by Ray Stedman:

God has given gifts. Paul calls them "graces," and we have different gifts, according to the specific gift of grace that is given to us. I like that term for gifts because it indicates something about them. Graces are graceful. Something that is graceful is a delight to watch, and this is true about a spiritual gift. A gift is an ability God has given you because he wants you to function along this line. It enables you to do this thing so naturally, smoothly, and beautifully that others will take note of it and ask you to do it and enjoy watching you do it. You will enjoy it, too. When you are using your spiritual gift you are fulfilled. It is called a "grace" because it is not a difficult, painful thing to do; it is something you delight in doing. And you can improve in it as you do it. Therefore it is one of the things that will make life interesting and fulfilling for you.[1]

We must slightly modify Stedman's description, for those who watch us use our gifts might not always enjoy them. For example, those who speak prophetically might not always be appreciated because their words are indicting. Upon due reflection, however, the people of God who are seeking to listen to God will be grateful for the gifts of the prophets.

The main point of Stedman's explanation, however, is a freeing insight. Just as the two flautists sounded glad to use their musical abilities, so we experience great delight when we use our grace-gifts. Two of the ways in which we discover our gifts are through our own sense of fulfillment and Hilarity and through the Hilarity of those who observe and benefit from our stewardship of our grace-gifts.

After the words "but having grace-gifts," Paul continues with "according to the grace." This phrase is precisely singular after the full plural of the term *grace-gifts*. God's

---

1. Ray C. Stedman, *From Guilt to Glory*, vol. 2: *Reveling in God's Salvation* (Portland, OR: Multnomah Press, 1978), p. 113.

grace is all of one kind: totally undeserved, never to be repaid, never to be earned, always fully flowing, never coming in a trickle or in spurts, but always perfectly free and abundant and moving. Moreover, that grace is always the same, never arbitrary, nor anything but holy and perfect.

Because of this character, how dare we question the way grace dispenses its gifts? The same grace that gave gifts to you also gave gifts to me. The same fullness in your gifts is wholeness for me. Never does grace slight; never does grace treat unfairly. Grace's gifts are always totally grace-full.

Such a concept eliminates any possibility for jealousy in the Body of Christ. There is no such thing as being more or less gifted than another. All persons are gifted with a fullness of grace, though that grace takes different manifestations in particular individuals. Still the grace is the same.

That we are all equal before grace has been the thrust of the entire book of Romans. Ultimately, Jews and Greeks are no different in the sight of God. Both are desperately in need of grace, and both are equally brought by grace into the family of God. But in God's wisdom grace comes to and through individuals in differing ways.

Nevertheless, the grace has been decisively given. The verb is a passive aorist (which means once-and-for-all) participle modifying the word *grace.* God is the agent of that action. He has given decisively, thoroughly, fairly.

Grace-gifts are given. We cannot seize them from someone else. We cannot demand them, or expect them, or crank them up; but they are a fact.

However, we err again if we think that this decisive action means that we are given our gifts once, unalterably, for the rest of our lives. That such is not the case seems to be indicated by the Greek construction of this whole phrase. Literally, the order is: "But having grace-gifts according to the grace which has been given to us different."

The word we translate "different" appears at the end of

the phrase, in the most significant position. This is the major emphasis of the phrase: that the grace-gifts are different. The Body is characterized by having them, given by grace, different. The plural form of the Greek adjective shows us clearly that the word modifies the noun *grace-gifts* — they are different. But its position after the participle seems to indicate that the whole phrase, including the fact of the giving, is to be marked with this difference.

Its position at the end of the phrase sets off the importance of that difference. This seems to open up our horizons, as if Paul were reminding us that we can never pin such a thing down. We can never figure out how the Giver of grace-gifts does the dispensing. His work is never the same.

He gives to each of us different combinations of gifts. Furthermore, he gives us each different gifts for different times. The appropriateness of the gifts for our ministries is borne out by our practical experience. Probably all of us have realized stages in our lives when one or another of the grace-gifts predominated, according to our situations.

When I was an English teacher at the University of Idaho, my primary task in faith was evangelism. My classes in Literature of the Bible brought many students to my office to ask questions about the personal significance of that literature and the meaning of Christianity.

Next, I worked for a congregation in campus ministry and was no longer called so much to be an evangelist as to equip others for evangelism. Then I moved into a parish situation, where my work centered on developing Bible study programs and youth choirs. Then my doctoral work took me into an entirely different sphere and the need for different gifts. Now, having returned to free-lancing and going into new places frequently, I work more like a spark, to kindle fires in people's faiths and ministries. I'm not sure how to name the gift that is the primary focus of my ministry now.

I'm not really worried that I cannot pin it down. For

each conference or retreat situation the needs are different, and so must be my service. God's grace works in unique ways appropriate to the circumstances, which I am so grateful not to have to try to figure out. Grace has already been given; we are privileged to serve as channels for its flowing.

Finally, we must fight the superficial cop-out from responsibilities expressed in the words, "I can't do that. It's not my gift." The fact that we all belong to each other in the Christian community will prevent us from avoiding the drudgery that we might want to escape. Furthermore, God might surprise us with the changes that he brings in the ways in which we can serve the community. We dare not give in to that terrible human tendency to pin God down, to think we have figured him out.

Much of the Hilarity of the Christian life gets lost if we have to have everything so tightly defined. This verse explodes our boundaries. Grace is in charge, and grace pours out its abundance as freely as it is infinite.

Look at each of these phrases briefly again in the Greek text's order and remember these emphases:

"*having* grace-gifts" — we continually possess a variety of possibilities and have a choice concerning how to respond;

"having *grace-gifts*" — they are gifts from grace, to manifest grace, in order to impart grace;

"according to the *grace* which has been given to us" — grace is a singular unity, equally bestowed, thoroughly lavished, manifested differently in different persons, but always the same;

"the grace which *has been given*" — decisively bestowed, thoroughly unearned or created by us;

"to us" — all of us together as a Body, each of us uniquely as a particular member with specific functions in that community;

"different" — never the same, always unique to our personhood, changing with the times and circumstances and needs and growth of the community; always *different*.

What a kaleidoscopic picture! All the bits and pieces of color pattern each of us; all the designs and combinations make the Body. And with every turn of the kaleidoscope's circle, new visions of the grace of God emerge.

What Hilarity to realize that we are a precious part of it, an essential steward of the grace entrusted to us! Having that, now how will we respond?

Therefore:

1. How does the concept of "having" increase our wonder at the grace of God?

2. What is grace?

3. What is the meaning of having grace-gifts?

4. What is the importance of reminding ourselves and others that our grace-gifts are given according to grace?

5. How have we manifested different gifts at different times?

6. What gifts have others noticed in us?

7. How does it increase the Hilarity of the community when we experience the fullness of our grace-gifts in the unity and diversity of Christ's Body?

12. The Grace-Gift of Forthtelling

. . . whether prophecy — according to the agreement
of the faith!

— ROMANS 12:6b

ONE OF THE FASTEST changes of attitude in all of the
Scriptures occurs when Jesus speaks in the synagogue
in his hometown of Nazareth after he has begun his preaching and healing ministry in Galilee. The scene is vividly
described in Luke 4:16-30.

When Jesus enters the synagogue, everyone wonders
about him. Favorable stories of his teaching and miracles were
being spread all over; everyone was praising him. Thus, as he
enters the house of worship according to his Sabbath custom,
the expectations of the hometown people are surely on edge.

Luke stresses emphatically that Jesus habitually observed the Sabbath by teaching in the synagogue. Throughout
Luke's Gospel we catch glimpses that Jesus was not rebellious
but highly orthodox in his observation of Jewish practices. His
proclamation of the Word came out of faithfulness.

He stands up to read the lesson for the day — a section
from the prophet Isaiah. Significantly, Jesus cuts off the quo-

tation from Isaiah 61 before reading the phrase "the day of vengeance of our God," and ends instead with "to proclaim the year of Yahweh's favor." His prophetic ministry emphasizes God's love; he initiates it in the Hebrew-Scripture terms of the Jubilee.

Still the people are on his side. When he sits down to begin his discourse, the eyes of everyone in the synagogue are "fastened on him" (Luke 4:20, NIV). Even after he says, "Today this scripture is fulfilled in your hearing," the people are still speaking well of him. Luke stresses that they are amazed "at the gracious words that came from his lips" (v. 22). How could this be? "Isn't this Joseph's son?" they are asking.

Yet within six verses a dramatic reversal takes place. By verse 28, "All the people in the synagogue were furious. . . . They got up, drove him out of the town, and took him to the brow of the hill on which the town was built to throw him down the cliff." But Jesus walks right through the crowd and goes "on his way" (v. 30, NIV). Luke implies the same control over his destiny that John makes explicit in Jesus' phrase "My time has not yet come" (John 2:4b).

What causes this sudden rush of anger in his neighbors? All Jesus does in the intervening verses is explain that "no prophet is accepted in his home town" (Luke 4:24, NIV). He makes it clear to the adoring crowds that they must truly understand the nature of his ministry. Its basic task of preaching good news to the poor is a critically relevant message that is still causing furor toward the prophets who proclaim it in twentieth-century churches.

Jesus simply explained to the synagogue crowds, eager to check out this hometown boy, that God's love would continue to flow even toward the Gentiles when it was rejected by God's very own people, Israel. Their furious response was exactly what Jesus had just predicted. To be a prophet is a painful task.

Why, then, would anyone undertake the task? Simply,

one must be faithful to God in the "having" of the prophetic gift.

Paul underscores the simplicity of gift-response by the style of the next seven verses in Romans 12. To present each item on his list of grace-gifts, beginning with prophecy, he uses no verbs and a simple structure in the Greek, composed of the word *eite* (best translated "whether"), followed by the noun naming the grace-gift and a prepositional phrase describing its use. We might reproduce his epigrammatic style with this translation of verses 6 to 13:

> Now as having *charismata* according to the grace given to us different: whether prophecy — according to the agreement of the faith! whether service — in that service! whether the one teaching, in the act of teaching! whether the one exhorting — in the exhortation! the one imparting — in simplicity! the one presiding — in diligence! the one extending mercy — in Hilarity!
>
> The love — not hypocritical! Abhorring the wicked thing! Glued to the good thing! In friendship love — tenderly affectioned toward each other! In the honor — leading each other! In the diligence — not poky! In the spirit — boiling! In the Lord — slaving! In the hope — rejoicing! In the tribulation — remaining under! In the prayer — continuing steadfast! In the needs of the saints — sharing in common! The hospitality — pursuing it![1]

The dramatic terseness of Paul's style intensely underscores his point. Whatever our gifts might be, the only response is to use them. Instead of getting jammed up in ourselves trying to figure out what to do or be or how to

---

1. This translation is my own, but the idea for this structure in copying Paul's cryptic style came from R. C. H. Lenski, *The Interpretation of St. Paul's Epistle to the Romans* (Minneapolis: Augsburg, 1936), pp. 758-59.

respond, we are free simply to do what we are gifted to do, and we don't have to worry so much about how something will come out or why we are doing it.

That last sentence does not advocate lack of thought and foresight; rather, it urges us to learn to respond more simply to God's grace-gifting. The slogan "Whatever you do, do it with all your might" suggests the kind of whole-hearted "throwing ourselves into it for all we're worth" that could characterize the Hilarity of the Christian community. Indeed, we can only discover the truth of our lives when we explore it full tilt.

Those who enter full tilt into faith are thought to be fanatics; being so consumed by one's beliefs seems un-balanced. Paul's style in these exhortations is meant to call us into a healthy kind of imbalance. We will use our gifts without the human hesitations that destroy God's power, if we can be consumed by the intense desire to give of our giftedness for all we're worth. Think about the Hilarious adventure of such freedom!

Paul first advocates full tiltedness in using the gift of prophecy — a good one to begin our study of the charisms since it is the one most frequently misunderstood. Too often the word *prophecy* is associated with slightly odd persons who predict such things as the collapse of the field-house roof at the University of Georgia, a "prophecy" given the year that my brother went there.

Unfortunately, some Christian sects and not-so-Christian cults have added to the bad connotations of the term by claiming that particular passages of the Scriptures are fulfilled in specific events of the present times. The danger lies in their being so certain.

Discussions about the "end times" especially distort biblical truth. Spiritual power for the work to which God calls us is lost through worrying about signs that count down the calendar to "prove" that Jesus is coming again soon.

Certainly Jesus might come again soon. On the other hand, he also said specifically that we are not to know the times and the seasons (Acts 1:7). Furthermore, he warned us against chasing after such things (Luke 21:8). The Gospel of Luke clearly records the words of Jesus about various signs of the age — signs like earthquakes, human hearts failing for fear, wars and rumors of wars, and so forth. However, these events, as signs of this age, have been happening ever since Jesus was here — and before his first coming. Indeed, such things will continue to happen until he comes again. "But the end is still to come," Jesus says explicitly, and again, "All these are the beginning of birth pains" (Matt. 24:6 and 8, NIV).

These signs don't occur with any greater frequency or power now than before, though specific ones might predominate at various points in history. Certainly our culture is better now at recording their occurrences. However, just as the enemy armies actually surrounding the city marked the fall of Jerusalem (Luke 21:20), similarly Jesus tells us explicitly that his coming in the clouds marks the end of time (v. 27). In other words, we will have absolutely no knowledge of when the end is coming until the end is here. Meanwhile, the signs of the times keep occurring to remind us that someday Jesus will come back and to urge us to invite everyone to believe in him.

We must read our Bibles carefully and not waste time trying to figure out things we cannot — and should not — know. Those who are so busy pinning down predictions of the end usually lose their balance for dealing with the present times. The Church desperately needs a new emphasis on the prophetic gift because true prophecy equips us for being God's people in the present.

Genuine prophecy entails applying the message of God, usually from the Scriptures, to the situations of our times. Rather than merely foretelling, it can be better defined as "forthtelling." The latter might give rise to the former if a person observes circumstances thoughtfully enough to recognize what events might follow. Especially if a person carefully reads the Scriptures, he or she will know that particular styles of life lead to inevitable consequences. The function of a prophet, then, is to speak out against these destructive elements in order to warn participants of their dangers.

An excellent example of such a contemporary prophet is the sociologist and lay theologian Jacques Ellul, who saw forty years ago the direction in which the technological milieu was taking our society. When he first wrote *The Technological Society*, fellow sociologists lambasted him for his "pessimism," but developments have borne out his claims. His insights into the truth about contemporary reality (founded on his extensive study of the Scriptures) enabled him correctly to predict many of the outcomes of social tendencies.

A resurgence of true prophecy would cause the Church to take firmer stands against the signs of the times that we see manifested in the promiscuity, unfaithfulness, and sexual libertinism of our age. God's people would speak against the graft, backbiting, lying, and other practices that corrupt business and government and churches. Our righteous anger would rage against injustices toward the poor, sexism, racism, ageism, classism, homophobia, and inequity in the distribution of the world's resources. More than anything else in the Church today we need persons with gifts of prophecy, who can speak into new situations in ways that indict and convict, set free and transform.

We must especially keep in mind throughout our study of the grace-gifts that they are given to the *Church*, for the strengthening of the community. Prophets speak first not to the world, but to the Church, which has fallen into the world's patterns — its immorality, greed, injustice, oppression. If prophets among us exercise their desperately needed gifts, the Church will be changed — and then it has the right to offer its alternatives to the surrounding society. As we truly learn to function as members of one another, furthermore, the life-style of Hilarity that we manifest will challenge the culture around us. However, we must recognize that the world does not owe the Church's prophets a hearing and might not listen. Only as we become a Christian community with a truly biblical life-style can our prophetic words carry the credibility of a demonstrated alternative to the society around us.

Manifestations of prophetic gifts usually flow from a deep knowledge of the Scriptures. As Jesus promises in the Gospel of John, the Holy Spirit brings to our remembrance what we have already learned from him (14:26). In order for the Spirit to do that work, however, the Scriptures must be already in our minds. Therefore, Paul's words about prophecy are a strong stimulation for daily personal devotional habits and corporate study of the Bible.

One practical aspect of the Church's life that needs immensely the gift of prophecy is the stewardship of possessions. Indeed, in many ways the Church has succumbed severely to the temptations of money and power.[2] God's Word, however, is very clear; both Testaments constantly emphasize God's special concern for the poor. We cannot simply spiritualize the task of Jesus to preach good news to the poor. The Greek word used literally means "the begging poor." Nor does "to preach good news" to them consist solely in announcing to them a "salvation message." The text must be taken literally and seriously: we are called to care for the poor in practical ways. To choose the values of God we can do no less than rethink our priorities.

Tragically, very few Christian communities are doing a thorough job of caring seriously for the poor in their

2. See Jacques Ellul's *Money and Power*, trans. LaVonne Neff (Downers Grove, IL: InterVarsity Press, 1984).

budgetary allotments. Therefore, we need prophets among us to call Christians back to more obedient discipleship in their concern for the hungry and malnourished and jobless and homeless.

Such a task would be terribly scary except for the prepositional phrase Paul uses to define this gift's use. He says literally, "whether prophecy, according to the agreement of the faith." The Greek word is *analogia,* which emphasizes a right relationship or proper proportion. I prefer the term *agreement* because of our all-too-human tendency to make that proportion a fractional one, such as two-thirds — or, more likely, one-eighth or so. We take a very small proportion of our faith and are willing to stick our necks out only that far. The result is a lack of power in our prophecy. The proportion of Paul's exhortation, however, is total agreement or one hundred percent. In the exercising of this gift we dare not hold back in any way but can enter full tilt into any situation wherein we are called to proclaim the message of the Scriptures. We are challenged to be as bold as faith can be.

Remember what faith is. It isn't feelings, nor is it experience. Yet if we confuse the three, we will perhaps fail to utter a prophetic word because we are afraid or because we do not envision that it will do any good.

However, if the gift of prophecy is exercised according to the faith, then we realize that we are often called to proclaim the Word precisely when we don't feel like it or when a situation seems to be absolutely a lost cause. The Greek noun for *faith* in this case specifically has the article *the* with it, so Paul's emphasis seems to be on the specific content of the Christian faith. One who is a prophet proclaims the truths of the Christian faith.

This leads to the recognition that the most difficult problem in being a prophet is making sure that one is forthtelling *God's message* in *God's way.* Some people glibly declare what they think is God's Word without the constant check of the community to discern the spirits (1 John 4:1-6). Others who think they are prophets and lambaste others with "the Word of the Lord" are actually suffering from an acute case of tactlessness.

Thus, the task of the prophet is to listen constantly — to God and to the Christian community. Out of silence and solitude and careful meditation and corporate conversation comes boldness to utter truly and lovingly a prophetic challenge.

Notice that the preceding paragraphs plunge us directly back into the need for constant habits of study and for a community of faithful believers. God calls us to prophetic work out of our immersion in the Bible by which we hear and hear again and then hear more effectively still the messages that we should bring to others. Then, in full-tilt proportion to the faith that we possess together with the rest of the Body and with the courage that comes from the community's support, we can boldly announce the messages God gives.

Within its space limitations this book cannot thoroughly survey the biblical description of prophecy. It encompasses all the teaching of the Hebrew prophets — from Moses and Elijah through the major and minor prophets — and the work of the Prophet Jesus and his prophetic followers.

A lifetime task of studying the Scriptures is necessary to learn what God would say to the Christian community in our world. By studying the prophets we learn God's values. By studying the world we learn how to apply God's truth to the reality of contemporary life situations. Our prophetic work requires a careful balance of intense study of the Bible and a deep relationship with the Lord, with ourselves, with the Church, and with our world in order to forthtell accurately God's messages for the situations of our times.

Sometimes prophecy is an act of the moment, a message to be spoken immediately for a particular situation.

More often, however, prophetic messages grow out of diligent faithfulness in preparing oneself. In the second letter to Timothy concerning his call and gifts, he is urged to "be diligent to present yourself approved to God as a workman who does not need to be ashamed, handling accurately the word of truth" (2 Tim. 2:15). As each of us seeks faithfully to study the Scriptures, God might empower us with the gift of prophecy for the upbuilding of the Christian community and the restoration of its Hilarity. The Church needs us to enter full tilt into the exercising of that gift — in full proportion to the faith which God has given.

Therefore:

1. What is the purpose of Paul's cryptic style in Romans 12:6-13?

2. How have we observed a misunderstanding of the concept of prophecy?

3. What does forthtelling the Word of God mean?

4. In what situations might we be called to forthtell God's message?

5. Why are prophets so needed in the contemporary Christian community?

6. What is the proportion of our faith — and how does it add Hilarity to one's task to prophesy according to it?

7. How could the Christian community become more open to the prophets in our midst? How would it add to our Hilarity to listen to their Word?

13. The Grace-Gifts of Serving and Teaching

> . . . whether service — in that service! whether the one
> teaching, in the act of teaching!
>
> — ROMANS 12:7

OUR CEM SECRETARY SANDY has the biggest servant's
heart one could ever imagine. How many secretaries
do you know who wash the dishes for their boss, paint the
walls, dust and clean, mow the lawn, run errands, and even
"snake" the malfunctioning toilet, in addition to the secretarial
duties of duplicating teaching tapes, handling the corporate
finances, and preparing the book orders for mailing?
She is crazy — crazy about being a servant. If anyone asks
her why she does so much, she invariably answers, "Because
I love it."

Being a servant is certainly one of Sandy's greatest gifts.
She serves everybody with the same gusto, though for
several years when we lived in the same city much of her
time was spent doing work for CEM and for me. I cannot
imagine how I could have gotten along without her. I hope

that using her for an example in this chapter will more thoroughly show her my deep gratitude to God for the gift of her and for all his gifts of grace to me through her.

In the previous chapter we began to define the *charismata*. They are the grace-gifts, given to us by grace and serving as vehicles through which God's grace is poured out to others. In this chapter, as we continue to define spiritual gifts and how they function together in the Christian community, we pause to observe the Hilarious freedom a person experiences when using his or her gifts — as is well illustrated by Sandy's enthusiasm for serving. She has often told me that she is happiest when serving other people.

The description of the prophetic gift in the previous chapter might have sounded as if possessing it is a heavy burden. To use any gift is absolutely impossible without the power of the Holy Spirit, upon whose grace we utterly depend, but under the Spirit's inspiration and guidance and empowerment every grace-gift is a source of freedom and delight — the true Hilarity of effective ministry and of being who we were created to be. Moreover, the Hilarity that we experience in using our gifts helps us to know that we are right in the center of God's will for our particular place in the Christian community.

The Church needs to note more thoroughly that one mark of grace-giftedness is freedom. That can be a clue to help us discover that we don't have the gifts for certain functions. (Remember our discussion of the participle *having* in Chapter 11.) We cannot respond with the use of what we don't have. We do ourselves and the community and the world a favor when we are realistic about not having certain gifts. We are free to say no to tasks that require gifts we don't possess.

We have been taught by our society not to say no. When first writing this book, I worked one day with a brilliant friend who frequently comes up with innovative ideas for ministry. Creating a fascinating ministry idea, he said, "Let's do it and go halves on the costs and the work." To be able to say no was terribly difficult for me. I loved the idea, but realistically I knew that my task at the time was to finish working on this book manuscript. I valued his idea but could not be the one to do it.

On the other hand, we dare not use an assumed lack of giftedness as a cop-out from the dirty work. A constant vigilance for how God might use us and develop new gifts in us is inherent in the plurality of the word *charismata* and in the fact that the word *different* takes the place of emphasis in verse 6 (see Chapter 11). Our gifts might change, so we dare not dogmatically exclude some function from our repertoire just because the gift for it wasn't there yesterday.

Once again this points to a need for constant prayer and meditation and conversation with other members of the Christian community. We certainly want to be as faithful as possible in using the gifts that God has given us. We want to keep exploring the nature of our gifts, though we do not have to panic about them or pinpoint them too closely, as we have previously discussed. If we are faithfully listening to the Lord with the help of the community and trying to discern his will, he will constantly be showing us who we are and how he can best use us. That gives us the freedom, then, to decline tasks that take us too far out of the spheres of our gifts.

We will be misunderstood in such a freedom. Therefore, in our relationships within the community we also need careful communication of what we are trying to do and to be. The urgency of that communication is especially poignant to me because of a painful encounter with the CEM Board ten years ago. I had botched a situation in the ministry of our crisis house, and the board rightly wanted me to deal firmly with the problem. Only after a lot of explanation and tears did we resolve the issue; we finally realized that I was not being insubordinate to the board's decision, but that I had become terribly bogged down trying to do something outside the lines of my gifts. Subsequently, we closed that ministry so that I could focus on teaching and writing — and the needs for care were soon met through the founding of a Catholic Worker house.

Notice the importance of balance in accepting roles in the Christian community for which we are gifted and in refusing those that take us away from our primary tasks. We can only discover that balance for our individual lives in a moment-by-moment testing and by a continual process within the Christian community. We want to be open constantly to God's revelation of how we can best serve him in a particular situation at a given moment.

All of these phrases in Romans 12 describing the grace-gifts, phrases that have no verb in the Greek, are translated in the TEV with the verb *must* or *should*. That inaccuracy is very destructive because the choice of the word *should* makes our use of the grace-gifts an onerous duty rather than a source of Hilarity. Verse 7, for example, is rendered, "If it is to serve, we must serve. If it is to teach, we must teach." The legalism of these phrases destroys our freedom. We do not use gifts because we have to; we rejoice in the task. One who has the gift of serving, like Sandy, does not serve because she must, but because she can hardly exist without choosing to do what her gifts excite her to do.

What, then, is the gift of serving? Some English versions (most notably the JB and the NEB) translate the Greek word *diakonia* as "administration," probably because the official title *deacon* comes from this Greek concept. In Acts 6, the title was first applied to those who were chosen to "serve tables" (i.e., to administer the food distribution to widows) so that the apostles could be set free to concentrate on their preaching of the Word and prayers.

Paul, however, seems to be using the term here more in the sense of any kind of lowly service, especially because in the next verse he speaks about the gift of those who are ruling (see Chapter 15, "The Grace-Gifts of Leadership and Hilarious Mercy") and because in 1 Corinthians 12:5 he writes about the "varieties of service" that all have the same Lord. Rather than emphasizing the leadership of the Christian community here, the phrase seems to concentrate on those who perform necessary functions in order to enable others to use their gifts. Sandy is such a good example because she does so many things to set me free to concentrate on other tasks.

Some people have this gift to an extraordinary degree, but all of us have many more opportunities for service than we usually realize. Perhaps the question we should ask is not whether we have the gift of serving, but whether we are letting grace empower each of us in our opportunities to serve.

The problems associated with the serving gifts are very different from the problems in being a prophet. In connection with the charism of prophecy, gifted ones wrestle with knowing when a message is truly God's Word and deal with the criticism and sometimes violent reaction of listeners.

One frequent problem in being a servant is that the person so gifted does not realize how important that gift is and therefore hesitates to offer it or seeks other gifts instead. Churches place entirely too much emphasis on the upfront gifts, like teaching or prophesying. Yet the silent people who do the behind-the-scenes serving are equally important for making the ministry of a congregation happen. Perhaps we mouth such a sentiment, but rarely does the Body of Christ truly incorporate that awareness into daily community life.

Who is more important — the speaker at a conference or the person who drove her there? Why is only the former applauded? Because of physical and visual disabilities, I cannot do ministry without those who serve as drivers. When will we start demonstrating in the Christian community the equality of the grace-gifts and the importance of each person's particular contribution?

In Acts 6 the early church ordained persons to the ministry of "the daily serving of food." For that calling they were very seriously anointed and commissioned, just as were the apostles, who then could focus on their teaching and prayer. I long for the day when our churches will ordain persons to their ministries of janitoring, dishwashing, errand running, lawn mowing, typing, bulletin distributing, and shut-in visiting. Without the unnoticed ministry of those who serve, the "people behind the church,"[1] we lose our Hilarity because we cannot function as a community that is whole.

The other grace-gift mentioned in Romans 12:7 is teaching. Paul says that the one with this gift exercises it in the sphere of his or her teaching. To survey entirely the biblical meaning of this gift is impossible here because the term includes so many dimensions and is used so extensively in the Scriptures. Above all, three main points about teaching are emphasized.

First, the Scriptures constantly call those who teach to teach the truth. Obviously, anyone's particular skills in teaching will bear no fruit if the content of those efforts is false. Remember again the injunction to Timothy to handle rightly the word of truth (2 Tim. 2:15; see the previous chapter).

This injunction is especially important in our day when people seek out those who will tickle their ears (2 Tim. 4:3). Too many teachers are bending over backwards to give people what they want instead of what they need.

---

1. Clint Eastman uses this phrase to describe the kinds of hidden service that help churches function in his article "The People Behind the Church," *Decision* 32, 6 (June 1991): 16-17.

Our society can best be characterized as an "age of entertainment," and, tragically, in many instances Christian congregations are conforming to the patterns of this age. We need in the Church those with gifts of humor and those who draw people to Christianity by the delight their presentations create. However, if Christian programs offer only superficial fun, no deep development of faith — and thus no Hilarity — can unfold. We need substance to grow toward maturity. Mere entertainment is not enough for discipleship.

The effects of a technological entertainment society are visible throughout the Christian community. Too often "famous" speakers at mass conventions (especially for teenagers) specialize in humorous or emotional sensationalism but offer little more for their listeners to think about. Many Christians remain immature in their faith because they invest their time in television and other vacuous pleasures instead of making an effort to develop devotional and study disciplines. Christian bookstore shelves often feature a plethora of superficial stuff. I am not at all rejecting fantasy or discounting the value of good story; fiction is an excellent tool for communicating deep truth, as are biographical and historical materials. I do object to the propensity to overindulge in mere froth in Christian literature. If we settle for shallow entertainment, we won't invest ourselves in diligent study for growth.

Critically, the main focus for teaching in the Church must be the Bible. When we study the Scriptures, we will become "rooted and grounded" so that we can always be in the process of growing from that firm planting.

That leads to this second point: those gifted to be teachers are responsible, therefore, to do the best job they can of preparation so that they can give their students as much substance as possible. The styles and the kinds of content vary, of course, but each teacher must be accountable to the community for his or her best.

We shortchange our students if we don't prepare as well as we possibly can. Sometimes circumstances interfere, and certainly the Holy Spirit still operates with power through the gift that has been given. But we dare not excuse ourselves and waste so much time that our preparation is reduced. Christian teaching is no place for too much "flying by the seat of one's pants." We are called to diligence in our study.

Third, those who are teachers use their gifts best when they are genuine about what they teach — when they "walk their talk." (I write about this with repentance because I fail so often to practice what I preach.) We have no right to talk about the Scriptures unless we are willing to be confronted by them and to invest our lives in doing what they say.

The final outcome of our teaching of the Scriptures should be that others would want to put them into practice in their own lives, and we all know that the best way for persons to learn is through the models of those who do that. Therefore, to be called to teach challenges individuals to great responsibility. James stresses this when he writes that not many should desire to be teachers because they are judged more strictly (3:1).

Again, these cautions point out the impossibility of exercising gifts without the empowerment of the Holy Spirit. Grace fills the teacher with Hilarity and surely enables the teacher to use the gift that grace confers.

Teachers realize that they cannot cram knowledge down anyone's throat. Rather, they want to create an atmosphere in which learning is desirable. Then they can demonstrate the importance of biblical application through the congruent sharing of how the Scriptures are transforming their own lives and of what struggles and victories they have experienced in wrestling with them. To lead students into the challenges of the Bible so that it can become more alive in their lives, too, is a privilege filled with Hilarity.

The Scriptures are such a treasure — bursting with new things to discover, the working of God to observe, his love to experience in new ways. Romans 12:7 challenges teachers to be constantly growing in faith so that in faithfulness and Hilarity they can more clearly see and pass on to others in the community the truths of God.

Teachers offer the stewardship of their gift "in teaching," Paul says. That sphere of responsibility involves the necessity of always teaching the truth, the requirement of careful preparation, and the challenge of modeling what one teaches. These three dimensions underscore the recognition that our gifts of teaching are exercised solely by the grace which has conferred them.

Each of us teaches at various times. You who are parents are constantly teaching. How much more thoroughly you can teach your children when God's power makes your inculcating and modeling of values more effective. You who teach in Sunday school or any other form of Christian education have the specific challenges of your particular class and subject matter. Every one of us has the opportunity to teach whenever another person is observing our modeling of whatever subject matter is important to us. We all need, therefore, to take seriously the critical nature of our constant teaching so that we can be, more effectively and with more Hilarity, the models God desires us to be. The thought-for-life questions below will help us meditate upon our places of serving and teaching in the community.

Therefore:

1. In the use of what particular gifts do we experience the deepest freedom and Hilarity?

2. How can we grow in courage to refuse to participate in tasks that are not part of, or that lead us away from, our calling?

3. How have we failed to limit ourselves to our own gifts? How have we used the lack of gifts as a cop-out?

4. How have we benefited from the grace-gift of serving in others? How can we express to them more thoroughly our appreciation?

5. In what situations could we have served more effectively if we had relied on God's grace-gifting power instead of on our own capabilities?

6. In what situations have we been called to be teachers?

7. How can we be more effective in our teaching, whatever forms that might take? How effectively do our lives model what we teach?

14. The Grace-Gifts of Encouraging and Sharing

> . . . whether the one exhorting — in the exhortation!
> the one imparting — in simplicity!
> — ROMANS 12:8a-b

WHY ARE PEOPLE more successful at losing weight when they join a club for it? Usually groups like Weight Watchers or Overeaters Anonymous stress highly the encouragement that members give to one another. The club's existence, furthermore, demands an accountability that is hard to escape. When dieters know they have to report in, they stick to their disciplines more faithfully.

An enormous variety of guilds, clubs, associations, and leagues clamor for our participation. We can join an organization to secure political rights, to share our various miseries, to discuss books, to support the arts, to be a better parent, or to cope more effectively with singleness or marriage.

Why are we better at things when we share them with others? The answer to that question is the key to the next item in Paul's list of grace-gifts in Romans 12. Paul is modeling the very thing that he urges, for this whole section of his letter demonstrates exhortation, and here specifically he urges those who have that gift to exercise it in encouraging others.

The word that Paul chooses here to describe the action of this grace-gift comes from the verb with which he began this section of Romans when he "urged" his readers to present their bodies as living and holy sacrifices pleasing to God (12:1). The concept seems to be a favorite with Paul, for he uses it extensively at the beginning of 2 Corinthians, which inspires us to comfort one another with the comfort with which we have been comforted (1:4). The word possesses an enormous field of meanings, including to encourage, comfort, urge, entreat, warn, admonish, or exhort. It seems that we should not pin the word down to one particular meaning in this passage in Romans, for Paul probably chose it specifically to express the range of activities that are involved when members of the Christian community use their spiritual gifts to uphold one another. The concept gives us a striking picture of what our relationships with others in the Body of Christ can be and how much more effective our encouragement of one another in the community is when it is empowered by the Holy Spirit.

Our yard offered a vivid demonstration of that when I was first writing this book. Three friends came down from Seattle to spend a day off with Julie and me. One friend, Bob, is an artist, too, so he and Julie put up easels and spent the afternoon helping each other experiment with new media for painting. Meanwhile, the other three of us chopped wood, mowed the lawn, and went for a walk. Each of us could more easily stick to the chore of wood splitting when others encouraged persistence. One friend even went with me to practice the organ for the worship service the next morning; her personal interest motivated better practice, and I enjoyed playing for worship even more the next day as a result. All five of us urged each other on as we made an Indian dinner that evening, and then another friend came to add still more exhilaration as we gathered around the piano for a songfest. All day long the inspiration of the others had enfolded each of us in Hilarity and supported our work.

Work is not the only thing that requires the support of others. We need others to console us especially in our times of grief and pain. A while ago I called very dear friends in Nebraska to help me work through the sense of loss I'm experiencing as I face life in a leg brace that prevents me from engaging in all my favorite sports. A great part of the Hilarity of the Christian community is knowing that we can turn to each other for comfort in our distress! (We will discuss this more thoroughly in Chapter 24, which explicates verse 17, but here we can begin to establish a deeper theology of exhortation.)

One great problem when Christians minister to one another is that too easily we dump the gospel on them and think that we have done our duty. Frequently, when members of the Body of Christ are going through terrible times of deep discouragement and despair, many well-meaning Christian friends quote the Scriptures at them and think that they should feel better.

Such courses as Parent Effectiveness Training have made me more aware of the destructiveness of not listening to those who are hurting. Our simple pat answers make the persons receiving the quick solution feel that they must be really stupid not to see the answer so clearly. However, life's problems are not like that. They involve many complex factors that no one else can know except the person involved in them all. For an outsider to give a simple solution for another's problem or a quick remedy for someone else's pain is totally inappropriate. Such answers increase the pain intensely because then the one suffering has to struggle not only with the facts of the situation themselves but also with the loneliness of being terribly misunderstood.

Many years ago, when my whole sense of self had crumbled in rejection and desertion, people hurt me more by quoting Romans 8:28 to me. At the time I couldn't see that "all things work together for good," and, knowing that Bible verse well, I felt all the more guilty that I was having such trouble believing it.

The verb that Paul chooses here in Romans 12:8 offers a much better way to upbuild. When others are hurting, the greatest grace we can bring is to comfort or encourage them right in the midst of whatever they are suffering. A person doesn't need empty words, but the freedom to crawl inside a hug and feel the embrace of God. In pain we need others to listen to our grief and fears, to help us sort them out, to encourage us by their presence not to lose hope.

Exhorting another can take a wide variety of forms, as is indicated by the multiplicity of translations given to this Greek participle. The KJV and the RSV both use the term *exhortation;* the JBP paraphrases, "and if our gift be the stimulating of the faith of others let us set ourselves to it." Other renderings stress the act of "encouraging" (TEV and NIV). A few English versions limit the concept to preaching (the LB and the JB), but such confining of the word is not warranted by the cotext of this entire chapter of Romans, which addresses the Christian community as a whole and not just its leaders.

Furthermore, we want to avoid any definitions of this gift that smack of pushiness or adamant goading. Rather, throughout the Scriptures the gift seems to be characterized by gentleness. Its proper functioning within the community might involve admonition or rebuking, but these are done with tenderness in order to build up the one who needs to be criticized and to enable that individual to change. Perhaps the most needful kind of exhortation in contemporary congregations is that which criticizes constructively, reproves, calls back from error, or disciplines. We will consider this further in connection with the phrase "Hate what is evil" (v. 9b) in Chapter 17.

The terms *encouragement* and *exhortation* stress well the profound need in our communities for lifting up one another, for motivational prodding. How we do such stimulation is critically important because both discouragement and lack of personal discipline are problems in the Church. We don't want our prodding to cause the other to feel guilty for not being able to perform according to our expectations. Such legalistic performance principles destroy the Hilarity of being God's people. On the other hand, fellow believers who are betraying the values of the community need to be challenged to repent and change.

An enormous amount of grace is required to be an encouraging person. One who is exhorting well, however, will be tenderly and fruitfully passing on the love of God as the motivation for someone else's life and ministry.

Each of us is called at times to exercise the gift of encouragement. However, we are all aware of certain persons whom God has especially gifted at passing on his love in this way. Think about the people who have touched your life with this charism. Perhaps you have experienced their special comforting or constructively critical care recently. Perhaps this chapter can prod you to express your gratitude to them for the extraordinary ways in which they have been a vessel for God's grace to enfold you.

Or perhaps this grace-gift has been manifested deeply in you. Then your response to Paul's exhortation might be to assess the needs of those around you, to discover who might need your encouragement in their struggles, or your exhortations toward deeper service, or your rebuke for their movement away from God's love, or your comfort to remind them of the Hilarity of his grace.

The next gift that Paul mentions in his list is probably the most often overlooked. We superficially assume that his injunction to be generous is meant only for those who have lots of money to give away. Sadly, that misunderstanding causes many people to miss all the Hilarity of being generous.

To understand the concept correctly we must stress again that grace is the basis for these gifts. One who is gifted with liberality gives generously not because he or she has much to give, but because that individual has a freer understanding of possessions and their importance.

Because the Greek word *metadidomi* is perhaps best translated "to share with someone else what one has" or "to impart," its object is not limited simply to financial resources. God invites us to be liberal with many other things.

Especially this matters in connection with the Christian community's care for the needs of the poor and oppressed. Often our money is not the best thing we could give them. More urgently they might need your farming skills, your medical expertise, or your time to help refugees resettle in a strange land. What is called for here is not necessarily financial generosity, but — vastly more important — an attitude of heart that says, "Whatever is mine is yours."

The concept is well summarized by the Hebrew word *Shalom,* which is used in a diversity of ways to connote everything from peace as an absence of war to the peace of having enough. The term carries a range of meanings such as prosperity, contentment, fulfillment, satisfaction, a sense of well-being, health, wholeness. When Jewish people seriously say *Shalom* to one another, they commit themselves to do all they can to insure that the other individual experiences such wholeness. Thus, if we say *Shalom* to hungry persons, we are committed to sharing our lunch with them and to giving them whatever we can to help them feed themselves in the future. (See James 2, especially v. 16.)

We can't say that word lightly, therefore, in an age when three-fourths of the people in the world go to bed hungry each night. Our world has such an enormous need for the use of this grace-gift as it is described by the NEB translation: "If you give [to the needs of others], give with all your heart."

Other translations describe the process as giving "freely" (JBP), "generously" (TEV and NIV), or with "liberality" (RSV). All of these terms effectively picture the open-heartedness of the gift. Moreover, an open heart produces open purse strings and open refrigerators and open clocks.

Writing about this gift, I am ashamed that I am so stingy with my time. A former pastoral colleague has a great gift of giving time with generosity. As he listens to persons, he always gives the impression that he has all the time in the world to devote to them. As a result, he expresses much more compassion and genuine care than those who seem busy and begrudging of time.

Similarly, my friend Sandy, described in the previous chapter, has a gift for giving. One night she invited Julie and me for dinner with her family simply because she had "such a big ham"; several times she welcomed me home from speaking trips with flowers from her garden. Now that I live elsewhere, she cares for me generously every time I go to Olympia for CEM board meetings.

The Greek word translated "generously" here in Romans 12:8 also conveys the notion of "sincerity as an expression of singleness of purpose" or "purity of motive." Paul seems to intend these ideas, too, in his choice of the word, for in the Christian community the gift of giving requires such singleness and purity in order to remain constructive. To keep a simple, pure heart prevents one from being generous for ulterior motives that manipulate or that destroy the dignity of the recipient. Furthermore, we are not rightly generous if we give away all we have and then depend on others for our provision. Rather, with singleness of purpose (namely, to serve God!), we are invited to live with as little as we need in order to share as much as we can with others.

Unless our giving is from a simple singleness of heart, we are like the religious leaders so often criticized by Jesus for their ostentation. We remember his praise instead for the widow who gave all she had in total trust. Yet she did it unobtrusively in humble simplicity and true Hilarity. Consequently, her offering of her whole life continues to be a grace-gift that reaches out of the pages of our Bibles to encourage us still today.

This grace-gift makes us realize again how important the Christian community is. I have heard it said that "Individuals can resist injustice, but only in community can we do justice." Individuals might take a stand against various ills in our society, but only as a group can we change them. The tasks of justice-building are too large for us alone. Only as we join together in giving generously can God's people generate enough resources to tackle the tasks. Consider the tremendous efforts of such outstanding communities as MAP International, Heifer Project International, or Prison Fellowship.

However, the generosity called for is not limited to giving only to those in need of charity. (JB errs in limiting the gift to almsgiving.) God's people have the privilege of sharing whatever we have that someone else might need.

One extraordinary example still stands out in my mind. A dozen years ago I wanted very much to attend a reunion for the college choir in which I had traveled around the world. I gave up the idea of going because I couldn't afford the plane fare to Chicago, though I longed for the opportunity to be with those who had experienced the profound effects of that mission tour and to talk with the choir director, who had been a spiritual mentor to me.

One day a travel agent called to ask for the dates on

which I wanted to fly to and from Chicago. I was baffled. Somebody had anonymously bought a round-trip ticket for me so that I could go to the reunion. To this day I am enormously grateful for such amazing generosity. Not only did that financial liberality enable me to attend the reunion, but that friend also gave me an invaluable picture of how richly my heavenly Father loves his children and provides for their emotional, spiritual, and psychological, as well as material, needs.

The simplicity and Hilarity and generosity of my benefactor's gift stir in me a deeper desire to give to others in turn. That person contributed what I needed in order to experience *Shalom*. How can each of us and all of us together be more generous, more purposeful givers of such Hilarity?

Therefore:

1. Who in our Christian community needs encouragement or admonition?

2. What is the best way for us to care about each one of those persons?

3. How have we hurt people in the past by dumping the gospel on them?

4. How can we in the Christian community increase the Hilarity that equips us to minister more effectively to those in need of upbuilding?

5. What do we have that we could give away more generously?

6. How does an increase in Hilarity enable us to become more generous?

7. How can our attitudes be changed so that we can become more simple and openhearted in our giving?

15. *The Grace-Gifts of Leadership and Hilarious Mercy*

... the one presiding — in diligence! the one extending
mercy — in Hilarity!

— ROMANS 12:8c-d

EVERYONE WAS TALKING at once; we were making no
progress on the assigned project. All the youth board
members were participating in a game designed to help us
see how leadership emerges. Suddenly one pastor in the
group began to speak. His deep voice and mellow pace
broke through the din and caused us all to pay attention.
We followed his advice, and the project proceeded to com-
pletion. His leadership gifts were clearly evident. We all
realized why he had always been the unanimous choice for
chairman of the board.

Not everyone has the necessary gifts for certain tasks;
no one else commanded the respect that our chairman did.
Gladly we all let him be the one to lead meetings and guide
the directions the board pursued. Our exercise in discovering leadership gifts set the rest of us free to serve the com-

mittee in other ways. The more precisely we know what are not our gifts but someone else's, the more surely we can move in those directions God has chosen for us.

This sixth function on Paul's list of grace-gifts also has a broad field of meanings as it is used in the New Testament. The Greek verb *prohistemi,* from which Paul derives the participle used here, literally means "to stand before" and thus is defined as so to "influence others as to cause them to follow a recommended course of action" — "to guide, to direct, to lead." This leads to a secondary meaning, "to be engaged in helping or aiding." Furthermore, in some instances in the New Testament the verb stresses engaging "in something with intense devotion." Our English translations catch the varied significances of this verb with widely divergent renderings. Our consideration of the word within the entire cotext of Romans 12 helps us to interpret it carefully.

Since this section of Romans is discussing the working together of the whole body of the Church, the gift of leadership enumerated here probably should not be confined specifically to officials (as in the JB); nor does the secondary meaning of aid seem appropriate (as in the RSV) since the next gift in the list of seven focuses more on the dispensing of mercy. Rather, it seems here that Paul is intending to encourage those who bear within themselves an inherent authority that gives them legitimacy as leaders in the community. You probably know certain persons to whom we gladly defer because we know that under their leadership our community's particular projects will flourish.

As each of our chapters about Paul's list of grace-gifts in Romans 12 has added new insights about the *charismata,* it is important to add at this point the frequent coalescence of corollary gifts within individuals or in a group of persons within the community. For example, 1 Timothy 5:17 uses the same verb as Romans 12:8 when it urges, "Let the elders who *rule* well be considered worthy of double honor, especially those who labor in preaching and teaching" (RSV, emphasis added). This combination of leadership with two other grace-gifts shows how interrelated they often are. Many times a person manifests one grace-gift in order to use others more effectively, or a team of persons possesses correlative gifts.

Once a regional board asked me to devise a three-week course for youth workers that involved overviewing the content of the Scriptures, learning how to lead Bible studies, and participating in training workshops for many dimensions of youth ministry. Normally I would gladly let someone else do all the detailed administration of setting up the whole project and planning the food, the housing, and the logistics of the training days. This time, however, I experienced God's empowerment (the grace-gift of leadership) for the planning as a correlative to the gift of teaching the Bible studies.

This example serves well to underscore again the centrality of grace in the gifts. We cannot ever manufacture *charismata* for ourselves, but when God's gifts are available to us, we can recognize and appreciate them and use them appropriately to channel grace into whatever situation called them forth.

Paul says that a person's gift of administration or leadership should be used "to work hard," to govern "with intense effort and motivation," "to do one's best." The Greek noun carries a field of meaning best associated with words like "eagerness" or "readiness to expend energy and effort." Because Paul focuses in Romans 12 on members of the community learning that they all are necessary to one another and belong to one another, it seems that here he chooses the term to combine care with eagerness, a special urgency and intensity about the leadership tasks. The attitude necessary for such leadership involves the idea of readiness of heart to seek the community's well-being.

Often leadership is destroyed by mixed motives. Our ambition is sinfully directed if we who are in charge manipulate others so that our administration creates personal benefits or increases power. If our eyes are fixed instead on God's purposes and our sole intent is to fulfill them, then our Hilarity will not wane nor will our governing be marred by self-centeredness.

Certainly our motives are always a bit mixed. However, our constant prayer and goal in spiritual growth as individuals and in the community is that we might eliminate the lack of passion that keeps us from thoroughness of vision, that saps our vitality, that mars our efforts and reduces their power.

The more single-minded we become, the more thoroughly committed to God all our efforts will be, the more his purposes can be accomplished in them, and the greater Hilarity we will experience. Our tendency to slip so easily into manipulation of others for our own ends is one of the greatest destroyers of genuine community, but to recognize our constant battle for purity of motive enables us to keep growing toward maturity in our faith and in the Body.

The need for diligence is critical in this age of extremes. A caring zeal enables us to find a balance in leadership between the overproductivity that characterizes workaholics and the mediocrity of those who limit their work to just enough to get by. Members of the community of God's people can offer to the world the alternative of an excellence in leadership that calls forth the gifts of all the members of the Body. This highlights one of the unique problems of the grace-gift of administration. Those who govern must be especially sensitive to the fact that their diligence in leadership serves as a model for the zeal of the whole community.

How often parish projects peter out for lack of leadership. Such situations invite the community to question whether an undertaking is no longer appropriate and ought to die a natural death. If a program deserves still to be nourished, the community is challenged to find members who have been gifted for its leadership. Those who get burned out are perhaps exerting a leadership they don't possess. Certainly the Church could have an atmosphere in which those with the grace-gift of administration will take seriously their "having" of it and delight in using it for the benefit of the whole community.

Furthermore, the functions of leadership are mistakenly localized in one individual — often the local parish pastor. Rather, the function of a pastor must be understood in terms of shepherding. When those called to the pastoral care of the community get so bogged down in "administrivia" that they are taken away from their study of the Scriptures and prayer, then they are able neither to care for the spiritual needs of the parishioners nor to preach the Word with power and sensitivity. Others gifted in leadership could set them free by administering the affairs of the congregation. This is indeed a critical case in which attendant gifts reside in a team of people so that each is freed to specialize in his or her particular concerns. Those who exercise tender pastoral care are not usually the best ones to function as administrators.

Our study of Paul's list reveals the interlocking nature of the grace-gifts. Often several of them exist together in one person, and the various gifts reinforce each other in that person's total ministry. At other times the attendant gifts necessarily reside in two or more persons close together so that the work of each can reinforce the work of the other. My secretary Sandy and I keep enjoying the Hilarity of that correlation in our teamwork. Her gifts of serving and giving and administration set me free to spend my time studying, teaching, and writing. Correlatively, she says my teaching motivates her to use her gifts more effectively. We both thoroughly need each other, and when we work together God's power can be more than multiplied.

Paul lists as the seventh grace-gift in Romans 12 the charism of mercy or kindness to those sorrowing or in need. Again, the position of the phrases in Paul's entire discourse is significant, because the very next admonition — to keep love from being hypocritical (v. 9) — is an essential qualifier for the way in which concern is dispensed. We don't offer gifts of mercy only when we feel like being helpful to those in distress, but we must also remember that acts of mercy done without appropriate compassion are empty and hypocritical.

Furthermore, verse 8 stresses that acts of mercy are to be done with glad Hilarity. As emphasized in the preface to this book, we don't want to make the anachronistic mistake of interpreting the Greek *hilarotēs* with our contemporary understanding of its English derivative *hilarity*. But the word does blast all the old stereotypes of dour-faced, serious-miened women dispensing soup for the poor. What better witness to the Hilarity we have because of our relationship with Jesus Christ if such acts of mercy are done with eager cheerfulness!

A wonderful example of true mercy with Hilarity in the biblical sense of that word is a woman who serves in the program of Broadway Christian Parish in South Bend, Indiana, to feed the neighborhood on Sunday noons. Once as she, her husband, her two sons, and I served dinner for the day's festivities, I was astounded by the scope of her project. She had prepared turkey, dressing, gravy, mashed potatoes, and pumpkin pie with candy canes for about ninety people! I asked her how she managed so much work, and she answered that she just loved to provide a special meal for those who usually couldn't afford it.

If only such Hilarity could characterize our use of all

135

the grace-gifts! No one really does anything well unless she or he enjoys the process of doing it. To be persons of Hilarity is all the more appealing because we live in such an age of pain and overwhelming confusion. Human beings live in fear of nuclear war, terminal illness, and economic chaos. We do not superficially ignore those problems when we live Hilariously, but we reveal the uniqueness of the Christian life, which is founded upon a wholly different basis for existence.

Throughout this book I am using the word *Hilarity* in its biblical sense, which differs from the superficial "noisy merriment" or "boisterous gaiety" of the contemporary world. Rather, the profound gladness this word signifies arises from a deep sense of the rich treasure of God's grace for us, from an awareness that God's love sets us free to enjoy being truly ourselves, and from trusting the Grace-Giver to work through his gifts to us. Hilarity in the Christian community comes from being transformed rather than conformed. It expresses itself in eager and generous love for others (as explicated in all the chapters that follow). It depends upon the renewal of the mind, though that doesn't hamper its spontaneity. As such it is the focus of everything we desire in the community of God's people and thus brings together all the concepts of this book.

Hilarity takes possession of our beings, enables them always to be growing toward greater wholeness (Shalom), *and springs out of us as a fountain of life reaching out to others. Hilarity is the freedom to be truly ourselves.*

We have seen in Paul's list of the seven gifts a wide variety of ways in which God's grace is passed on to others. At various times and in various ways appropriate to our personal situations and arising out of our particular relationship with the Lord, we are unique bearers of that grace. Each time, the power and freedom of doing what God has called us to do fills us with Hilarity, an immense cheer and exultant gladness for the privilege of serving him in whatever way he chooses and out of our truest selves.

Focusing particularly on the grace-gift of showing mercy, we recognize that God's people often do not link doing deeds of mercy with gladness. Somehow the cheer gets lost between our study of the Scriptures and the practical application. Or maybe we don't study the Scriptures deeply enough and consequently don't experience the constant Hilarity that could mark our lives.

This takes us back to the initial *therefore* with which we began our study of Romans 12. In the first chapter we hoped that all of our responses to Paul's exhortations about our behavior would come out of a deep sense of God's love and grace. When we are thoroughly involved in the passing on of that great love to others, we will become more and more aware of the immense privilege that we have to serve the Lord as we do with his power and direction and freedom. Then our acts of love and mercy, as well as our exercising of whatever gifts God bestows, will all be characterized by this grand Hilarity, the Joy of being what God intended us to be — uniquely gifted and immeasurably important as participants in the Body of Christ.

As Paul says later in his letter to the Romans, the kingdom of God is "righteousness and peace and joy in the Holy Spirit" (14:17). The word *righteousness* defines our right standing with God by means of our faith and trust in him. Peace marks our relationships with others because of the mutual love and acceptance that we will explore in the next chapters of this book. And Joy marks our relationship with ourselves, as we live out the reality of God's purposes in our lives and the extension of his grace to others through the use of our gifts. Being truly ourselves is Hilariously delightful.

Moreover, our joyful Hilarity is heightened because we celebrate it together with the other members of the Christian community. Our sense of belonging to one another sets us free to be truly ourselves, each one characterized by grace-gifts valuable to the community and not burdened by responsibilities for which others possess the gifts. Our togetherness sets us all free to use our gifts with more Hilarity.

Life is not all roses if we are Christians. We still mourn and struggle. However, underneath all the responsibility and grief will always be the deep sense of wholeness, the Hilarity of being in a community of caring, the profound knowledge of the truth that God is God — and a grace-giving God at that.

Therefore:

1. In what areas of life in our parish or family is each of us called to leadership?

2. Is our leadership characterized by diligence (whatever form that might take in us), or are we struggling with burnout? If we are burned out, what leadership functions might we have taken on ourselves that are not a part of our calling?

3. What motivates us to be eager or intent on our purpose? How can we grow to be more focused in our callings and as a community together?

4. Who that we know needs our acts of mercy?

5. What are some ways in which our Christian community can offer mercy to our world — in our local community? in a more global sense?

6. Does Hilarity characterize our mercifulness or do we dispense mercy with an air of superiority or condescension or duty?

7. Who are models for us of Hilarity in their use of gifts? How can their example be helpful to us in increasing the Joy with which we serve the Lord? How can we avoid making our service in Hilarity too legalistic?

16. Agapē without Hypocrisy

The love — not hypocritical!

—ROMANS 12:9a

THE CHINESE TRAIN was terribly overcrowded. My friend Chi Ping realized that the sodden, drunken, bedraggled man was heading for his seat, and there was no escape. Chi Ping leaned as close to the window as he could.

He could not escape the stench either. The man reeked as though he had not had a bath in years. Chi Ping held himself tightly, not wanting to come even close to touching the man for fear of the lice that his body must carry and out of disdain for his ghastly odor and appearance.

Nevertheless, as he pulled away, my friend was tormented by the fact that he should love this man, too. A new Christian, Chi Ping was only beginning to learn the meaning of Christ's love. Sharing that love with his family and friends was difficult since they were still all Buddhists as he had been till not long before this event. He began to think about Jesus' love for the outcasts and lepers of his time. He began to pray that God would fill him with the Holy Spirit's perfect love for this despicable creature, who had invaded his piety

139

with a realistic need. No phony demonstration of love was possible; this object of God's love was too overwhelmingly undesirable to charm a false show of acceptance. Any demonstration of care must be a supernatural power.

Over twenty years ago I heard Chi Ping describe how, contrary to his very emotions and thought, he felt his arm being raised and, to his great surprise, found himself putting it around the man's shoulders and drawing him close. The poor man wept as he received Chi Ping's genuine expression of care.

I don't remember any of the other details of the story (they probably included taking the man home for food, a bath, clothes, and shelter), but I was too overjoyed by the raising of the arm to get the rest of the story straight. Chi Ping did what he would not have desired to do because, willing to be loving, he had prayed that God would somehow create love in him for the invader of his quietude.

The love that Chi Ping showed to that man on the crowded Chinese train was Hilariously not hypocritical. Surely it demonstrates vividly the first part of Romans 12:9, which the Living Bible paraphrases, "Don't just pretend that you love others; really love them." To do that is absolutely impossible without supernatural empowering. On the other hand, to do so is also absolutely necessary for our Christian witness and vital for our own realization of the power of God at work through us. To love genuinely is the message of the rest of the twelfth chapter of Romans. All the verses that remain will illustrate for us different ways in which the reality of our love in Christ is manifested.

Besides being an introductory statement for the rest of Paul's exhortations, this verse also connects us very closely with the ideas from which we have just come. If we pause here to review the progression of the discourse to this point, we will realize how integrally the various exhortations of this chapter work together to give us a picture of how our

Christian communities can experience greater Hilarity in being the people that God has designed and called us to be.

Paul began his injunctions by urging the Romans and us to offer ourselves as sacrifices, living and holy and acceptable to God, and he challenged us to continue to be transformed by the renewing of our minds. Then he called us to discover more deeply the meaning of the Body of Christ and our place in it by stressing that we each have different gifts to contribute Hilariously to the upbuilding and outreach of that Body. Now he helps us to understand that the exercising of those gifts in response to God's grace ("therefore") will be characterized by attitudes and actions of genuine love.

As he moves from the naming of gifts that particular individuals might hold within the Christian community to virtues that are to characterize all the members, this universalizing is underscored by the additions of the specific article *the*. In the verse we are examining in this chapter, Paul declares: "The love" that marks those who belong to Christ is "unhypocritical."

This progression, which creates the fundamental sense of the whole discourse, is paralleled by the general thrust of Paul's letters. Compare, for example, the great love chapter of 1 Corinthians 13 and its setting. Right in the midst of explanations about speaking in tongues and the exercise of other gifts, Paul asserts that the greatest thing of all is love and that without love everything else is empty. Always we must be aware of the hollowness of using gifts without love, so that our service for Christ is continuously lived out in the context of our relationship with him, in the Hilarity of his grace.

However, as we explore the concepts of love and affection in the next several chapters, we must also remember that a great diversity of manifestations of these virtues characterizes the unity of the Christian community. As Chapter 8 stressed, each of us is called to be faithful to our own particular standard of faith, not to be compared with the measure of others. Let's avoid the danger of making certain expressions of love normative in Christian circles.

By God's gifting some persons are more outgoing and warmly affectionate; others demonstrate his love in quiet ways that are just as genuine. Some persons are more suited to hospitality (Rom. 12:13) or are more able to pursue peace (v. 18). Others are able to be deeply compassionate in sharing the emotions of others (v. 15) or are empowered for fervent prayer (v. 12). Though the rest of Romans 12 describes attributes that we all want to incorporate more thoroughly into our lives, we dare not become legalistic in expecting all of these traits to take the same forms or to be equally manifested in each of us.

This is why we must be careful to notice that Paul's description of the fruit of the Spirit in Galatians 5:22-23 is decisively singular. The fruit of the Spirit is manifested in nine different ways, including love, patience, and peace, but that one fruit is the life of Christ within us. Some persons are more loving as Christ lives through them; others are more self-controlled, and still others, more gentle. Our proportions of the nine manifestations are uniquely different, though we all want more and more to reflect each of the qualities. Furthermore, together the Christian community manifests them all.

Therefore, when Paul urges affectionate love in Romans 12:10 or hospitality in verse 13, some will be better than others at demonstrating these dimensions of God's grace. We dare not impose certain norms on all Christians that would squeeze them into molds rather than letting the Spirit transform each of us according to the uniquenesses of our special creation and the renewal processes in our individual minds. Hilarity thrives in freedom.

The friend who pointed out to me the need for this

warning is not an outwardly affectionate person, so she doesn't fit into the mold of the gushy, huggy Christian. Yet when I was going through a time of discouragement and depression several years ago, she was the one who stood beside me most effectively with reminders of God's grace and its sufficiency for my needs. Her gentle care and affection are no less genuine expressions of love than the hugging displays that seem to be demanded in some Christian fellowships.

Now specifically in Romans 12:9, the fact that love can be hypocritical makes this exhortation to sincerity necessary. In order to follow all the rest of the twelfth chapter's injunctions appropriately, we must get this one down: our love dare not be a "pretense" (JB) or "imitation" (JBP).

Recall times when persons have loved you with a phony love. So easily we recognize that false lovers only want to get something out of us or that they are merely fulfilling a duty. Sometimes that sugary-sweet, sticky love is so apparent that it is repulsive. We detest the slick Christian, who oils his way into our consciousness and obstructs us with the pretense of his godliness. Super-piety is easily recognized for the self-centered lovelessness that it really is. Of course, you and I have observed false love not only in other Christians but also in ourselves.

So how can we avoid a phony love? The secret lies in understanding the true meaning of the Greek term *agapē*. In our society the idea of love is distorted into "I love hamburgers" and the sort of romantic love that seizes pleasure but does not stay committed. Our English language is deficient in that it lacks specific words for sexual, friendship, disinterested, and family love.

Before its extensive use in the New Testament, the word *agapē* had been a weak term in classical Greek. Decisively, however, the early Christians strengthened the word by using it to describe God's unique love. As they took over a term that had signified an insipid, disinterested love, its application to God emphasized his being able to give love wisely, thoroughly, without any demand of return, freely. Such love allows what is truly best for us and what is completely appropriate for God's perfect purposes. Thus, when we pass that love on to others, it is the intelligent, purposeful love which God creates in us and which flows through us to minister to the needs of the person loved. Let us heavily accentuate the intelligence of this love, its specific direction toward the needs of the other, and its source in the Hilarity of knowing how thoroughly God has loved us first.

This intelligent love, Paul writes curtly, is to be without pretense. As in this whole section (see the translation in this epigrammatic style in Chapter 12, p. 103), the phrase has no verb. Paul simply writes, "The *agapē* — unhypocritical." His very terseness underscores this as the most essential quality of the love that the Christian community displays. Absolutely without pretense, it is to be instead a genuine expression of the love of God at work in and through us.

Agapē is also intensely practical. Paul begins at this point to describe more thoroughly the love that is to characterize the Christian community. Integral to his whole message is that love is the core of all the gifts in the Body, all the living sacrifices, all the offerings of our lives. As Francis Schaeffer entitled his little booklet, love is "the mark of the Christian."[1]

Consequently, this verse convicts us with its challenge: we are ashamed of the hypocrisy of our love. Indeed, we would be destroyed by grief at our failure if it were not for the fact that this phrase, too, like everything else in Romans 12, is hinged on that great word *therefore*. Our understanding of giftedness, of "body-ness," of being holy sacrifices, of

1. Francis Schaeffer, *The Mark of the Christian* (Downers Grove, IL: InterVarsity Press, 1970).

being transformed, and now of love is based all on the same grace. "With eyes wide open to the mercies of God," we recognize that he wants to fill us with his perfect love.

Our understanding of the nature of love in the Christian community is heightened by paying careful attention to this complementary passage:

> And I pray that you, being rooted and established in love, may have power, together with all the saints, to grasp how wide and long and high and deep is the love of Christ, and to know this love that surpasses knowledge — that you may be filled to the measure of all the fullness of God. (Eph. 3:17b-19, NIV)

Notice this paradox: God's love is unknowable in its infinity, and yet we can know it because we actually become filled with it! Ephesians describes it in four dimensions (wide, long, high, and deep) even though we live in a three-dimensional world. This use of four terms carries us beyond the sphere of human experience into a love that transcends the natural. Thus, we know this love powerfully and supernaturally because we recognize it in ourselves and because, "together with all the saints," we experience it Hilariously in community. This incredible prayer has even more incredible implications.

The major implication is the release that this theology gives us from any efforts to manufacture our own love. How often we have tried somehow to love somebody that we can't stand! The harder we try to love, the more difficult it becomes. We get super-frustrated and angry at the other person for making love so difficult. All our human efforts to try to love others are bound to fail because the more we put ourselves under a performance principle, the more our failures make us feel guilty and cause us to love less. This is the corollary to the central message of God's freeing love throughout the discourse of the book of Romans: that all human efforts, all performance principles, will only bring failure and despair. Only when we are set free from the demands of the law can we discover the Hilarity of living in love through faith. Indeed, this is not of ourselves, but a gift of grace.

Central to our theology, then, is giving up our attempts to love. This does not imply a giving up of self-discipline. Much to the contrary, what I am suggesting demands greater self-discipline. However, we choose discipline freely as a response to God's love. The Hilarity of God's immense grace for us makes us *want* to grow to be more loving and to love without hypocrisy.

The First Epistle of John essentially describes how love can be without hypocrisy in this gentle invitation: "Beloved, let us love one another, for love is from God; and everyone who loves is born of God and knows God. The one who does not love does not know God, for God is love" (1 John 4:7-8).

By logical syllogism we deduce a very important fact. If a person is not loving, John says, he or she does not know God. How will that individual become more loving, then? Can we grow in love by trying to love more? No, our attempts to love will only end in more frustration and less love. The solution, John implies, is to know God better. This is so simple that we miss it all the time: our means for becoming more loving is to know God better.

Then, as Paul asserts in 2 Corinthians 3:18, we will become more like him as we reflect his character from one degree of glory to another. Remember how Chi Ping prayed for God's love to flow through him toward the bum. The more he thought about the compassion of Jesus for outcasts, the more he became filled with the very fullness of that love. He began to know that love which "surpasses knowledge" because it was flowing through him grace-fully.

Some might dismiss this idea as too simplistic or as a rejection of discipline, but greater spiritual discipline is needed to approach things God's way than to keep up our own efforts. God's way, however, is to set us free from performance principles and to fill us with the Hilarity of his presence.

Our love gets hypocritical because we attempt to love out of our human capacities. That will never work. Rather, when we spend our efforts in the spiritual disciplines of getting to know God better, then his love can flow through us more effectively. We are transformed by the renewing of our minds.

This concept is the essence of Christianity and an overturning of the way we always do things as human beings. Can we fully appreciate the privilege? That God should so deign to work through us drives us to our knees in gratitude. Moreover, the result of our wonder and sense of privilege will always be a deepened love and a greater desire for God to fill us. Imagine with me what could happen in the Body of Christ if we could get this straight! Just dream of how the Church would affect the world if we would become a Hilarious community filled with the very love of God pulsating through us to others.

When we catch visions of the love that persons around us need so desperately, we are driven by an intense desire to share more thoroughly that love which fills us to overflowing. We need to discipline ourselves, to immerse ourselves in the Scriptures (as we are doing in this study of Romans 12), so that we can know God and his love better together with all the saints. The challenge before us is an awesome one, but one that we can seize together with Hilarity.

Therefore:

1. What is Paul's progression of thought in this twelfth chapter of Romans? How does understanding the sense of the whole discourse enable us to grasp more deeply the meaning of each particular phrase?

2. Why is love the most important attribute of all? Why does Paul write about it right after his explications of the grace-gifts in the Christian community?

3. Why does the Body of Christ lose its Hilarity when it is not characterized by love overall?

4. What other passages in the Scriptures speak of the pre-eminence of love?

5. How shall we define the love that we want to characterize our community?

6. How have we experienced God's love through us lately?

7. How have we experienced genuine love from other persons in the Christian community?

8. How have we experienced the fact that love is not our production, but a gift from God which fills us — and works through us — till we know it?

9. What should we do when we have trouble loving someone? How can we prevent this theology from becoming too simplistic?

10. How can we understand the "surpassing knowledge" love of God? What is the importance in Ephesians 3:14-21 of the phrase "together with all the saints"?

11. How can we as a Christian community and each of us specifically as an individual member of that community bring God's love to the world around us?

12. What is the connection of love and Hilarity in the Christian community?

17. Love by Abhorring and Cherishing

Abhorring the wicked thing! Glued to the good thing!

— ROMANS 12:9b

ON A SUNNY DAY western Washington is the most beautiful countryside in the world. But even a gorgeous, beflowered, sun-dazzling, sparkling-blue-ocean day can be spoiled by a slug.

Slugs surely are the most gruesome of all creatures; they are long (up to six inches in length), brown/yellow/gray giant snails without the shell. My first exposure to their gross ugliness was quite traumatic when someone (helpfully!) held my head right next to their slimy, sticky trail on a tree branch. They eat the best plants in the garden — almost whole tomatoes and the forget-me-nots I brought back from Alaska — and don't do anything constructive. Why did God make them? Perhaps to remind me that he loves the unlovable, including me.

One value of slugs is that they provide such a superb illustration for the first part of the phrase to be studied in this chapter: "Hate what is evil." We should abhor what is wicked as intensely as I detest slugs.

The connection of this injunction with the previous exhortation to let love be without hypocrisy is important. We strengthen our unhypocritical love by not letting it be spoiled by any involvement in evil. If we compromise our principles in any way, our love is made impure. We are to stand firm against even the appearance of evil and not let love be weakened by any contamination.

Imperatively we detest whatever is evil in ourselves and in a brother's life-style or attitudes. The phrase "loving the sinner and hating the sin" expresses excellently this sequence in Paul's exhortations. Our love for the person committing wrong should be genuine, not pretended in any way; but in true love we will abhor the evil that can only harm our sister.

God's love is like that. The freedom we have because we are loved by God is wonderfully summarized in this sentence: "God loves us so much that he accepts us just as we are, but he also loves us too much to let us stay that way." He certainly loves us without any phoniness and with total acceptance, but he cannot stand anything in us contrary to his purposes and is working constantly to purge that from us and to transform our lives by the renewing of our minds into the Hilarity of living in the image of Christ.

Consequently, this is the nature of the love that we are to have for each other in the Christian community. We will exhibit compassion toward the one suffering from guilt, but we will not condone the errors that cause it. Furthermore, we can learn to deal with ourselves that way also. By faith we are learning to love ourselves with a genuine and proper love, but the more our faith matures the more we grow to hate everything in us that is evil. We want to walk as far away from it as possible in order to purify our love.

Throughout the centuries theologians have wrestled

with this terrible question of theodicy: if God is all powerful and God is good, why is there evil in the world? No one can thoroughly explain why evil exists, though we know that loving God out of freedom necessitates the possibility to choose not to love him. Furthermore, human choices that reject God's will throughout history have resulted in that which is apart from him — namely, evil.

Our response to evil, then, is to hate it — to abhor or detest it — and to flee from it (see 2 Tim. 2:22). The Amplified Bible expands Romans 12:9b with "loathe all ungodliness, turn in horror from wickedness." That addition captures the deep sense of Paul's exhortation: from everything that is evil (in us and in others whom we love) we are to shrink as if from a slug.

This injunction guides our reactions to the practical realities of daily life. We must realize that whenever we dabble with evil in the slightest way, our love is spoiled. If we fudge truth just a little in talking to a friend, the relationship is marred. The community is made unclean by the slightest bit of gossip. The smallest trace of games, pretensions, or manipulations in our care for others makes our love less than whole or holy. We want to hate with a perfect hatred all those little jabs that puncture our love.

We need the terseness of this description: Abhorring the evil! One day in a car I suddenly reached over and turned off the radio. My teenaged companion was shocked. But the rock station had begun playing a song that I knew to be grossly immoral, and I didn't want to corrupt our minds with its suggestions. We need to abhor evil. We can turn off our radios and television sets (my husband and I have chosen not to own one) when they bombard us with garbage. We can protest the proliferation of raw sex and violence in movies and seek alternatives to false values of power and self-centered exploitation.

This is not to make our Hilarity prudish or provincial.

151

But we want to be pure. Hilarity is destroyed by immorality. Truly the only way to be growing toward purity in our culture is to be outraged by that which is impure.

I read recently of a man who in a tragic accident lost from memory his seven most recent years, which included the time of his marriage and the birth of his children. As he was adjusting again to life with his family, one night he watched television with them and was absolutely astounded by the immorality in the programs. Remembering only the state of television seven years before, he could not understand why his family members were not horrified by the values they were viewing. Just as a frog immersed in lukewarm water that is gradually heated to boiling does not jump out when it begins to cook him, we have become immune to the increasing corruption of the mass media in our society.

Think of all the dimensions of life in which we compromise our biblical principles. Think of the impingement of our society's values upon us in the ways we speak to one another, the things we do, the methods we use. Shouldn't we be shrinking a lot more with abhorrence so that our love and the Hilarity of our community aren't dirtied by the corruptions of our culture?

Invariably when I speak strongly about this in teaching situations, someone responds, "But we can't do that as much as you can, Marva. You don't have children, and you don't live in the real world with the kinds of job commitments and family situations that we face." Indeed, my circumstances of home and work avoid many dimensions of evil that you might confront. That is why we need the Hilarity of the Christian community so desperately — and why our Hilarity needs so much to be strengthened! We need the encouragement and support of our fellow believers to have the courage to abhor the evil of our world. Certainly for each of us a greater shrinking from evil is not just wishful thinking, but a disciplined possibility and an urgent necessity.

I know there are many taints and tints of evil in my life that I could weed out. Why don't I? Why don't you? Two of my goals for this chapter are simply to stimulate awareness of the need for the Christian community to fight evil more actively and to intensify our desire to be more faithful to who we are as the people of God. God is at work in us to renew us. One of the ways in which we cooperate in that renewal is by a growing refusal to let our minds and lives be polluted by the garbage that surrounds us.

Furthermore, one of the best ways to withstand the assault of the corruption of our society is to fill our minds and lives instead with the good — as Paul advocates, to be "clinging" to what is good. The same verb is used in Luke 10:11 to describe dust that "sticks" to our feet. Just as love and Hilarity are spoiled when they are polluted by evil, contrarily both are deepened by close association with what is good. Since we defined good in Chapter 7, now we can simply concentrate on the benefits of clinging to it. We can rejoice together in the effects of purity on our love.

Paul doesn't present these two attitudes and life-styles with imperative verbs, urging "do this and don't do that." Rather, he uses present participles, adjectives that characterize our existence in continuous action. These describe God's people as those who are "abhorring the evil; glued to the good." Constant vigilance against evil is necessary; daily we renew our commitment to what is good. Our lives are constant processes of weeding out negative influences and clinging as tightly as we can to what is upbuilding.

The first time that I had to rescue a lad who had gotten into trouble in the deep water of the lake where I was a lifeguard, I saw the terror in his eyes as I swam toward him. Talking to him gently to ease his panic, I gave him instructions for holding on to my arm so that I could bring him back to the shore. He clung for all he was worth.

In the same way we are to hold fast to what is good —

not to crush it in a false attempt to possess it, but to be so close to it that its good can influence us and be of benefit to us. This is especially important in our choice of models for our growth in Christian faith and for the selection of our friends, co-workers, and marriage partners.

For example, I appreciate profoundly one friend from graduate school days whose commitment to excellence as a classical pianist encouraged my own striving for depth in Bible study preparation. Another friend models patience and compassion. Other friendships with men and women, young and old offer insight into God's peace or wisdom, strength or faithfulness. Each of these gifts of friendship offers aspects of good in the total model of love that I need.

Just as evil influences impinge too much on our Christian lives, so, on the other hand, we fail to cling enough to what is good. We do not expend extra effort to develop relationships that will nurture traits of good within us. We back down when the good gets threatened; we don't fight for principles when they are under attack. We don't cling to the Hilarity of goodness.

Once again Paul's participial structure helps to remind us that we are to be in a constant state of clinging to what is good. This does not advocate a style of love with the negative connotations of a stifling stickiness that alienates or suffocates, but a love that remains committed and intimately faithful. My choice of the word *glued* at the beginning of this chapter is intended to emphasize the unbreakable closeness of such a positive *clinging*.

This devotion to the good can be operative on several different levels in our lives. Seeking to understand how commitment to the good deepens our love in the Christian community, we realize that it refers not only to relationships with people but also to many other aspects of our personalities. For example, I try to teach others about classical music because it so wonderfully uplifts our spirits, stimulates our

intellect, heightens our sense of well-being, and ushers us
into the presence of God. Just as we want to abhor the evil
of violence, sexual immorality, and meaninglessness in
much modern music, so we want to cling to music that will
deepen our love for others. Similarly, I want to learn more
about art from Myron because a deeper understanding of it
will increase my sensitivity and powers of observation. Also,
my husband's love of the soil and delight in gardening keep
beckoning me to a greater awareness of God's creative
beauty. All good things increase our Hilarity as they effect
the growth of our ability to love others and to love God.

On another level, clinging to the good involves striving
for excellence and craftsmanship. One mark of a Christian
in this age of mediocrity might be our intent as God's people
to be as much like him as we can in the way we do everything, no matter what our roles or gifts. To cling to what is
good is to love those we serve and, consequently, to be
responsible about how we fulfill our tasks and spend our
time. Our Hilarity will issue in good work.

All sorts of enrichments, all kinds of positive values,
all healthy disciplines of body and mind and spirit are the
good to which we are invited to cling. Especially I want to
inspire holding fast to the good in each moment. To recover
a sense of delight, to appreciate the flavors or fragrances or
colors of beauties that surround us at particular moments,
to feel things with our inmost being, and thereby to be
sensitive to God's presence in multitudes of little ways —
these, too, are ways in which our love and Hilarity in the
Christian community can be strengthened by our devotion
to that which is good.

Finally, we must address the contemporary tragedy of
lack of commitment. Recently when I spoke on sexual morality to seven "Family Living" classes at a public high school
in Omaha, the question that the students raised most often
was "How can you be so sure of Myron — how do you know

that your marriage will last the rest of your life?" The way the students asked the question made apparent their deep longing for some sort of assurance that love can truly be permanent, that a marriage partner can really be faithful.

The lack of commitment that characterizes contemporary society leads to so much instability for children, so much heartbreak and pain. Spouses not committed to each other for a permanent relationship according to God's plan all too easily leave if somebody seemingly better comes along. Similarly, kids in school not committed to anything fumble around with no sense of purpose or direction. Members of the Body of Christ are not committed to each other with a genuine and thorough love that is applied to the needs of others.

How desperately the world needs the alternative that the Church can offer as it demonstrates the Hilarity of commitment in the gladness of our love for one another. During some of the toughest times of my many years of singleness one of my best friends was a youth worker and musician with whom I could talk deeply about the meaning and working out of our ministries. Moreover, one of the greatest aspects of that friendship was that man's constant assurance of commitment to me. When I had trouble believing in myself, Tim encouraged me because he believed in God's work through me. When I felt confused and alone, he stood beside me to remind me of God's steadfast love and faithfulness.

When I told Tim that I wanted to use him as an illustration for this chapter, he agreed — but only if I emphasized that God's love, and not his abilities or strength, created the good things in our friendship. In fact, that is why the friendship is such a solid illustration. If persons are committed to each other under the love of God, we can cling to that, because we know that his love will never fail even though human loyalty and our abilities to love do.

Many years ago the top-selling single for months was

"Cherish" by the Association. That word describes well the commitment that Paul urges. When we learn to cherish the good, we gain appreciation for the treasure that all things from God are. To cherish the good fills us with Hilarity over God's blessings.

Daily that with which we are associated will change us. Each moment the choice is ours how we will be changed. Will we conform to the influences of evil or will we abhor it? Will we cling to the good and learn to cherish it? Will we let our Hilarity be marred by evil or will it be increased by good?

Therefore:

1. What are some of the evil influences from the surrounding culture — or even within our Christian communities — that adversely affect our lives?

2. How can we grow to hate them and to flee from them more?

3. How can we abhor the evil practices of persons and yet care for the persons?

4. What are some of the good things to which we want to cling?

5. How can we increase the good in our corporate life? How does it deepen the Hilarity of our community to become more committed to the good?

6. What are some of the values that we hold but don't live out? How can we rectify that inconsistency?

7. How can we cling to persons who are good for us without becoming possessive or clinging so tightly that we suffocate or alienate them?

18. *Tenderly Affectionate Devotion*

In friendship love — tenderly affectioned toward each other!

— ROMANS 12:10a

PSYCHOLOGICAL WISDOM gives us the following "statistic":

It takes four hugs a day to survive;
eight hugs a day to maintain;
twelve hugs a day to grow.

Have you received your quotient of hugs today?

Or do you remember the bumper sticker that queried, "Have you hugged your kid today?" And then one came out that asked, "Have you hugged your parents today?" Long ago I had a button that declared, "Hugs improve my appearance."

In spite of all the idolatry of sex in our culture, social scientists have discovered that our society is grossly deficient in genuine expressions of affection. They conclude that the major reason for the rampaging rise in persons living together, in pregnancy out of wedlock, and in abortions is the frightening lack of true affection that most persons experience.

Jacques Ellul offers the most helpful insights for understanding the lack of intimacy in our culture when he juxtaposes technology and intimacy as dichotomous poles on an axis. As technology takes over more and more aspects of life, its tools channel us increasingly into solo activities — such as playing games on our personal computer, listening (with earphones) to our own radio, or passively watching videos that don't even have advertisements to give time to talk to companions. Gone are old-fashioned activities, such as doing dishes or chores together, that fostered communication skills.

Furthermore, as technology decreases our abilities to be intimate with others, we reverse the poles and technologize our intimacy to make it more efficient. Instead of sexual intercourse being the celebrative culmination of a long process of growing intimacy and an expression of a lifelong commitment within the bond of a marriage covenant, now sexual union is the way for persons to get to know each other — and one-timers need a technological manual in order to do it well. How the Hilarity of true intimacy is annihilated!

On the other hand, since we suffer from the deficiency of intimacy, we also reverse the poles in the opposite direction and try to make our technology more intimate. The latest technological toys are advertised with sexy models. We create pink telephones and urge their use with a propagandistic appeal: "Reach out and touch someone." This lie confuses us about our connection with others — certainly it is wonderful to hear the voices of loved ones, but we don't particularly like the touch of a cold instrument; it doesn't hug us well. Computers have advanced the technological encroachment on intimacy because now we can simply send messages over the modem and not even hear the voice of our loved one.

In such a society, what is the role of the Church in

demonstrating the affection of Jesus? We dare not be overly simplistic, but Christians can address the rampant sexual immorality of our times by offering an alternative, the preventative medicine of the true devotion in tender affection that Paul encourages us to learn. We who follow Jesus are certainly struck as we read the Gospels by his extraordinary affection in drawing persons away from their immorality and setting them free to love in godly ways. I long for the Church to become more intentional in ministering with his kind of loving care.

One problem is that love in churches gets so superficial. I'm tired of the "I love you, brother/sister" jargon that has no substance behind it.

I am not issuing this challenge to the Church out of frustration that my own needs aren't being met. (My pastor's appeal during the prayer time in yesterday's worship service for drivers to take me to Portland for cancer tests and laser therapy for my eye resulted in an outpouring of offers and expressions of care.) On the contrary, in my teaching travels I observe vast numbers of lonely sisters and brothers of all ages withering without affection. Once an elderly widower in our congregation suffered so much in his loneliness that he talked to me about it one Sunday while I was playing the organ before worship. Serving on a task force to develop a more effective singles ministry in the Lutheran Church several years ago, I became much more aware that there are specific things the Christian community could do about the lack of care.

Part of the problem is that we Christians often don't have a healthy sense of our own social sexuality. For example, in the past my own longings made me terribly afraid that my needs for affection were inordinate, that somehow I should be able to put them down and handle life by myself. Nowhere in the Church did I ever hear teaching about godly affection in relationships. Nor did I experience in many

160

churches the kind of small-group closeness that allows care in the community to develop very deeply. Many of the circles in which I teach do not place much emphasis on fellowship groups that are small enough for real love to grow. The kind of friendly affection about which Paul writes in this verse cannot easily happen in the great assembly.

Many single persons in our communities have been deserted or widowed, or have desired to marry but never had the opportunity; many have been deeply hurt in relationships or have made major mistakes out of the desperation of their loneliness. Moreover, many who live in families suffer from tragic loneliness, too, especially in families in which not all the members are committed to Christ. Also, some have chosen singleness for the sake of the kingdom of God and would like the support and affirmation of their community in their desire to remain celibate. How is the Church ministering to these persons?

Many lonely persons simply drop out of our congregations. They do not feel at home there. A single person in Seattle who is a friend of mine once went to a potluck dinner at which the host said, "Everyone please stand and tell who you are and with whom you came." My friend felt like an oddball because he'd come alone, so he rose at his turn and said, "I'm Bob, and I came with the ice cream."

His funny line was painfully true. Our society desperately needs the churches' emphasis on upbuilding families, but this can make singles feel out of place.

Because all sorts of single persons have all sorts of needs, the typical singles groups often do not really minister to them either. Too easily such groups degenerate into cliques or places where people look desperately for someone to fill their needs and turn desperately away because everyone else is too lonely to give them any help. Since statistics show that single persons compose perhaps forty percent of the U.S. adult population, are part of the fastest growing life-style, and remain the most disillusioned of people, the Church could more directly address the problems and needs of this group of persons.

I deliberately choose the phrase "group of persons" rather than the word *people* because our strategies must focus on learning about the personhood of individuals and on recovering in the Church both a genuine care for them and a deeper corporate sense of ourselves as a community in which to enfold them. One way to begin is to listen carefully to the words of Paul in Romans 12:10.

The verse begins literally "in friendship love — toward one another tenderly affectionate." The Greek language makes use of several words for love: *erōs* (sexual love); *storgē* (natural affection); *philia* (brotherly/friendship love); and *agapē* (disinterested/Christian love, as defined in Chapter 16). This verse begins with *philia*, the kind of love that friends have toward one another because of mutual interests. But the second noun is a combination of *philia* and *storgē*, and this is the only occurrence of that word in the New Testament. Literally, then, the progression in this verse moves Christians from simply being friends with each other to loving each other with family love. Leon Morris points out the uniqueness of this kind of love as follows:

> [T]he idea of *brotherly love* in such groups [the Essenes or various religious societies] is not found anywhere but among the Christians. They saw themselves as a family in a special sense. God was their Father and they were all brothers and sisters. Therefore they were united in a love that other people saw only in those of a natural family.[1]

Because in the Christian community we have a primary common goal to love God, we can respond to the Hilarity

---

1. Morris, *The Epistle to the Romans* (Grand Rapids: William B. Eerdmans, 1988), p. 444.

of God's immense love for us ("therefore") by caring more deeply — and more expressively — for each other.

Part of the difficulty in today's society, however, lies in the fact that people don't know how to be friends and to express intimacy because they have not learned how to be affectionate in their families. Various factors contribute to that malaise — such as fathers and mothers working away from home much of the time, children involved in myriads of social activities, television creating an entertainment society in which interpersonal communication has been lost, and so forth. Sadly, part of the problem arises simply because we are afraid. Because we fear rejection, or do not understand homosexuality, or remember incest, abuse, or other perversions, we run away from affection altogether, often thereby creating the very perversions and rejections we fear.[2]

Several years ago my brother Glen came from New York City to my home in Tumwater, Washington, for a two-week visit. We had been separated by great distance for more than a dozen years and had both gone through great and difficult changes in our life's directions in those years, so we did not really know each other very well. Consequently, we decided when he came to be carefully intentional about our relationship. Hugging each other was an important part of our days and helped us recover a lost sense of "family-ness." Glen also brought tender affection, gentle encouragement,

2. A very important recent sociological study confirmed my long-standing distrust of overusing the modern notion of a static homosexual orientation. David Greenberg's *The Construction of Homosexuality* (Chicago: University of Chicago Press, 1989) demonstrates how urbanization, science, medicine, bureaucracy, and other social forces have developed the social logics that create such an identity. It seems that often the basic feelings of deep affection and friendship for a person of the same sex are perceived (because of the cultural supports) as a homosexual orientation since our society is no longer a milieu which fosters intimate (but non-genital) same-sex friendships.

and new Hilarity to all the other residents of my house, including several guests in our crisis ministry.

Two weeks later my parents came from Ohio for Christmas and brought my grandparents from Wisconsin. Glen had taught me the value of expressing care, which became increasingly important with my grandparents, whom I rarely saw in those days. One time as I hugged Grandma and said, "I'm so glad you're here," she laughingly responded, "I know; you keep telling me." I answered, "I want you to know that forever. When you get home and I can't hug you physically, I want you to find happiness in remembering all the times I hugged you and how much I love you." In later years when I was able to visit her more often I could express my affection more concretely by praying with her and reading to her in German. Recently Grandma died, and I remember with happy gratitude her twinkling eyes when she was kissed and hugged after German bedtime prayers.

In Romans 12:10 Paul exhorts us to "be devoted to one another" (NIV) in the family of Christ. The phrase — literally to be "tenderly affectionate" — means to have a heartfelt love and gentle care toward each other. It is time for the Church to stop being afraid of true affection and to be set free from the distortions of the society around us. We need to learn to express community concern in wholesome, pure ways that will enfold lonely persons in genuine love so that they do not try to get their needs met in cheap affection or one-night stands.

When I was single, a member in my home church had an exceptional gift for expressing genuine care and sensitive concern to those who were hurting. One day, struggling terribly with my aloneness and back in my home city after several weekends away for speaking engagements, I saw Bill and his family at the grocery store. He walked right up to me in the aisle, said "I've missed you," and gave me a warm hug and a kiss on the cheek. His brotherly affection helped me to experience the reality of the Christian community as my family. The Hilarity of that enfolding kept me warm for days!

Around that same time an older widow from a duplex across the street came over to talk about the garbage can problem. Actually she came because she had nothing else to do and no one to care for her. As she left she said, "Come over and talk when you have some spare time." Have we visited a lonely person lately? What would happen in the Church and in the world if we all visited lonely persons on a regular basis? Think of the Hilarity we would create!

One spring during a pastors' conference in Victoria, British Columbia, an intern pastor and I, walking around a park, noticed a lot of elderly folk sitting alone, each one on a separate park bench. So we began introducing them to each other, asking them questions, and being silly. Then they would sit down together and start to talk. We had great fun watching them communicate with each other, even if their only subject of conversation was our craziness as we continued to turn cartwheels on the lawn and play tug-of-war games.

The memory of that experience makes me want to do such things more often. To be a catalyst for people getting together and being affectionate toward one another is a critically important ministry these days. However, we dare not be superficial or simplistic. The source of our desire to help others is the Hilarity that we ourselves experience in the love of the Christian community.

Once, when I was still single, during an intense time of work and loneliness, I misunderstood a friend's comment. After stewing about it an entire evening, I drove back to his house the next day to clear up the missed communication. His explanation was gift enough, but then he added, "Marva, you are so afraid of rejection. I'm not going to run away or drop our friendship without talking things through. I am committed to our friendship."

That word of commitment made a huge difference in

my feelings about myself and about life, and I am eternally grateful to God for giving such a sign of his grace. How imperative it is for the Church to realize that hurting and lonely persons need affectionate friends to be committed to them. My sisters and brothers, how can we deepen our care for one another? How can we learn to express tenderhearted affection in the Christian community?

Instead of fearing our relationships with persons of the opposite sex in the Church, we could love each other enough to push past those fears into understanding. *A Single Person's Identity*, an excellent little booklet by John Fischer and Liz Fuller O'Neil, urges individuals to love each other *more* rather than less to learn wholesome means for expressing and receiving affection, to find personally a healthy sense of one's own sexuality.[3]

Why can't we concentrate in our churches on caring for individuals, on helping persons to become more committed to each other so that no one ever has to go through trials alone? Why don't we form small, caring groups in our churches to pray and study together to grow in family affection? Why don't we pray for one another more deeply? Why can't we be more real about expressing our care in ways that bring warmth and glad Hilarity to those who are hurting?

Much of the emptiness and perversions and violence of our culture could be dealt with more effectively if we understood our sexuality in healthy ways. The greatest need of the lonely is not for genital sex but for the security of knowing that they are cared for. They need the gentleness of an assuring touch and the warmth of someone's affirming affection. Those tired of struggling alone, of having to be solely responsible, and of carrying all their problems by themselves are helped if they can crawl into a good strong hug.

3. John Fischer and Liz Fuller O'Neil, *A Single Person's Identity* (Palo Alto, CA: Discovery Papers, 1973).

A forceful argument for working at creating more closeness is the plea of Jesus to his disciples the night he agonized in Gethsemane. He wanted them to be with him, but they deserted him in sleep. We can hardly imagine that Jesus suffered even more intensely than we do from the pangs of loneliness, but, especially when he cried from the cross, "My God, my God, why have you forsaken me?" (Matt. 27:46, NIV), we recognize the depths of loneliness to which he went. Now, because he experienced that hell, we can be sure in our own times of sadness or despair that he understands — and he has promised to be with us!

His love, however, needs to be incarnated. When persons are lonely, they can't easily remember that Jesus cares. When our brothers and sisters hug us, we can feel his presence more personally. In our friendship love for one another, we can incarnate the love of Christ with all the tender affection that he displayed toward the people around him. The apostle Paul told his close friends, the Philippians, "God can testify how I long for all of you with the affection of Christ Jesus" (Phil. 1:8, NIV).

I long for the Christian community to discover such intimate affection and to practice it. Then we would draw the lonely back into the Hilarity of the community and make real for them the steadfast love and tender faithfulness of our God.

Therefore:

1. How has the Hilarity of affection strengthened us for life and ministry?

2. How could we be more affectionate toward lonely persons?

3. What could our community do to bring more affection to the lonely?

4. How would the Hilarity of greater affection strengthen the Church's ministry to the world around us?

5. How could greater affection that is pure and true change some of the immorality and perversion of the culture in which we live?

6. What could we do to create a healthier sense of sexuality in those we love?

7. How could our community foster a more positive self-image in lonely persons? How can we affirm them more and create wholeness within them?

19. Honoring the Valuable Everyone

In the honor — leading each other!
— ROMANS 12:10b

WE WERE GUESTS at a potluck dinner, and I was extraordinarily hungry. As people began moving through the dinner line, I got increasingly frustrated with my companion who kept holding back. "Come on," I said. "I'm so hungry."

"So is everybody else," he answered, and then he explained that he was waiting for the end of the line to make sure there would be enough food for everybody. There wasn't — most unusual for a potluck — and I was ashamed that to be more concerned for others had never even entered my head. My friend's selflessness indicted my failure to observe this second half of Romans 12:10.

We must beware lest the need in this book to separate the ideas of Romans 12 into such small units in order to explore their practical ramifications causes us to miss the close connection between the subject of this chapter and the emphasis of the last, to learn to express tenderhearted affection toward one another. The second half of verse 10, exhorting us in the Christian community to honor one another, gives us means for preventing that tender affection from becoming impure. As long as our relationships are held in godly honor, the deep intimacy that is expressed will remain holy.

The idea of "honor" was much stronger in Roman society than it is in contemporary cultures. Paul chose in Romans 12:10 to use the Greek word *timē*, which signified the concrete worth or merit of something and thus, secondarily, its price. As a result, the noun's meaning grew to include the reverence, status, and respect we accord to that object or person of value. The term here acknowledges the worth of all members of the Body of Christ and underscores the honor and respect with which the Christian community cares.

To hold others in honor prevents us from doing anything to hurt them or our relationship with them. Thus, if someone's expression of affection were to become disruptive to another's family life, then careful restraint is in order. If one's motives for caring about others become manipulative, one's honor for them necessitates repentance and restructuring. Communication, obviously, is imperative for clarification. Only with growing sensitivity can we "have a profound respect for each other" (JB).

Furthermore, this verse invites us to be urgent about it. The participle that Paul chooses is used only here in the entire New Testament so the way in which his readers would understand it is more difficult to ascertain. The verb might mean "to do something with eagerness" or "to exhibit a type of behavior far above the norm," as in to "honor one another to an exceptional degree." Both possibilities challenge us to be more concerned about others than about ourselves and emphasize that zeal to show honor should consume us.

We are to be "eager" to show respect (TEV), to "take delight" in it (LB). These paraphrases attempt to define what it means to excel in deferring to another. The phrase does not suggest (as does the RSV) that we should try to "outdo" one another in showing honor as if we were in a competition with other members of the Christian community. Instead, its invitation to give preference to each other especially frees us from any sense of an onerous burden of duty in caring about one another. Remember always that Paul's exhortations come out of the *therefore* which began our study. We don't show honor because we have to, but because we want to. We treat each other with respect as part of our Hilarity, because we delight in preferring to make other persons glad.

Obviously, that is not our normal human reaction (at least, I know it is not mine). Such a characteristic must be imparted by faith, created by God's love flowing through us. Our tender heavenly Father loved us first and showed us the greatest honor of all by giving up his Son to reconcile us to himself.

We honor someone because we think that person is valuable. God goes to great lengths to reveal to us how valuable we are to him. For example, the three "lost" parables of Luke 15 describe God's love in terms of a tender shepherd searching for one lost lamb, a woman scouring the house for a lost coin, and a waiting father embracing and welcoming home his prodigal son.

The literary device of a parable is designed to turn the listener's world upside down in order to call forth a response. The picture in Jesus' first story is completely contrary to the character of normal Semitic shepherds. That is why Jesus' parable is so profoundly effective. When he asks who of his listeners, having one hundred sheep, would leave the ninety-nine in the wilderness to go after the lost one, any good Jew familiar with shepherding would answer, "None of us would." That is a crazy way to be a shepherd.

The second picture no doubt rattled his listeners because Jesus used the figure of a woman to describe the love of God. Still today we need to hear the freshness of God's searching love illustrated in feminine terms.

Finally, no genteel Jewish senior citizen would *run* to welcome a son who had asked for his inheritance (which is to ask for the father's death!) and then wasted it, and he certainly would not immediately restore that son to full participation in the family. Yet the love of our heavenly Father is crazy like that. He values us so much that he completely overthrows all sense of decorum in his zeal to make us his. What Hilarity that gives to our lives!

Not by our worthiness but by his choice God values us so profoundly. This, then, is the honor we are to have for one another in the Christian community: a deep awareness of how valuable each individual is to God and therefore of how valuable we can be to each other in his family.

Such an honor especially creates a proper kind of affectionate love among those who show godly respect. How rich and deep God's love can be between those who make him the top priority in their lives and in the relationship! Tender community love and godly honor mutually depend upon one another.

Related to our valuing each other in the Body of Christ is the importance of our ministry to each other's need for affirmation. Though ideally a mature faith would receive the affirmation of God as sufficient to ameliorate our insecurities and inferiorities, reality is very much different. Those of us who have experienced various kinds of hurts and rejections that make us doubt ourselves need others in the Christian community to help us know our worth.

Significantly, we find that worth as children of God, uniquely created by him for special purposes. To simply affirm one another for human traits is insufficient because our physical beauties pass away, we make mistakes, or we experience failure, and then our sense of self-esteem is shattered once again. We are much more comforted by the assurance of our eminent worth because of who God is, for nothing can ever change his characteristic valuing of us.

Recognizing the difficulty most people have in valuing themselves, our present society offers all kinds of programs (technological fixes) to help persons grow in self-esteem. We who are the people of God know what is truly the basis for a lasting sense of self-worth. From the Creator who made us, the Savior who sacrificed himself for us, and the Holy Spirit who inhabits us we discover genuine value, and this is reinforced by recognizing how priceless we are to the Church, which depends upon the unity of our diversities for its Hilarity.

When I formerly taught "Effectiveness Training" classes, I grew to appreciate greatly how much those courses emphasize skills of affirming one another. Our relationship with God gives us a holy basis for doing that. How much more effectively we would show to those around us the love of God if we more carefully nurtured each other. Our esteem and honor for others enfolds them experientially in the value we have in the eyes of God and of his community.

Such a life-style is so different from the patterns of our culture. Think how much our society is characterized by "machoism" or pushing oneself to be number one. The mark of intelligence in our society is expertise in putting others down and, consequently, in proving oneself to be the best of all.

We must find a very careful balance in our understanding of the principle of honoring. For example, we who are God's people certainly endorse heartily the goal of equality in human rights. Especially we who are white owe great debts to blacks and other minority groups that have been oppressed by our culture's racism and supremacism. However, various liberation movements of our times sometimes swing the pendulum too far in the other direction in their pushing for rights. When a movement urges women to demand their bodily rights to the exclusion of the rights of an unborn child, that hastens the development of a society that does not welcome children into the world. The great

173

privilege of being a mother offers the opportunity to give up certain rights in order to nurture a child's emotional, physical, intellectual, and spiritual growth. On the other hand, families ought not to expect — or demand — that she always give up her rights. That would abuse her offering. Romans 12:10 challenges God's people to be characterized by an absolute lack of pushiness to be number one and by an eagerness to give place so that others can be affirmed and find in themselves a deeper sense of worth.

If our personal goal in life is to reflect the character of Jesus Christ, then, as Paul urges us in Philippians, we want to have his mind. The mark of his attitude was an unwilling-ness to grasp at equality with God, even though that was his right. Instead, he humbled himself and became a servant, even to the point of dying the most ignoble of all deaths (see Phil. 2:5-11). That is the style of honoring others above our-selves that is our model.

Such a stirring challenge is made even more difficult for us because so much of our culture is built upon the opposite attitude. For us as Christians really to follow this exhortation from Paul calls us to a life-style that moves strongly against the currents of our times. Therefore, it is imperative that we encourage each other and stand by each other in the Christian community to give one another sup-port in pursuing the mind of Jesus.

We must appreciate how radical this statement from Paul is — as radical as the whole ministry of Jesus, who spent his time affirming the sinners and honoring the out-casts of society. And he was killed for it.

To put this exhortation into practice will demand sacri-fice. To live this principle requires careful choices. But that is the whole point: what and whom do we value? If we esteem our relationship with God more than anything, then our honor and reverence for him will issue in a deeper honor and respect for life and, particularly, for the lives of those we love.

That leads to a final point that must be stressed because of the situation of the world in which we live. When so many of our neighbors in the world are starving, when so many are poor and oppressed, what does valuing others more highly than ourselves mean? Certainly it challenges us to sacrifice the luxury in our life-style in order that others might have enough.

We who are God's people know that the world is a global community. To offer it the Hilarity of our Christian fellowship is to choose gladly a more simple life-style in order to respond to the needs of others. Some would respond, "But we have worked hard all our lives, and now we deserve to enjoy our possessions." Does anybody ever deserve to enjoy rich extras when others suffer without the basics? What does honoring others above ourselves mean in light of our possessions and comfort and the needs of the world for our care?

These questions must seriously be asked by each of us as individuals and in our churches as communities. What can we do to show honor, not only for our brothers and sisters who worship together with us, but for our neighbors in our communities, and for the Church at large, and for a suffering world?

Therefore:

1. How will our honoring of our brothers and sisters keep our relationships with them pure?

2. What does the term *honor* mean in our culture? How can we restore a deeper sense of honor in a society characterized instead by the lack of genuine respect and reverence?

3. How does our Hilarity set us free to strive to show honor without getting competitive?

4. How can we more effectively affirm certain individuals in our community or family for whom we have special concern?

5. How does the Hilarity of the Christian community enable us to pursue equality for all without becoming pushy for our personal rights?

6. How can we be more involved in honoring the rest of the world above ourselves?

7. What specific steps do we want to take beginning today to put this verse more into action in our personal lives and in the life of the Church?

20. *Zeal and Fervor in the Right Lordship*

In the diligence — not poky! In the spirit — boiling! In
the Lord — slaving!

— ROMANS 12:11

I COULD NEVER HIKE uphill well. My body just cannot
make its energy available to the cells fast enough, but
Julie was patient with me. Now we had made steady progress for a few hours and were enjoying immensely the gorgeous view of the mountains, the lovely wildflowers, and
the dazzling rocks.

After we had climbed almost five miles and the path
began to be covered with snow, however, the going got
harder. Sometimes when I could barely keep on walking,
the hope of victory over my physical handicaps always
stirred me into motion again. Every time my strength and
courage started to wane, the thought of coming this far and
then missing our goal of seeing the lake at the top of the
trail was too disappointing. So we kept on.

The goal was eminently worth the effort. The end of

the trail brought us to the most placid lake, surrounded by avalanche lilies almost hidden in places by the snow. As we sat down on a rock to eat our lunch, I breathed in the accomplishment with great gulps of zesty cold air. For the first time in my life, I had climbed a trail to the top of a mountain.

Three days later I hiked another ten-mile trip to a different lake, above Lake Chelan in north central Washington, and there, in the exuberance of having made it, I dove into the glacier-fed water in all my clothes and celebrated with a twenty-minute swim. The exhilaration of all the beauty filled me with poems, and my hike down the path was often delayed while I scribbled down lines that danced in my head. What had kept me going whenever the way got too rough was the vision of the goals. I still taste the grand mountain Hilarity as I remember those moments more than ten years later.

The same process illustrated by my hikes is the point of this eleventh verse from Romans 12. The goal before us is what enables us to keep on keeping on, no matter what befalls us, as we seek to offer ourselves as living and holy sacrifices, to be transformed by the renewing of our minds, to use our gifts for the upbuilding of the community, to love with the genuine love of Christ, and to express that love in affectionate and honoring ways. The goal is expressed in the final idea of this eleventh verse, and all three of its phrases work together to show how we aim toward that goal as we continue growing in our desire to serve the Lord as part of the Christian community.

Once again we must begin by recalling the essential fact of God's love. Without its infinity we could not possibly go on without ever flagging in zeal or with continually fervent spirits. Sometimes, after all, serving the Lord gets harder than that mountain climb. Hilarity does not mean cozy easiness.

God's pre-eminent love sustains us in times when our faith is tested. When first writing this chapter, I was struggling to accept certain aspects of my life and ministry, and real battle in my spirit ensued. At one point I complained, "I'm so tired of all the turmoil. Why can't God let me alone for awhile?" Deep in my mind I knew I was grateful for the tasks God gives me, but I was feeling terribly burned out at that time from bearing all the responsibility alone. In such moments of dim faith Paul's exhortation never to be poky in diligence or lacking in zeal seems impossible to follow.

That same day a friend's letter reminded me that God promises to carry us through the difficult times. (What Spirit-led timing — she hadn't known that I was having such a struggle!) This description of God's character manifested in the Suffering Servant is marvelously fulfilled in the incarnation of Jesus: "A bruised reed He will not break, and a dimly burning wick He will not extinguish" (Isa. 42:3). When we are wounded, he will not let us be destroyed. When our zeal is barely smoldering, he will not allow it to be snuffed out.

We must understand as we begin that Romans 12:11 is not a command hanging over our heads. It is instead a description of — and an invitation to participate in — the power that is available to us when we present our bodies as living and holy and acceptable sacrifices. God wants to transform the Christian community into a people with these characteristics as we keep our eyes fixed on Jesus, the Author and Perfecter of our faith (Heb. 12:2).

In addition, we must again remember Paul's cryptic style, which makes it seem that he is proclaiming with great exuberance these traits which will mark our lives as we offer them in sacrifice and are transformed. Each of the three phrases in this eleventh verse relates to our Hilarity in community.

The first noun, *diligence*, occurring here in the dative case (so we add our English preposition *in*), is the same one that we encountered in verse 8 as the description for the way in which leadership should be conducted. Recall that we discussed then its meaning as "eagerness" or "doing one's best" (see Chapter 15, p. 132). Paul's repetition of a key noun associated with his previous listing of the grace-gifts invites us to remember that only by God's empowerment can we exhibit this trait of diligence in our community life.

Now Paul urges *all* the members of the Christian community to keep that eager and attentive steadiness up, with no waning of its exuberance or power. The Greek adjective might imply "lack of ambition" or even laziness. How can we continue to work with such an "untiring effort" (JB), with "unflagging energy" (NEB)? As J. B. Phillips puts it, "Let us not allow slackness to spoil our work." That is an awfully large order when the going gets tough.

When zeal wanes, we certainly can't crank up more. Indeed, a great danger of trying harder is that we get burned out even faster. We dare not let this exhortation become a demand over us because the harder we try to force a diligence that isn't there, the more we will hate our work and the less we will be able to be genuinely earnest about it. We will lose all our Hilarity.

The secret lies in always remembering our goal. We are not diligent for merely human reasons. Our enthusiasm is not empty because we are not serving that which will soon wither and fade. Rather, we know true Hilarity because of the eternal purposes involved. We have infinite power at our disposal; incredible wisdom lies behind it all. That makes the strain worthwhile.

In fact, our traveling up the hill in our spiritual lives has two major advantages over the goal that encouraged my mountain climbing. First, on the trail I had no assurance that I would eventually make it to the top. I could guess at the sense of accomplishment during the grueling climb, but I didn't really know if I could make it until I actually did.

In contrast, we know for sure, with great Hilarity, that we will reach the goal in our spiritual lives. We have that assurance because all the work has already been accomplished by Jesus Christ. Nothing that we do or fail to do can keep us from the goal which is being preserved for us. We are offered a clear affirmation of the sureness of this hope in 1 Peter 1:3-9. Paul, too, reminds us elsewhere in Romans (5:1-5) that our hope will not be disappointed.

Second, on my mountain hike I had to wait till I reached the top before I could see the lake. But on our spiritual journey, we don't have to wait until the end to see visions of our goal. The lake of God's gifts does not exist only at the top of the mountain. Rather, the great Hilarity of persisting in zeal is that we continue all along to catch glimpses of the ultimate triumph toward which we are moving. Someday we will know that victory in full, but meanwhile we experience bits and snatches of the Hilarity and hope to which our faith clings.

A good illustration for me has been writing this book. Sometimes hours at the computer become too arduous and long. First the pain from my shattered foot and broken leg and now the difficulty of seeing with only one eye have tempted me to wane in ardor. But just when my diligence gets poky, I receive some sort of encouragement from someone in the Christian community — a phone call, a letter, or the gift of a ride to the doctor. I realize afresh in the deepest core of my being that I passionately want to write about the Hilarity that the Christian community could experience if we treasured each other more and if we paid closer attention to the exhortations in the Scriptures.

If we keep relying on the Lord to keep our zeal from flagging, he will give us the strength. The Psalms stun us with their frequent references to Yahweh as our refuge, our fortress, the one who sustains and upholds us, and so forth. As long as we desire to continue steadfastly, God will keep us from indolence or laziness, according to his means, his timing, his best purposes.

One of the major means that God uses is the fellowship of believers. Each of us needs others to encourage us in our common desire to remain diligent in God's work. I experience that kind of encouragement daily when I go to an exercise club to work out. Sometimes I just want to give up, but other women who are exercising, too, keep encouraging me as they notice my struggle to do things in my leg brace. It seems that such groups as exercise clubs have taken the place of the Christian community in being the locus of intimacy and support. Certainly the members of the Church could become more intentional in their efforts to sustain one another in the strains of remaining diligent.

The next pair of key words in verse 11 — literally, "in spirit boiling" — is one of the most vivid pictures in the Scriptures for maintaining our spiritual glow. Too easily we who are God's people can become so immersed in our culture's rationalism and striving for self-satisfaction that we lose our fervency of spirit. In contrast, I remember with enormous gratitude the dedication and commitment and "boiling spirit" that my grandfather and my father after him manifested as they poured out their lives in utter devotion to their call as Lutheran school teachers and church musicians.

One of the great gifts of the charismatic movement in our times is its evident fervency of spirit. Many participants in charismatic prayer groups exhibit a boiling over of the spirit that draws others into their Hilarity. Worship services are characterized by a spiritual intensity that brightens the music, deepens the expression of affection, focuses the attention of listeners on the teaching of the Scriptures, and results in a life-style of goodness.

To have "a heart full of devotion" (TEV) in our service is the goal. With "great earnestness" (JB) or "ardour of spirit" (NEB), we are to "be aglow" (RSV). J. B. Phillips' vivid image, "Let us keep the fires of the spirit burning," captures well the warmth of our Hilarity.

Checking a woodstove at this point in my original writing of this chapter gave me a new insight: to keep me warm, the fire required a regular addition of logs. Similarly, our spirits require continuous input to keep boiling. What a strong motivation to have a daily devotional time and to participate in a mature community of believers! We need both the fuel of the Scriptures and the Hilarity of the community so that our spirits can remain fervent.

Only when our spirits are taken over by the Holy Spirit can they remain on fire. Thus once again we see that these exhortations cannot be fulfilled by our striving, but rather by our yielding. Our efforts cannot sustain a spiritual glow, but the presence of Christ's Spirit at work within us will.

This certainly is the case in my work as a Bible teacher. Trying to be enthusiastic under my own power wears me out. On the other hand, when the text is carrying me, my spirit has plenty of strength and eagerness. The Joy of discovering the truth of the Scriptures together with others always increases our fervency. The Hilarity of the community exhilarates us.

Now the last phrase of verse eleven reminds us to what end we want to have a non-poky diligence and a boiling spirit. Our purpose is always to be slaving "in the Lord." However, this purpose also is the means by which the whole verse can be experienced. Consequently, this phrase is not an "ought to" over our heads, but rather the good news of how God's love does indeed work through us. That good news is the basis of our Hilarity.

As with the other two phrases, the first noun here is in the dative case, so we usually translate it with the English preposition *in*. The ambiguity of the dative might allow us also to stress that it is *to* the Lord that our slaving is directed — a meaning which would be appropriate in this context because it certainly is the Lord that we serve. However, in the cotext of Romans 12 the emphasis seems to be more on how we serve each other to strengthen the whole community. Furthermore, the apostle Paul frequently uses the phrases "in the Lord" or "in Christ" to emphasize that as Christians we live in vital union with Jesus Christ our Lord. Thus, this phrase in verse 11 tells us not so much how our service is directed as how it is empowered. In vital connection with Christ, we serve God and each other. Our union with the Lord enables us to continue serving the community with true Hilarity.

The Greek verb for "serving" is not the same one that we encountered in verse 7. There the word from which we get our English term *deacon* connoted a particular grace-gift that some experience more than others. The verb used here means "to slave." Such a quality of life is available to everyone. Not specifying a particular gift, it refers to whether a person has made a choice.

The nature of that significant choice is implied in the initial noun, translated "in the Lord." Who is our Lord? How have we decided? If our Lord is Jesus, then our service of others will be empowered and inspired and directed by him. If we make ourselves our own lords, then we will try to serve ourselves out of our own abilities and for our own ends. That is the choice we must constantly make in all the situations of our daily lives. Whenever we choose to do our serving "in the Lord," we will experience the empowerment of Hilarity. Then we will be able to remain diligent in our zeal, fervent in our spirit.

Thus, one of the most important goals for our spiritual growth is to become more and more aware of the constancy of that choice so that we will learn in every situation to practice the presence of God. Then, no matter what we might encounter, we will choose with Hilarity to slave in the Lord.

We want that decision to guide the way we eat and sleep, walk around and do our chores, grow together with friends and love our enemies, and use our gifts.

We certainly can never be perfect at always choosing the Lordship of Jesus. But that is the direction in which we want to be moving. That is another reason why we so much need each other in the Christian community — to remind one another of the source of our motivation, to encourage a deeper reliance on the Lord's empowerment for all our slaving. Then we will be moving in that direction together — more often with a diligence that does not get quenched, a spirit that remains aglow with his presence, and the Hilarity that can only be had by slaving for, with, in, and through the Lord.

Therefore:

1. In what areas of our personal and corporate lives do we experience the Lordship of Christ? How does that increase our Hilarity?

2. In what areas of our lives have we not yet let him take control? Why not?

3. What circumstances cause our zeal to flag, our diligence to get poky?

4. How can we experience renewal of our eagerness?

5. For what reasons do our spirits cease to boil?

6. How can we add fuel to the fire so that our spirit — personally and corporately — will more steadily remain aglow?

7. How have we experienced the empowerment of the Hilarity of slaving in the Lord when we have served others?

185

21. Handling the Serious with Joy and the Hopeless with Patience

In the hope — rejoicing! In the tribulation — remaining under!

— ROMANS 12:12a-b

SOME THINGS are serious, but not hopeless; other things are hopeless, but not serious." Though I heard that distinction secondhand and don't know exactly what the original speaker meant by those phrases, they summarize well the two major kinds of difficult life experiences under the grace and love of God.

Some things are serious. They involve a lot of discouraging factors; they might be bleak situations or relationships that seem irreparably broken or needs that feel too profound to be filled. But those things are not hopeless. Always a touch of promise carries us through the death-shadow.

Other things are hopeless, but that is not serious. These things ultimately don't matter. Though the hopeless things can be profoundly painful, they cannot destroy us because their place in our lives is secondary.

186

Because we know that God in his wisdom will not let us be tempted above what we are able to bear (1 Cor. 10:13) and that our present sufferings aren't worth comparing to the glory that will be revealed in us (Rom. 8:18), we can trust that the serious things in our lives will never be hopeless. On the other hand, because we know that God brings all things together for our good (Rom. 8:28), we can trust that the things which are hopeless will not affect us seriously. Indeed, God is in charge no matter what our circumstances.

This distinction between the serious and the hopeless introduces us to the first two phrases of Romans 12:12. The way to deal with those things that are serious but not hopeless is to remain joyful in the hope. In the affliction of those things that are hopeless but not serious, we are invited to remain patient.

Paul continues his epigrammatic style. The Greek text says literally, "in the hope rejoicing." This time, however, the noun appearing in the dative case adds the definite article *the* to make it particular, a specific hope. Moreover, the verb participle is in the present or continuing tense. We don't rejoice just once in awhile. Joy — Hilarity — can be the constant state of our hearts when we understand the nature of our hope.

The biblical pictures of Joy delight us with their fullness and reality. If we would refer to such passages time and again, the Hilarity in our lives as the people of God would be renewed. Why does the attribute of Joy-full Hilarity seem so often to be missing from our lives and worship and service?

This afternoon I was translating the Hebrew text of the first few verses of Isaiah 9. Listen to this description of the Hilarity the Messiah brings:

> You have enlarged the nation,
>   you have made great their Joy;

they rejoice before you
    like a woman rejoicing at the harvest,
as men rejoice
    when dividing the plunder.

(Isa. 9:2)

Or consider this picture from the fifty-first chapter of Isaiah:

The ransomed of the LORD will return.
    They will enter Zion with singing;
    everlasting joy will crown their heads.
Gladness and joy will overtake them,
    and sorrow and sighing will flee away.

(Isa. 51:11, NIV)

The latter passage always brings to my mind the commercials in which a child receives a crown when he bites into his bread spread with a certain margarine. Just so we receive a magnificent crown of Joy when we taste and see the goodness of the Lord. The powers of evil keep harassing us and taking potshots at our crown, but they have no right to remove it. Sorrow and sighing must flee away in the end. We lose our Hilarity only if we remove the crown ourselves and refuse to receive its gift.

The reason for such rejoicing in the book of Isaiah and in our lives is the hope for ultimate deliverance from suffering and pain. Paul has already been quite specific in writing about hope to the Romans. In chapter 5 he constructs carefully a theology of hope focusing on the verb *to boast*, in the sense of exulting or rejoicing. Studying that sequence in Romans 5 enlightens our understanding of this phrase in Romans 12 since the latter merely calls to mind what Paul has already more fully explained in the former. Notice that Romans 5 deals with many of the same themes that we have been considering in this book. The two passages together make clear how we can make our boasting and rejoicing a holy exulting, a sacred Hilarity.

Verse 1 of Romans 5 also begins with that great word *therefore*, after which Paul summarizes to what the connector is referring in this instance. In the previous chapter he had explained the fact that by faith we receive the reconciliation that God's love makes possible. So now he summarizes that doctrine of justification by grace through faith in order that we might link it with the implications he is about to present. The first implication, in verse 1, is that we have peace with God by means of our relationship with our Lord Jesus Christ. Notice that he uses the full title there for God's Son and thus underscores his deity (Christ), his humanity (Jesus), and his rule in our lives (Lord). When Christ is our Lord, he reconciles us with God the Father.

The second implication of justification by faith, Paul says, is that we "have gained access" by that same faith into the "grace in which we now stand" (5:2a, NIV). That expression fills us with Hilarity because of its assurance that we can with great boldness walk right up to the throne of the Creator of the universe and the Judge of the world to receive his love. We do not have to fear his wrath, though we deserve it, but we can stand with confidence under his gracious love and know that it forgives and frees and fashions us.

Deliberately, Paul places the two verbs in the phrases quoted above in the perfect tense, which means that a particular decisive action once and for all caused a lasting change which continues thereafter. Thus the verbs stress that gaining access and coming to stand in grace will continue always to be the case. It is the nature of God's love: once we accept God's gifts we shall continually receive them (unless we obstruct the Giver and refuse his grace).

The third implication of justification by faith, according to Romans 5:2b, is that we rejoice in the hope of the "glory" of God or the full realization of all his promises to us. We know that someday all that God is will be fully revealed to us and we will fully enjoy his presence. Therefore, we can rejoice now in anticipation of, and confidence in (that is, hope of), that final fulfillment. Thus, our hope is a double one — both for now and also for eternity. This old aeon is hopelessly lost to the powers of violence and destruction and death, but a new age has come smashing into it with the accomplishment of Christ's work of restoration, so we already experience the fulfillment of that hope to a small extent and anticipate its ultimate realization more profoundly as we wait for the second coming of Christ.

This comment about our rejoicing in hope is the first in a sequence of three boastings in which Paul describes a deepening of maturity in faith. First of all, we exult in our "hope of glory," in the basic fact of our deliverance with all its temporal and eternal implications (Rom. 5:1-2). Next, Paul goes on to say that we can rejoice even in our sufferings (5:3-5).

This is not a masochistic rejoicing because we are being hurt. Rather, we exult because we know the outcome of such suffering. We know that suffering produces perseverance (the theme also of Rom. 12:12b), perseverance produces character, and character produces hope. There we are, back at hope again, but this time the hope is deeper than the hope of glory. This is the hope of suffering, the ability to know, regardless of the circumstances, that our God is able to take all the strands of our existence and weave them together into that which is good for us. Some of the good things that he creates even out of the struggles of our lives are these increasingly more mature qualities in our faith life: perseverance, character, and hope.

Now Paul expands this theme to prove that such hope will not disappoint us (5:6-8). The evidence he enjoins is twofold — subjective and objective.

First, the subjective verification that hope will not disappoint us is that we know God's love from its very existence within us. Second, the cross of Christ gives us objective verification of God's love. The cross is the absolute assurance that hope cannot disappoint.

Why the cross is such sure proof Paul continues to explain. It is the supreme verification because Christ died at such a significant time — when we were still powerless, ungodly, unrighteous sinners, enemies. With these four terms Romans 5:6-10 describes our state when Christ died for us. In contrast, Paul reasons, in human situations we don't expect that anyone would die for someone else; that other person would have to be tremendously good for anyone to be willing to die. In fact, Paul asserts, very rarely will anyone die for a righteous person. But this is the incredible demonstration of God's love for us: Christ died while we were still unbelievers. He didn't demand that first we change and become righteous and good. Of course, we know we would never have passed the test if he had demanded that we become holy first. Instead, Christ died at this majestic time: while we were still powerless (having lost our power when we tried to do things our own ineffective ways), ungodly, sinners — yes, even enemies! What a cause for Hilarity!

Now Paul capsulizes his argument in his awe-inspiring "how much more" phrases (5:9-10, NIV). First he declares, "Since we have now been justified by his blood, how much more shall we be saved from God's wrath through him!" And second, if we were reconciled when we were still enemies by means of the death of Christ, "how much more, having been reconciled, shall we be saved through his life!"

Dramatically, Paul piles up a mountain of factors that contribute to our ability to rejoice in our sufferings, for all these proofs of God's love enable us to trust him for his purposes also in our afflictions. In fact, the apostle continues, we can trust him so much that we move on to a still deeper level of spiritual maturity. At this level we no longer need even the assurance of the good that God will bring out of this present state of affairs. Rather, at this third level of boasting, we exult simply in the fact that God exists and has revealed himself to us through Jesus. In other words, the work of Christ has brought us into such a relationship with God that whatever happens in anything no longer matters. All that really matters is that God is our God. We rejoice and find our Hilarity simply in him.

This is why anything that is serious can never be hopeless: because in everything that is serious, God will be there to accomplish his purposes and to be our God. What a grand climax this sequence has reached: God alone is worthy of our greatest exultation and boasting and is the source of our Hilarity.

Thus, we can continually rejoice in our hope (which carries us ahead now to chapter 12 of Romans), for our hope will not disappoint us. It cannot, for it is founded on a deeper reality than hope — the very fact of God himself. Paul will build on this again at the end of his letter to the Romans where he names God with the title "God of hope" and reminds his readers that this God is able to "fill you with all joy and peace as you trust in him, so that you may overflow with hope by the power of the Holy Spirit" (Rom. 15:13, NIV).

The fullness of that hope is incomprehensible, but in mysterious ways we sometimes experience its overflowing. One night many years ago I saw only hopelessness in my personal life. I couldn't find any reason to go on living; any purpose was clouded over by bleakness in every direction. Yet when I read my Bible that night in a thick fog of despair and depression, this incredible fact broke through: God loves me, no matter what I am like. That he is God and that he is *my* God are reasons enough to go on. Even though I couldn't see any hope in anything because of the grief that still engulfed me, yet I felt a strange exultation — even a wild Hilarity — because God is God and I am his.

Obviously, the biblical concept of Joy is much different

from the idea of happiness. Happiness is dependent to a great extent on one's external circumstances. At many points in daily life God gives us gifts of happiness: the taste of clean mountain air, the fragrance of baking bread, the colors of a dazzling sunset, the songs of a meadowlark, the touch of someone who loves us. We are happy when work is going well, when we feel affirmed for who we are.

But many things in life also make us sad. We grieve when we lose a loved one. We feel the pain of illness or difficult circumstances. We weep from fear and frustration at what seems like fate. We cry out at the world's evil.

Yet Joy remains Joy through it all. No matter whether our circumstances are conducive to happiness or sadness, darkness or light, our Joy remains firm because it is based in our hope and in the One who is deeper than hope.

Three of my favorite sayings summarize this concept: "Joy is the infallible sign of the presence of God"; "Joy is not the absence of suffering, but the presence of God"; and "Joy is the flag that is flown o'er the castle of our hearts when the King is in residence there." All three sentences stress the same point: because God is with us, we can continually rejoice. His presence makes possible our hope — hope for how he will create good from even the negative elements in our lives (Rom. 8:28) and hope for how we will discover that the sufferings of this present time are not worth comparing to the fulfillment of God's promises as they will be revealed to us (8:18).

Moreover, this hope does not disappoint. God has proved his love to us time and again, through the subjective witness of our own hearts and through the objective fact of the death of Christ on our behalf. Can there be any doubt? We might encounter serious circumstances, but they are not hopeless. The King is still in residence here.

On the other hand, some things are hopeless, but not serious. In such tribulations, Paul exhorts us to remain patient. We need careful definitions of both of the major words in this second phrase from Romans 12:12, because we do not naturally remain patient in troubles.

The afflictions spoken of here are tribulations that come from the outside. The Greek noun *thlipsis* is related to a verb that means "to press upon" or "to press together." Thus, the noun Paul chooses means to be oppressed or afflicted from the outside of oneself, to become restricted or forced into narrow circumstances. Such trouble involves direct suffering. That very accurately describes the struggles that we experience as circumstances press us into tight places, confinements from which we cannot escape. Delightfully, one of the strongest words for salvation in the Hebrew Scriptures actually means to bring one to a spacious place, to give a person plenty of room.

We all suffer from various kinds of tribulations from the outside. Pressures come from our peers, who urge us to live in ways contrary to our Scriptural principles. Restrictions originate in demands upon us in our work or at home or, sad to say, even in our churches. Afflictions arise from accidents or hazards of nature or other forces over which we have no control.

For a day I helped a farmer in eastern Washington one week after Mount St. Helens erupted for the first time and distributed generous amounts of volcanic ash in a wide swathe across the farmland. As I struggled to move irrigation pipes in the ash, my friend climbed off his tractor and said, "I've never been beaten before, but this stuff is beating me." He could do nothing about the thick layer of ash. The situation was hopeless; there was no way to get rid of it.

What can we do when something is hopeless? The second phrase from Romans 12:12 reminds us that such situations are not serious. We are invited by Paul to keep remaining under them because we will not be destroyed by them. Most English translations render the Greek participle with the concept of patience. However, that word has become so watered down in our society that it no longer expresses the original strength of the Greek word, which literally means "to remain under." In our culture *patience* designates a brief wait till the aspirin takes hold, till the television program gets resolved, till the microwave heats the instant dinner. In our technological milieu's craving for efficiency, we have lost the biblical meaning of patience.

The idea is to remain steadfast instead of fleeing, to hold out, standing one's ground, enduring in the face of all sorts of trouble. As Ernst Käsemann points out, "Trials are not to be suffered passively. They must be carried like a burden on firm shoulders."[1]

Notice the connection between this method for dealing with hopeless but not serious situations and our previous consideration of dealing with those that are serious but not hopeless. With a clear perspective on what gives us hope, we can remain under the things that are hopeless. Not resigned to those situations, we bear them confidently because we firmly know their value as less than ultimate.

A farmer facing the ash problem, for example, could simply accept the fact that the ash had nowhere to go so it wasn't worth wasting energy worrying about it. Such serenity and calmness come from the realization that our God will not let us be destroyed by our situations. He is faithful to provide for his people and can bring good even out of the dumping of a volcano.

In fact, God did. Farmers in eastern Washington had the best apple crop in years because the volcanic ash effectively held moisture in the ground.

Paul's second letter to the Corinthians contains many sections of tremendous comfort for times of affliction in

1. Käsemann, *Commentary on Romans,* trans. and ed. Geoffrey W. Bromiley (Grand Rapids: William B. Eerdmans, 1980), p. 346.

which we must remain patient with firm shoulders. These words show us why that which seems hopeless is not serious:

> Blessed be the God and Father of our Lord Jesus Christ, the Father of mercies and God of all comfort, who comforts us in all our affliction so that we may be able to comfort those who are in any affliction with the comfort with which we ourselves are comforted by God. For just as the sufferings of Christ are ours in abundance, so also our comfort is abundant through Christ. But if we are afflicted, it is for your comfort and salvation; or if we are comforted, it is for your comfort, which is effective in the patient enduring of the same sufferings which we also suffer; and our hope for you is firmly grounded, knowing that as you are sharers of our sufferings, so also you are sharers of our comfort. (2 Cor. 1:3-7)

This paragraph especially demonstrates the importance of the community in our learning to endure tribulations. Not only are we helped by the comfort that we can share with one another, but also the desire to let our sufferings benefit others gives us a purpose in enduring them.

Again Paul reminds the Corinthians:

> But we have this treasure in earthen vessels, that the surpassing greatness of the power may be of God and not from ourselves; we are afflicted in every way, but not crushed; perplexed, but not despairing; persecuted, but not forsaken; struck down, but not destroyed; always carrying about in the body the dying of Jesus, that the life of Jesus also may be manifested in our body. (2 Cor. 4:7-10)

Because we have become sensitized in this book to Paul's use of the word *body* to signify both the personal physical body and the corporate body of the Church, we might

196

wonder if he intends that double emphasis here. Since in the first passage quoted above Paul writes of the Corinthians sharing his sufferings, we can also expect the second passage to emphasize the unity of the Christian community. Indeed, the life of Jesus is more thoroughly displayed when the Christian community bears his sufferings together.

Finally, Paul declares that it is possible to exult in one's tribulations because they teach us the hope of the sufficiency of grace. He describes in this passage the discovery of that truth which grounds his Hilarity:

> And because of the surpassing greatness of the revelations, for this reason, to keep me from exalting myself, there was given me a thorn in the flesh, a messenger of Satan to buffet me — to keep me from exalting myself! Concerning this I entreated the Lord three times that it might depart from me. And He has said to me, "My grace is sufficient for you, for power is perfected in weakness." Most gladly, therefore, I will rather boast about my weaknesses, that the power of Christ may dwell in me. Therefore I am well content with weaknesses, with insults, with distresses, with persecutions, with difficulties, for Christ's sake; for when I am weak, then I am strong. (2 Cor. 12:7-10)

Some situations are hopeless in human terms, but we can remain under and endure them because our hope lies elsewhere. Instead of despairing over such situations, we find our Hilarity in that which really matters. This is a victory of a different sort. We don't overcome the situations, but we overcome ourselves and learn to rest in God's grace, which is sufficient to carry us through the tribulations that don't ultimately matter. In the things that do, our hope is sure to give us Joy.

Therefore:

1. How do we experience the difference between happiness and Joy?

2. How could we describe the Joy of our hope of glory, the Joy of suffering, and the Joy in God himself as presented by Romans 5:1-11?

3. How can we know Hilarity when we are not happy? Is it phony to be Joy-full when we are encountering sadness in our lives?

4. What other sections of the Scriptures are our favorite descriptions of Joy, exulting in God, Hilarity?

5. How has God encouraged us personally to know that hope will not disappoint us? How has the Christian community been a source of comfort and hope?

6. What things in our lives are serious, but not hopeless? What things are hopeless, but not serious?

7. How in the Christian community could we help each other to develop the mind-set to be able not to worry about those things that are hopeless, but don't really matter ultimately?

22. Constancy in Prayer

In the prayer — continuing steadfast!

— ROMANS 12:12c

PERHAPS YOU STRUGGLE as I do to improve your prayer life. I frequently learn new methods and try new tools, yet prayer continues to be the weakest part of my spiritual life. Paul's exhortation to be continually steadfast in prayer reveals our individual and community need for constant renewal.

In just one chapter we could not pretend to deal adequately with the subject of prayer when so many entire books are devoted to the topic. (See the section entitled "Resources on Prayer" in the bibliography for recommendations.) Hopefully this chapter can at least stimulate a deeper desire in us to grow in our personal and corporate prayer lives.

Again, because this book's chapters have had to divide the text into such small portions, we must deliberately notice the link between the phrase we are studying now and its preceding cotext. Consequently, we begin our consideration of prayer by realizing that through its power we both discover the Hilarity of our hope and find the courage to keep remaining under the tribulations that afflict us (Rom. 12:12a-b). We must also hinge prayer to the ideas of all the other chapters in this book, for it is a vital means for discovering and experiencing the Hilarity of the Christian community. Prayer is the basis for our service, our zeal and commitment, our love, our use of gifts, and our offering of ourselves together as a holy, living sacrifice.

Prayer is critically central to all that we are and do as God's people. We should be bothered, therefore, if it is not having much of an effect in our lives and if it is not a mainstay of our community's life together. If this is the case, we don't understand its nature, its practice, and its power.

One of the main ideas in all of Paul's writings about prayer is his recognition that it is wrought in us by the Holy Spirit. Definitely it is a "Therefore." Just like faith itself, prayer is a gift from God and is not dependent upon our efforts or any work on our part that could earn God's love — though the disciplines of prayer are a vital part of our active involvement in the process. Thus, the whole theme of Romans — that we are Hilariously free from performance principles because God has brought us into relationship with himself by his love — undergirds our study of prayer.

Two specific sections in Romans 8 give background cotext on Paul's sense of prayer for our study of chapter 12. Our vital intimacy with the Father as sons and daughters, who have been brought into this relationship with him by Jesus Christ, issues in expression to him of our needs and concerns (8:15-16). Furthermore, when we are not able to pray because of our weaknesses, the Holy Spirit is at work within us to intercede for us (8:26-27).

Keeping these things in mind, therefore, we realize that when Paul calls us to steadfastness in prayer in this verse he is calling us again to a deeper reliance upon God's actions. The perseverance in prayer that carries all the rest of Romans 12 with it into deeper spirituality is possible only as a gift.

It's such a frustrating paradox: if prayer is a gift, how can we do anything? And if we can't do anything about it, why does Paul exhort us to remain faithful in it? This paradox is part of the larger dialectic of faith. Our response to God is, indeed, entirely a gift from him (as emphasized throughout Romans and summarized well in Eph. 2:8-9). Yet we are active in the process; God cannot respond for us. Such an apparent contradiction — the activity and passivity of both faith and prayer — is difficult to comprehend.

A closer look at the Greek participle that Paul chooses in Romans 12:12 gives us some insight into keeping the dialectic in balance. The verb designates how we are "to continue to do something with intense effort, with the possible implication of despite difficulty." In Acts 2:42 the verb emphasizes that the members of the first Christian community were "continually devoting themselves to the apostles' teaching and to fellowship, to the breaking of bread and to prayer." Then in Acts 2:46 the verb underscores the persistence of the early Christians in gathering "with one mind" in the temple.

No mere continuing in prayer is advocated here. Rather, we are invited to spend much time in prayer, and that is the secret of the paradox. God is the one who prays through us, who stirs up our prayer, who makes it effective, but the choice is ours whether or not we will participate in it. Our response to this exhortation, then, can be a careful decision regarding the importance of prayer in our personal and corporate allocation of time.

Martin Luther commented on the translation of Paul's phrase "instant in prayer" as follows:

> [T]he word "instant" is a call to order and vigilance that everyone . . . must hear and fear. For it means that praying must be a constant effort . . . a labor that is harder than every other labor . . . for it requires a subdued and broken mind and a high and triumphant spirit. . . . Christians

must practice prayer frequently and with diligence. For "to be instant" does not only mean "to be constantly engaged in something" but it means also "to press on," "to quicken one's pace," "to demand earnestly." So then, as there is nothing that Christians must do more frequently than praying, so there is also nothing that requires more labor and effort and, for this reason, is more effective and more fruitful. . . . In my judgment, prayer is indeed a continuous violent action of the spirit as it is lifted up to God.[1]

Luther's words become even more powerful when we remember another statement which is credited to him. When we think of all that he did — his teaching, debating, writing, translating, training, struggling for the truth — we are amazed to learn that he also said, "I have so much to do that if I didn't spend at least three hours a day in prayer I would never get it all done."

Coming to the decision about time is the most critical aspect of our personal and corporate spiritual lives. We can read hundreds of books and attend scores of seminars, but our skill and power in prayer won't improve unless we simply take time to do it. If we believe that prayer is so important, why don't we value prayer enough to deepen its operation in our lives?

Sadly, it often takes a crisis or great need for us to begin to understand the power available to those who pray. Needing deeper prayer for direction in my professional life and for healing in my physical life, I am also especially eager to find ways to nurture the prayer life of our Christian communities. Perhaps some simple suggestions might touch off new ideas for you and your community. Hopefully the process of thinking about prayer will stimulate each of us to give it priority in our daily choices about time.

1. Martin Luther, *Lectures on Romans*, trans. and ed. Wilhelm Pauck (Philadelphia: Westminster Press, 1961), pp. 347-49.

We will utilize various subsets or kinds of prayer to think more widely about its possibilities and tools. We will consider both personal and corporate prayer as structured/planned and unstructured/spontaneous, verbal and active prayer.

Both individual Christians and communities often excuse their lack of structured prayer with the argument, "But we're actually praying all the time." Certainly we do frequently offer sentence prayers in the midst of situations, but we also need the structured times of prayer to give focus and direction and depth to the flash prayers and the actions of prayer. The Scriptures consistently urge us to pray, to lift up holy hands, or to gather for prayer in our assemblies. Especially we notice that Jesus, our Model for a life spent in perfect relation to the Father, frequently went away by himself for prayer. The Gospel of Luke particularly shows the significance of structured prayer times in Jesus' life. Consider, for example, how he spent the whole night in prayer before he chose the twelve apostles (6:12-16). We can't escape the need for a quality discipline, a habit of spending time in prayer.

Various structures give tools to discipline our corporate prayer life. Denominational assemblies specialize in planned prayers printed in liturgical books or spontaneous prayers offered by members of the Body. We need both in our community life — for planned prayers widen our horizons beyond the narrow interests of our group and spontaneous prayers make us more receptive to the immediate work of the Spirit and the immediate needs of our fellow saints.

In our personal prayer lives we are helped by such structures as Dick Eastman's twelve steps in prayer,[2] the

2. The twelve steps are praise, waiting, confession, Scripture promises, watching, intercession, petition, thanksgiving, singing, meditation, listening, and praise; see Dick Eastman's *The Hour that Changes the World* (Grand Rapids: Baker, 1978).

Billy Graham Association's prayer notebook,[3] a spiral prayer notebook arranged alphabetically,[4] a spontaneous response to Scripture reading, or such planned prayers as biblical passages themselves (especially the Psalms), hymns, or special books of prayers.[5]

Until twenty years ago I could never function with prayer lists; they always got boring as I tried to pray for the same persons time after time. All the petitions became so general that nothing seemed to matter. My struggling "God bless so-and-so and this-or-that and why-for-what" was not very effective. Christian teachers convicted me when they stressed the importance of prayer because I couldn't establish meaningful prayer disciplines for myself.

A change in those bad habits began at a youth conference where I promised an old friend that I would pray for him every day concerning a matter that deeply troubled him. Then I wondered how I would remember to do that.

Perhaps you will think that this idea is silly, but it has worked for me to link my various kinds of prayer with different health disciplines. More extended prayer is possible while I exercise or wait in doctors' offices; shorter intercessions are

3. This prayer guide structures a week's prayers under the daily categories of church/religion, the family/home, media, government, education, business/commerce, and arts/entertainment. The book also describes the needs of two nations per week so that in the course of the year an individual or group could pray for the whole world.

4. This enables us to pray for each person or category on the list regularly, but with great freedom to spend longer on any particular page. At the end of our prayer time, we can simply place a bookmark and return to the next part of the alphabet on the next day. We continually travel through the alphabet, adding new items, updating the situations, praising God for his answers, changing the pages for individual persons or categories of needs.

5. I especially like John Baillie's *A Diary of Private Prayer* (New York: Charles Scribner's Sons, 1949), which contains a month's prayers for morning and evening.

offered while I do mindless therapeutic routines or wait for my blood glucose meter to finish its countdown. Once a peridontist said that my gum tissues were doing much better. I laughed in reply, "That's because my prayer list is getting longer!" I have found that it helps me immensely in coping with the pain of doctors' procedures to focus instead on the needs of others in my Christian community. And the discipline certainly deepens my relationship with them and the Hilarity of our care for each other.

Our specific structures of prayer enable us to notice more God's definite answers to our intercessions and petitions. Also, we will increasingly discover how much God is changing us in those hours. As we employ various disciplines God will faithfully show us concrete courses of action for our lives and particular insights into the needs of our friends and enemies. Finally, the whole process will deepen our commitment to one another in the community. We will be more directly involved in others' lives as we take seriously their needs for prayer and share their Hilarity in God's answers.

One particular tool helpful for both personal and corporate prayer is to group lists of persons into categories. A specific time of prayer begins with the plea that God will bring to mind all the individuals for whom we should pray in the various categories. This practice has been especially exciting for me because often persons who are really in need of prayer come to my mind several times in different categories. These are the categories I use:

Praise

Confession

Thanksgiving and intercession for

　• persons I was with today — which brings to mind

promises I've made to pray for them and the concerns of those with whom I spent time;

- persons that I will be with tomorrow — to prepare me to be open for the possibilities of the day for ministry and nurture;
- persons with whom I live — thanksgiving for my treasured husband and concern for his needs;
- my extended family — including parents, brothers and sisters, grandparents, in-laws, cousins, aunts and uncles, nephews and nieces;
- my godchildren — I promised at their baptism to pray for them daily;
- members of the Christian congregation, St. John Lutheran Church, to which I belong;
- pastors and other professional teachers of the Scriptures;
- members of my small groups — Bible study and discipleship groups;
- friends involved in difficult ministries — to street kids and drug addicts in New York City, to a church in a racially tense neighborhood, to counselees in crisis;
- persons whose ministries we support financially;
- my work colleagues — the CEM Board and their families, pastors of churches where I am teaching, contact persons for speaking engagements, editors and publishers;
- specific friends with whom I share particular concerns;
- best friends — including those from past times and places;
- single persons who are lonely or who have special needs;
- prisoners — this includes the man to whom I write as well as such agencies as Chuck Colson's Prison Fellowship;
- the unemployed — since many of my friends are out

206

of work or serve in jobs that don't use their gifts I ask God to show me ways to encourage them, to bring healing to their spirits, to help them financially, or to assist them in finding a job;

- the hungry and homeless and agencies that work to meet their needs;
- persons who are ill and those who stand beside them — often the ones who assist or wait beside the sufferers are in even greater need of extra strength and courage and patience;
- the handicapped and chronically ill — special friends who are physically and mentally challenged and those who work with the disabled;
- peacemakers, justice builders;
- visionaries;
- teachers — my husband's colleagues and my college classmates;
- children — so many are being destroyed by our culture, and so many in the world are hungry and without a home;
- government and church leaders throughout the world, especially the many new leaders in Eastern Europe and South America;
- atheists and agnostics with whom I want to share my faith meaningfully;
- relationships that need deeper insight.

Personal petition and thanksgiving for

- immediate concerns — this category is SO much fun because it changes with the times. Over the years God has faithfully answered my petitions for such things as a new pen-name, a publisher, the selling of my house, my graduate work, my recent marriage, our new home, and new directions in my work. Presently my immediate concerns focus on health needs as I thank God for successful surgery to reconstruct my foot and the brace which supports my crooked leg and as I yearn for healing of my eyes;

* aspects of my work — specific problems that I might be encountering, my writing, speaking engagements that are coming up in the future;
* personal attitudes — toward people, situations, crises;
* allocation of my time — in personal projects and in the Christian community.

More praise.

It is crucial to remember in structured times that prayer is two-way communication. We must allow uncluttered time for God to speak to us. Often he brings new Hilarity to our lives and community when he changes our attitudes, deepens our insights, gives us specific guidance, or sets us free to adore him. I have to keep paper and pen handy for the insights of prayer time.

As our structured times become more careful, our flash prayers become more frequent and particular. If I've thought about some matter thoroughly during a meditation time while exercising, new awarenesses keep popping into my head throughout the day and stimulate brief sentence prayers. As we lay out the matters on our mind, even as Hezekiah spread out his concerns before Yahweh (Isa. 37:14-20), the insights gained in our disciplines enable us to make our prayers a larger part of all the moments of our days.

The apostle Paul frequently mentions in his letters that every time he thinks about his readers he prays for them. We cannot discount that merely as an exaggeration, that Paul really couldn't do so much praying. Obviously, he had developed a careful habit, so that whenever a person's name entered his head he would immediately respond to the thought with intercession and praise. He was grateful for each person and church and had learned to appreciate in constant thanksgiving how God used individuals and communities to enrich his life. Our experience of Hilarity in the community will be nourished by such habits of spontaneous, frequent prayer for others.

I want to learn also how to pray immediately about circumstances so that my "practice of the presence of God" would be more constant.[6] If we develop a total attitude of consistently placing whatever happens into God's safekeeping, then our actions will be more intimately connected at all times with his purposes and our relationship with him.

My verbal prayers became more meaningful when I first learned about the action of prayer. As a child, I worried when asked to pray for a sick person that maybe not enough people would pay attention to the request. What if the number of people required to convince God to heal that person didn't pray? Childishly I wondered how many prayers were necessary to change God's mind.

Not until I learned the concept of "putting legs on our prayers" did corporate prayer make much sense. Complete prayer does not mean simply throwing words about someone's needs up at God. After all, God already knows what all our needs are, and his perfect will is what is best for each of us. However, if we pray about concerns and say, "Thy will be done," we are actually promising, "Yes, Lord, here we are. Use us in whatever ways you want for the effecting of your will in this matter."

One of my college professors said, "If you ask God to feed the starving in India, you'd better duck; he might just send you over there to do it." (And, sure enough, the very next year I wound up in India on a mission concert tour that permanently changed my life by opening my eyes to the

6. Brother Lawrence uses this phrase to describe his habit of recognizing God's presence in every moment of the day. See his book *The Practice of the Presence of God* (London: Samuel Bagster and Sons, n.d.).

needs of the global community. I've been more careful how I pray since then!) Praying about the world hunger situation drives us to action; we must rethink our stewardship of money and our participation in groups that raise awareness and gather funds. If God's will to care for the poor and oppressed is going to be accomplished, he needs people willing to be vessels for his purposes in the world.

Similarly, if we pray for someone ill, then we must be open to ways in which God might use us in his processes of healing — to encourage that person by sending flowers or going for a visit, to ease the strain of medical appointments by providing transportation or child care, to release him from fears by paying his bills, to give her rest by preparing meals or cleaning her house. This is why we want the whole community to pray about a matter: more people offer all they can to free the person for healing. (The next chapter will especially discuss such sharing in the Christian community's needs.)

Furthermore, in most denominations we need to learn greater boldness in praying for healing — without succumbing to the dangers of demanding something from God or of presumptuously claiming that we know best in what ways God wants to heal. Many denominations that are more obedient in asking for healing limit the kind of healing God might do to only the physical.

The Christian community will certainly experience greater Hilarity as we become more involved in each other's lives through the intimacy of intercession and practical care. As we prioritize our time to allow longer periods for structured prayer, our spontaneous prayers will become more frequent and our sense of the presence of God more constant. Both our verbal and our incarnated prayers — personally and corporately — will issue in lives of caring, deepened relationships and Hilarious love.

Therefore:

1. How can we set aside more time for prayer in our daily lives and in the life of our Christian community? Why would that increase our Hilarity?

2. How effective are our structured times for prayer — both personally and corporately? Why and why not?

3. How have we experienced prayer as a gift of grace?

4. How can we make spontaneous prayers a more frequent habit of mind?

5. To whom do we want to make a deeper commitment of prayer?

6. How can our Christian community deepen its prayer life together?

7. How have we recently experienced the Hilarity of seeing God's answers to our prayers?

23. *Sharing in the Needs of the Saints and of the World*

> In the needs of the saints — sharing in common! The hospitality — pursuing it!
>
> — ROMANS 12:13

For about a year Christians Equipped for Ministry tried to sponsor a home for crisis care in Olympia, Washington. I had bought a large house, and our corporation hired a director as hostess for a ministry of hospitality. We soon discovered, however, that the needs were overwhelming — far beyond the potential we had for meeting them. We were besieged by calls from many who were homeless, abused, recovering from substance addictions, broken, or confused. We got overloaded. For a few days we had so many guests in the house that I slept on a chair in my study, which I wouldn't have minded at all, except that the guest staying in my bedroom would go up and down the nearby stairs in the middle of the night and turn on all the fluorescent lights where I was trying to sleep. She was so out of touch with reality that her presence threatened to destroy the positive

212

effects of our community on the lives of other guests. Needless to say, the whole situation quickly shattered our false idealism and taught us instead good lessons about God's provision.

After our house director resigned to go back to school, the CEM Board came to understand through much prayer and wrestling that our sponsoring such a house took us beyond the call for ministry that first led us to incorporate Christians Equipped for Ministry. One of Satan's best ways to render ineffective the ministry of God's people is to get them involved in too much that lies outside of their particular gifts so that they lose their Hilarity and the Holy Spirit's power in the areas in which they are gifted to serve.

Shortly after we gave up our attempt, a Catholic Worker house was established in Olympia which meets the needs of the community far better than we could. We experienced glad Hilarity as we gave them our extra beds and blankets as partners in a concern for which they were better equipped to deal directly. However, this battle still remains for me: how do I care for the needs of strangers and also be faithful to my own call to write and teach? The crisis ministry in which we were engaged burdened me forever with the pervasive need for open Christian homes. How can I motivate others and find ways myself to care about the wide variety of immense needs in our times?

The struggle is a good one. It forces me to search for ways to be hospitable within my own limitations — through financial support, through stirring up awareness in others by teaching and writing, by watching for the needs of others as I wait at airports and bus stations. Myron and I tried to create our wedding to be an alternative to the elaborate displays of contemporary society and thereby to include hospitality to strangers in our plans. We requested on our invitations that guests not bring presents for us and noted that we would instead take an offering for the hungry and homeless during the worship service. Relatives and friends eagerly responded to that suggestion; we were over-whelmed by how much money came in for Vancouver's SHARE House.

The thirteenth verse from Romans 12 involves two movements of caring — one within the community and one beyond it — and both are extremely relevant for our age. Furthermore, the interaction between them heightens them both. Perhaps you are already active in one or both of these types of caring; if so, I hope this chapter will commend you and encourage you to expand your vision. Perhaps you will respond to this chapter by developing a new ministry of an open heart and home. Prayerfully we will all respond to Paul's exhortation by becoming more eager to deepen the Hilarity of our communities through richer caring for each other and more effective reaching out to the world around us.

The first phrase in the Greek text says literally, "in the needs of the saints sharing in common." The word *saints* specifically designates members of the family of God. The name reminds us that God set apart each of us for special functions within the community and that the community is set apart from the world to be a blessing to it (as in Gen. 12:1-3). To fulfill our personal and corporate callings we need to be strengthened, equipped, and supported.

To "have the needs of the saints in common" involves a wide diversity of possibilities. We might provide material necessities — by paying bills for a fellow saint who is un-employed or by gathering money for missionaries to buy medicines for their clinics and gas for their motorcycles. We might assist someone with emotional or intellectual difficul-ties, run errands for someone with physical challenges, or offer spiritual aid — like the time my anonymous friend bought a round-trip plane ticket so that I could participate in the choir reunion. What a great gift that was at the time to refresh me for ministry!

214

The real power in the first phrase of Romans 12:13 lies in the participle "sharing-in-common," which is related to the Greek noun *koinōnia*, a term many churches use to describe their fellowship gatherings. The Greek root actually implies a sharing in something to such a degree that one claims a part in it for oneself. Thus, in verse 13 it involves being partners together in meeting the needs of the set-apart people of God. More than just a contribution to assist someone, more than just taking an interest in that person's need, *koinōnia* signifies actually becoming immersed in the other's situation.

Our English word *sharing* has become much too superficial (through overuse in such phrases as "I'd like to share . . .") to convey that kind of commitment to others. And our usage of the word *fellowship* so often simply means serving cookies and coffee in the narthex after worship.

When first working on this book many years ago, I wrote an Easter present poem for a special family in Seattle. Their friendship illustrates the kind of partnership in another's needs that Paul calls for here in Romans 12:13:

With Gratitude
You said,
    "Call us, any time you need us,"
    and I felt at home in your words.
I poured out my grief,
    and you hugged me.
I told you my fears,
    and you prayed that I would sleep protected.
I expressed my confusion,
    and you helped me sort out the parts.
I tried to face my ugly self,
    and you kept on caring.
I gave you my pain,
    and you gave me a kiss.

How can I thank you?
How do I express this awareness
    that I have found a home in your love,
    that I've been adopted by your grace?
It's like the Resurrection, promising life
    and healing and Hilarity.
It's just that Easter
    is incarnated in your care.

My particular need then as a single, traveling teacher was for some sort of rooting. This family provided that in many ways, such as making a bedroom in their home available to me whenever I was stranded or needed a break. They even put in the room a picture of a lion (the CEM logo at that time).

Because members of the Body of Christ are gifted with so many differing sensitivities, we are each more aware of certain kinds of needs and thus are more able to provide certain necessities for particular saints. Paul's exhortation encourages us to explore them and to find ways in which the call of this verse can be put into practical application in each of our lives.

What a wonderful picture the saints offer of the reality of God in our midst if those around us can see how deeply we love each other by our Hilarity as we minister to one another's needs! That takes commitment. To choose to be deeply involved with each other, even when we do not feel so eager to do that, throws us back again upon grace. God's perfect and thorough love for us is our empowerment and motivation and source of guidance. Under his direction we can choose those needs to which we can contribute, those ministries for which we are gifted, those persons with whom we can share. Our Christian congregations will remain just collections of disparate people unless we learn more directly, specifically, and practically to enter into the needs of others.

I have been experiencing the profound blessing of sharing within the community to a larger extent the past three years as I have undergone various hand surgeries, foot reconstruction, a broken leg, and laser treatment and surgery for my eyes. Several members of our congregation here in Vancouver have offered gentle words of encouragement, transportation to clinics in Portland, meals and housecleaning, crutches and a wheelchair for the years I was in braces and casts, and lots of prayers. Each kind of offering — from persons with various gifts — increases the Hilarity of our community. Myron and I wonder how we could ever have coped all these months without their aid.

The other thrust of Romans 12:13 involves hospitality to strangers, which seems to be sorely deficient in the Church in our times. In this age of loneliness and alienation, few strangers look for emotional and spiritual care in churches. Most seek it elsewhere — in bars, for example. Those who are down-and-out know that in a bar they will find a listening ear and companionship.

Obviously, the assemblies of Christian congregations are too large for thorough hospitality, although much warmth and welcoming friendliness can be demonstrated in the gatherings of believers. Here in Romans 12, however, Paul is addressing the greater need to welcome strangers into our homes and lives.

Right after the CEM Board's decision to close down our crisis ministry, I received several heartbreaking requests for a place for persons to stay. Similarly, while I was doing graduate work in South Bend, Indiana, several men slept in their cars in a parking lot beneath the bedroom window of my apartment and other people frequently went through my garbage can in the alley looking for food. Such incidents and the growing statistics make me more painfully aware of the huge number of persons that are homeless, on the road, without any security or love, in need of Christian community to enfold them.

Check out the data for the area in which you live. Call the YMCA or women's shelter or crisis lines, or go down to the "First Avenue" of your town and see how many persons have no home or no one to love them. Get involved in a soup kitchen or a resource center or a skid row mission or a ministry to drug addicts, abused women and children, AIDS victims, or runaway teenagers, and you will be overwhelmed with the needs. Look at the work of Mother Teresa in Calcutta, or consider the plight of the refugees. How many millions — billions? — of people in our world need the hospitality of Christians?

Paul says literally, "pursuing the kindness to strangers." The word translated "kindness to strangers" is built from the same root as the noun *philadelphia* or "friendship love" that we discussed in Chapter 18. Thus, the same kind of love we were encouraged to express in the Christian family with tender affection (v. 10) is the love God wants us to express toward strangers.

In Paul's day, this phrase would especially signify caring for Christians who might be traveling to do the Lord's work, since at that time, as Leon Morris explains, "it was not always possible or desirable to stay in inns." Thus, Paul "is not advocating a pleasant social exercise among friends, but the use of one's home to help even people we do not know, if that will advance God's cause."[1] However, we should not limit the phrase only to Christian strangers, for it invites us — in this twentieth-century world so characterized by injustice and oppression — to open our homes to all kinds of strangers in ways that serve God's purposes.

Furthermore, we won't merely express hospitality casually, whenever we can't avoid it, once in a while. The participle Paul chooses here means literally "to be pursuing." The verb

1. Morris, *The Epistle to the Romans* (Grand Rapids: William B. Eerdmans, 1988), p. 448.

is used often in the New Testament (in fact, in the very next verse of Romans 12) to mean persecution, so it signifies "to do something with intense effort and with definite purpose or goal." We aspire to hospitality with a holy ambition. We will become burdened — not weighed down unduly, but motivated — by the needs of the strangers around us.

This could be a devastating exhortation except that again we remember the *therefore* with which we began this book. We are thrown back into utter dependence upon God's loving grace. Can we ever be reminded of that enough? Nevertheless, this is true: the only way that we can possibly begin to minister to the needs of the world without being driven to despair by their immensity is if we are first of all undergirded by the Hilarity of God's love. Then, knowing full well that the world's needs will always be larger than we can handle, we will each select those ways in which we can serve most effectively and commit ourselves to the ministries to which we are called. It will be difficult to say no to other needs, but recognizing our place within a whole community of saints, in which each member meets specific needs, frees us from our savior complexes. We will serve best in those areas to which we have been called if we aren't distracted by the immensity of other needs for service outside our gifts.

That became very clear to me after our house director left, and I tried to continue the crisis ministry in addition to teaching and writing. Trying to do too many jobs, I didn't do any of them well, and my health suffered, too. How immense is the need for a strengthening of community life so that we can share in each other's needs (v. 13a) in order to set us all free to do what we each can do well in the ministry of hospitality to strangers. Certainly I am not gifted to administer a crisis home — but God has gifted others in the community to do so, and perhaps more opportunities will arise for me to support them financially or to stir up greater awareness of the needs for hospitality through teaching and writing.

World Vision International produced an eye-catching poster that helps to put these things in perspective. Against an all-black background the poster asks in stark white letters, "How do you feed two billion hungry people?" A small picture of a tiny boy and his rice bowl appears at the bottom of the poster with the caption, "One at a time."

We might not be gifted to administer a soup kitchen, but we can prepare sandwiches for it or drive delivery trucks. We certainly cannot care for everyone who is lonely, but we can invite a stranger home for dinner after Sunday worship. Jesus didn't heal everyone who was ill in Galilee, but he cared gently for each person who came to him — one at a time.

We cannot pursue kindness toward everyone, but each of us can find specific avenues for caring. The world has so many needs that each one of us is vitally significant for the meeting of those needs. It takes the global Christian community to respond to them all and to fight the structural injustice that escalates oppression. Consequently, both personally and corporately we must ask how we might most effectively minister to some of the needs and stir up the rest of the Church to consider the same question. The immensity of the world's needs directly challenges the people of God to become more truly a Christian community that is set free by its Hilarity to share and care.

Paul's exhortation invites us always to be open to new possibilities for becoming more hospitable. Karen Burton Mains' *Open Heart — Open Home* contains many excellent suggestions.[2] Our community prayer times and small-group discussions can become times of exploring opportunities for ministry so that we all — individually and to-

2. Karen Burton Mains, *Open Heart — Open Home* (Elgin, IL: David C. Cook, 1976).

gether — know more clearly how God would have us serve the world.[3]

One final point is critical for the freedom and Hilarity of our hospitality. We must remember that the quality of hospitality does not depend on the cost of the food we prepare or the elegance of the setting in which we provide care for those in need. True hospitality instead involves the investment of our lives in genuine kindness to those for whom we care. Perhaps the term *elegance*, then, can be applied to our spirit and might be part of our definition of the Christian community's Hilarity. Hospitality includes whatever makes the other person feel welcome, loved, affirmed. We all can grow in elegance of spirit, in Hilarity, as God's love empowers us together to be more concerned for the needs of the saints and more hospitable toward strangers.

Therefore:

1. What unmet needs have we noticed in the saints of our community?

2. How can we contribute more directly toward meeting those needs?

3. How has our sharing of ourselves been lacking in depth of commitment? How has our lack of Hilarity prevented us from sharing? What could we do about that?

4. In what ways are we particularly able to show kindness to strangers?

5. What are the needs of the local community in which we live?

---

3. One excellent tool is *A Covenant Group for Lifestyle Assessment*, by William E. Gibson and the Eco-Justice Task Force (New York: United Presbyterian Program Agency, 1981).

6. How can our congregation share its Hilarity by becoming more involved in caring for the needs of our local community?

7. How can the Church become more involved in caring for the needs of the world?

24. Caring for the Persecutors

Be blessing the ones persecuting you; be blessing and
do not be cursing.

— ROMANS 12:14

THE GRADUATE SCHOOL English professor had called me
into his office to threaten me. I had become the brunt
of all his jokes — and persecutions — because of my Christian faith, so I wondered what this next encounter might
entail. I was afraid of him, but, on the other hand, he seemed
so lonely that God had stirred in me a new concern.

The interview with him that day turned completely
around and became an opportunity genuinely to care about
his pain and struggles. After listening to his unhappiness, I
left his office sadly, wishing that he could believe what I did
about the love and grace of God instead of persecuting me
for it.

I grew up in an unusually sheltered and warmly religious environment, had gone to Lutheran schools for my
elementary and college education, and thought religious
persecution happened only in atheistic nations. I'll never
forget the first (and only!) time that I explained naively to a

graduate school professor that I hadn't finished a certain project yet because of an important meeting the previous night with my church community. I was genuinely surprised that she didn't accept that as a valid reason! Was I so stupid not to realize that the things of God are not the top priority in everyone's life?

We must begin this chapter by remembering that persecution, violent opposition to our beliefs, will be the likely lot of all who genuinely desire to be God's people in the world. The description to son-in-the-faith Timothy of the rigors of persecution Paul had suffered is concluded with this striking warning: "Indeed all who desire to live a godly life in Christ Jesus will be persecuted" (2 Tim. 3:12, RSV). But the key lies in the phrase "godly life," for some overzealous Christians deserve the persecution they get.

That last sentence may sound overly harsh, but probably you have also been confronted by religious behavior so obnoxious that it alienates all those who observe it. Our conversation and actions should not be tactless or pushy as we speak about our faith and seek to live out the Hilarity of God's love in daily situations. If our life-style is not genuine, then abuse is indeed deserved, even if it is unkind. We need one another in the Christian community to help us know when our expressions of faith are causing offense.

On the other hand, we must question the reality of our faith if we are never persecuted. The old saying indicts us: "If you were arrested for being a Christian, would there be enough evidence to convict you?" If we never experience any hassle from work colleagues, family members, neighbors, or perhaps persons in our churches who are offended by how radically we try to put God's love into practice, then we need to check out our godliness. A lack of persecution might indicate our failure to stand up truly for our principles.

The commitment of some contemporary high school

students who participate actively in Bible study and prayer groups makes me wish I had been like that. I was a faithful member of our congregational youth group, but we did not gather to become equipped for more intentional living out of God's love in our high school. I didn't clearly understand the difference that Christ could make if he were the center and focus of my existence until I became deathly ill in my junior year. Prior to that I believed that Jesus was my Savior, but I didn't fully understand the Hilarity of his Lordship in every aspect of life.

Consequently, I didn't run into any persecution till I was teaching a course on the literature of the Bible while I worked on my master's degree in English. Those years when my faith was frequently under attack were some of the most strongly maturing times I've ever experienced. How tragic that so many of us never experience the deep Hilarity that comes to faith from our confidence in God's grace until we have to struggle against crisis or tragedy or persecution!

How is our faith life now? Does our family see the glad Hilarity of grace at work in our daily interactions? Do our neighbors know that Christ is the center of our lives? Do colleagues see him in us, not in ways that are overbearing, but in ways that lead them to ask us to explain the hope that lies within us (1 Pet. 3:15)?

As we discover, one of the best results from times of persecution is the strengthening of our faith. When everything we hold dear is called into question, we will either recognize its utter supremacy or throw it overboard. In the face of pain we discover what is worth our devotion. Indeed, persecution is a purger and a pruner. It clears out of our faith whatever is nonessential and drives us back to the basic, absolute reality of God's love.

I learned the profound necessity of Christian fellowship, too, in my first times of persecution. Members of a high school Bible study group I was leading enfolded me in prayer and were a constantly encouraging and supportive community. Even though we are now separated by many miles and years, for some of us the great bond of love forged in pain is still strong.

Of course, this truth has been evident on a large scale throughout history: the times of persecution have always been great deepening times for the Church. Not only are doctrines often clarified and rid of the extra froth that has accrued, but also relationships are deepened as persons cling to each other for support and survival. As the communist world began breaking apart in 1989 and 1990, we could easily see how strong various Christian communities had become in Eastern Europe as they had suffered persecution and repression.

Persecution can also turn into a great benefit for the persecutors — if they can come to understand the significance of their actions. This lesson is very apparent in the Gospel of Luke, which dramatically shows that everywhere Jesus went he was a divider of the people. Everyone either loved him with adoring devotion or hated him with confused frustration. For example, at the end of the account of Jesus healing the woman bent over double, all the common people were rejoicing, but Jesus had put the religious leaders who opposed him to shame (Luke 13:17). When he spoke the truth, he alienated those who were not of the truth.

If persons react with hostility, then, when we speak the truth, their true character is revealed. If persons are offended by how we live as the people of God, then they are being convicted for their own lack of integrity.

Again, we must be careful that the stumbling block is genuinely the grace of God and not our offensive life-style. Nevertheless, we can be glad if the truth that we speak and live is convicting to others. Moreover, we will want to follow up on that conviction with a sensitivity and care that frees the one who hassles us to come to know and accept the truth.

That is why Paul urges us in Romans 12:14 to react to those who persecute us by blessing them, being a gift to them. The present imperative form of the verb commands us to make our giving of love a continual attitude and action.

It is striking that Paul here uses a verb for the first time since verse 5. Certainly the action to which he calls us must be unusually significant. What, then, does Paul mean by his challenge to us to bless our tormentors?

The Greek verb that Paul uses in this verse is all the more striking as we compare it with others in the same semantic field. Out of the entire range of verbs for how one speaks to or deals with another, Paul chooses *eulogeō*, which grew from a root meaning of praising or extolling others to signify "to ask God to bestow divine favor on, with the implication that the verbal act itself constitutes a significant benefit." To bless our persecutors, then, does not mean that we quietly wish them well within ourselves. Rather, we respond to them vocally with the desire that God would provide them with benefits. Thus the action is no mere empty formality; it demands a commitment of us.

Part of the reason why we are to respond to persecution with blessing is the principle of "heaping coals of fire," which we will study more thoroughly in Chapter 30. Nothing takes a would-be persecutor more by surprise than to be answered with love and kindness.

Yet the deeper reason for such a response lies in the nature of the one who is hassling us. As in the case of my friend from the English faculty, persecution seems usually to arise out of the persecutor's own pain. He was lonely and felt that nobody cared about him, so he lashed out against others for some sort of release. When Paul advocates a response of blessing, his exhortation invites us to assess very carefully our persecutor's needs.

We have come back again to the genuine love of Romans 12:9. The experience of persecution gives us a chance truly to minister to the hurts and griefs of those who afflict us. It offers us the opportunity, out of the Hilarity of faith, to love the unloveable, to speak the peace of Jesus to those who are reconciled neither with God, nor with others, nor — usually — with themselves.

As we bless them, then, we commend them to God for his loving care. This takes us back to Paul's words about persistence in prayer. When we have thoroughly prayed about our enemies' needs, we will more easily genuinely bless them to their face. Over the days following the confrontation described at the beginning of this chapter, God brought my persecutor to mind several times and created a profound concern for that man. I truly wanted to bring him happiness and care and the knowledge of God's love for him.

That was not my human reaction, however. The *therefore* of God's love was the strong empowerment in that situation. My usual reaction to being hassled is to get angry and lash out bitterly. Paul knew that we would have a hard time accepting this exhortation, so he said it twice in the same verse.

Nothing is repeated in the Scriptures just to fill up space. If instruction is repeated in a literary structure, its author knows his readers need to hear it again. Because our natural tendency is not to rejoice in difficult circumstances, Paul exhorts twice: "Rejoice in the Lord always. I will say it again: Rejoice!" (Phil. 4:4). Similarly, Romans 12:14 seems to say, "Bless those persecuting you. Yes, you heard me right; I really mean that you can respond to persecutions with the opposite of cursing — indeed, with praise and love."

How often in this book we have recognized how impossible Paul's words are for us, but for the love of God. Together we realize more and more that such is always the case in living out our Christian faith. We can never be unselfish enough to obey all these ethical exhortations. Only as God's love fills us with Hilarity to motivate us, empower us, and flow through us to others can we live out these principles in the midst of the difficulties of our daily lives.

Paul concludes this injunction with a specific command not to be cursing those who hassle us. God's purposes can never be accomplished if we react to our own pain by inflicting pain on others. Nor can we continue growing as the people of God if we seek vengeance on others. That spoils our reconciliation, not only with them, but also with God and with ourselves. To curse our persecutors is surely always more destructive to us than to them.

To set aside our natural inclinations in favor of the godly response will always produce good things for us, though not necessarily in the immediate situation. After months of making jokes about me in his classes and mocking me to my face, one person who hassled me the most in the English department came up to my office the day before I finished my work there and with great seriousness declared, "I really hate to tell you this — but I like you."

I like you, too, sir — so much that I still keep praying for you. . . .

Therefore:

1. From whom have we experienced persecutions?

2. Did we deserve their persecution because our behavior caused offense?

3. How can we in the Christian community help each other so that our life-styles do not offer any offense but the stumbling block of the truth?

4. What might be the personal needs that might have caused our persecutors to hassle us? How can we be sensitive to their needs and bring the Hilarity of the gospel to those persons?

5. Is our faith life active enough to arouse persecution?

6. How have we experienced the good things that come back upon us when we bless those who persecute us?

7. How will we add to our personal and corporate prayer life a greater concern for those in other countries who are being persecuted and tortured and killed for their faith?

25. "With-ness" in Human Emotions

To be rejoicing with the ones rejoicing; to be mourning with the ones mourning.

— ROMANS 12:15

M Y FAVORITE COLLEGE professor listened compassionately as I poured out the grief that was ripping apart my life. Finally, in desperation, I cried, "Whatever can I do with all the pain? It just stays there, a huge lump inside, killing me. How can I deal with all the spiritual pain?"

He took my face in his hands. "I don't know," he said softly, and I noticed the tears on his cheeks.

He didn't give me any answers, but I was immensely comforted that afternoon. I hadn't realized before I saw his tears how much he cared. Then suddenly I wasn't so terribly alone anymore.

My teacher entered into my pain so much that he wept with me. That helpful "with-ness" eased the burden, though nothing could take it away.

At first glance Romans 12:15 seems too easy, a simple

instruction to be happy with folks when they are happy and sad when they are sad. However, the depth of Paul's exhortation and its implications for the Hilarity of our communities easily escape us unless we pay closer attention to the obstacles that keep us from obeying it.

One difficulty with this text lies in its apparent contradiction with verse 9, which asserts that our love should be genuine. How can we be genuine in our ministry to others if we don't feel like rejoicing or mourning when they are happy or grieving? Our definition of the love in verse 9, however, sets us free from this problem. Remember that we recognized *agapē* as intelligent love, purposefully directed toward the needs of the other. Thus, when we are trying to minister to others in their present emotions, genuine love will care enough to enter with them into that state of mind and psyche.

Tragically, many Christians think instead that what we should do with persons who are sad is "cheer them up." In times of deep sorrow, it is profoundly aggravating when friends say such things as "Well, be happy" or "Come on, smile." Such roadblocks arouse our anger because they deny the reality of our emotions. They do not allow us to be ourselves, persons who at that point in time are sad and grieving.

Why are we so afraid of other persons' sadnesses and fears — and sometimes, surprisingly, even their happinesses? Why do some believers think that the Christian remedy for sadness is to talk about all the promises of God and how we who suffer should just be able to lift ourselves right up out of that depression because, after all, God loves us?

In an incident reported by a campus ministry, a committed Christian once thought she always had to show only the happiness of her faith to her college roommate. Whenever things were not going too well, she hid that from the non-Christian, but talked with her endlessly about how

Christ helped her through everything. Finally the roommate believed and became a Christian, too.

Two weeks later the roommate committed suicide. She left a note saying that she just couldn't be a Christian because she couldn't be happy all the time. That tragedy could so easily have been prevented if only the two women had understood better the place of human emotions in our faith.

The major point of this verse from Paul is to encourage us to be real with our emotions and to be real about them together with others. The Greek construction of these phrases literally says, "to be rejoicing with the ones rejoicing; to be mourning with the ones mourning." These two simple phrases (six simple words in Greek) show the reality of human existence with its ups and downs. Now how can we put this verse into practice effectively?

Larry Richards' book *69 Ways to Start a Study Group and Keep It Growing* offers an excellent schema that makes this verse more understandable. He describes these two dimensions of our Christian life: the static or human level that experiences failure and mistakes and pain, and the dynamic aspect of our existence that functions under the Lordship of Christ and experiences growth. Richards insists that Christian groups must talk with one another on both levels. We share on the static level so that we can identify with each other as fallible human beings, so that we don't make the mistake of the college coed and think that all Christians are super-heroes with no problems. On the other hand, we must also communicate on the dynamic level to remember the hope and Hilarity that faith brings to our existence. The Resurrection assures us that ultimately the outcome of everything is under God's love, that Jesus already has triumphed over principalities and powers and over our mistakes and pain.

If we relate to one another only on the dynamic level, we lose touch with human reality. If we relate only on the static level, we lose our hope. In our communities we can know each other on both levels in a healthy balance.[1]

Richards' insight enables us to put verse 15 more effectively into practice. To share on the static level with persons who are mourning is to participate in the pain of their humanity by grieving with them. That is not phony because, in our genuine love for them, we know intelligently that what they need is not someone to dump God's love on them with trite pious platitudes, but someone to incarnate God's love for them so that they are not alone in their pain. Moreover, at appropriate moments, we can remind them on the dynamic level that God is there, too, and that ultimately his love will prevail.

The emphasis is on the "with-ness." Our mourning with them dare not be in a condescending way, as if to say, "If you must cry, I'll put up with it this time, but really you must get stronger so that you can face things better."

What enables us to be genuine about the "with-ness" is the realization that we each have certain areas of weakness in which we need to be supported by the rest of the community. Paul began his discourse to the Romans with this assurance: "both you and I will be helped at the same time, you by my faith and I by yours" (1:12, TEV). The apostle knew that no one is greater or lesser among the people of God. We all have gifts to give to each other; we all have dimensions of maturity greater than others' as well as phases of our existence in which we are not so strong. Thus, our mourning with others is genuine because we mourn for ourselves, too, at the same time, and for all the pain people have suffered and do suffer and will suffer as long as we are human.

The key word for balance is the conjunction *with*. It

---

1. Lawrence O. Richards, *69 Ways to Start a Study Group and Keep It Growing* (Grand Rapids: Zondervan, 1973).

prevents any sort of condescension because we must place ourselves with others in their pain. However, the concept of "with-ness" also prevents us from thinking that we can perfectly understand another's situation. We are only *with* the other; we cannot *be* that person. A false understanding is as destructive as condescension.

For example, a woman who had suddenly lost a baby to crib death described her experience in a Christian magazine. Many persons had completely avoided her and failed utterly to be with her in any sense of the word. Others wrote notes admitting that they did not know what to say — which helped, she commented, because at least she knew they cared.

The ones that caused her the most pain were the inconsiderate folk who said things like, "I know just how you feel." "No way!" she would respond in her mind. "How can you know just how I feel? You've never lost a child."

We can never fully understand the pain of other persons; we can only be with them in it. This verse is most effectively applied when we realize our own limitations of perception.

Unquestionably, "with-ness" involves commitment to the other person. We can't know what an individual's rejoicing or grief is about unless we spend the time necessary to listen. This is perhaps our greatest area of failure.

Our culture is not characterized by persons taking time for one another. Many factors of our society militate against such an investment of ourselves, yet the sacrifice of time always proves to be well worth the effort. Social scientists have commented in recent years that the need for psychologists and psychiatrists would be greatly reduced if we would return to such former patterns of caring as lap time for a child, neighborhood gatherings over coffee, family play times, or couples swinging on the front porch on summer evenings.

We can't mourn hurriedly. Nor can we drink deeply of

the delights of our lives if we are always rushing through things. For "with-ness" to happen, we need to spend time in conversations, in worship, in wonder, in waiting.

Several aspects of our lives together as God's people in community will be changed by this text. First, this verse blasts the old "macho" image that a man is not supposed to cry. This attitude seems to be changing in many circles in our culture, but certainly the Christian community could release us all even more to express, and to share in, sadness. Somehow we human beings are afraid of that — perhaps because we think that grief will drag us down, or maybe because we are afraid it will open up some painful wounds in ourselves.

God gave me a powerful lesson about that one night in Juneau, right after the overwhelmingly affirming experience of the "therefore" cake described at the beginning of Chapter 1. Something I read in my studying later that night jogged my thoughts, and a huge bunch of painful memories surfaced. Usually my habit in such a situation is to push those memories back under and try to forget them so that I can go on with work. But that particular night I was feeling so deeply loved that I decided not to do that. It was time to face those bad memories and deal with them. The result was a wonderful time of grieving.

I'm surprised that I could ever write "a *wonderful* time of grieving," because previous personal mourning times had always been so painful that I would want to get over them as soon as possible. Yet that night, within the care of those Juneau friends, I felt safe. Weeping was cleansing, freeing, and good because it arose from a sense of well-being, the Hilarity of community.

When Paul calls us to mourn together, he is urging us to make use of one of the means God has for bringing us healing. In the closeness and security of one another's love, our mourning can be transformed into good grief.

236

A long time after that night in Juneau I finally discovered the difference between that good grieving in Alaska and other times of grief that had been terrifying and terrible. That night my grieving came out of community wholeness rather than solitary brokenness. I wept because things are not the way God intends them to be — the evil in the world violates his plans — but that fact didn't scare me at the moment. It was only a thing to be sad about, not something that could destroy me. Suddenly I saw that the personal situation over which I grieved might be hopeless, but it was not serious (as we discussed in Chapter 21).

One of the best things that we can do, then, for persons who are in despair is to create for them an enfolding and safe environment in which they will know so deeply that they are loved that they are set free to do their mourning work, to discover that their grief can be enfolded within the wholeness of the community, that they are not alone in their pain. Sometimes many months of caring are required to make a major breakthrough. Many people might invest many hours to let the grieving persons cry, to listen to their sadness, and thus to bring God's healing.

I cannot stress enough the essential need for the Christian community to be a safe environment. More often than not, it seems, we are not able to let those who mourn really mourn. We are too afraid of our brothers' and sisters' grieving! One Sunday between worship and Bible class several people asked me how I was doing, and I burst into tears. I had broken my leg after enduring fourteen months of a shattered foot, and it had just become further complicated by blisters that broke open and exposed me to the great danger of infection, which my body cannot fight very well. Because I'd been working on this book, I was overly prepared to notice how many people tried simply to pat me on the back and say, "There, there, it will be better someday." I am enormously grateful for one dear friend who made it safe for me to mourn, who accepted me for what I was at the moment — broken by what seemed an insurmountable pile of complications. In the security of her acceptance of my weakness, I could begin to hope again because I experienced tangibly — by means of her love in my Christian community — the acceptance and the "with-ness" and the care of God.

A second major area of change in the Christian community will be new growth in our ability to share our brothers' and sisters' Joys. When Paul says, "to be rejoicing with the ones rejoicing," he gives us the sure means of shared Hilarity for fighting jealousy and envy.

That convicted me one day during the time I lived in a Christian community, when I went upstairs to see the new skylight that two carpenters had installed in Julie's art studio. My human reaction was to be envious because now Julie's place for creativity was so bright and cheery, while I disliked the dark coldness and lack of view in my basement study. But when I focused on how vital this new atmosphere would be for Julie's work as an artist, when I rejoiced with her in the freedom and motivation the skylight would give her, then I wasn't jealous.

That might seem like a silly example, but often our relationships with others are marred because, instead of rejoicing with them in the gifts that come to their lives, we resent the fact that they don't come to us in quite the same ways. Consequently, we lose the Hilarity of the community.

Noticing the progression of the last several verses in Romans 12 helps us to understand the principle better. In verse 10 Paul invited us to love one another in the community with a family sort of love — so that we really care about one another as if we were natural brothers and sisters. Then in verses 11 and 12 he showed us that such love will be worked out in tangible actions such as serving the Lord, enduring in tribulations, and persevering in prayer. The challenge to be constantly praying for one another leads

directly into the emphasis in verse 13 on meeting the needs
of all the saints. Certainly as we pray for one another we
will observe more ways to meet each other's needs.

Verse 14 seems to break the continuity of these verses
by suddenly speaking about enemies. However, since the
word for *persecutors* comes from the same root as the word
for *pursue,* which characterizes the way we earnestly seek in
the Christian community to be hospitable, Paul's play on
words accentuates the way God's people pursue kindness
to strangers with as much effort as enemies expend to hurt
us. Furthermore, it makes great sense to return in verse 15
to the emotions of others, because a very important means
for preventing persons from becoming enemies is to share
in their emotions. If someone wants to hurt us and we react
by caring about that individual's pain, we join *with* the person instead of treating him or her as an enemy.

What an immense tragedy it is in our churches that
jealousy and envy cause Christian brothers and sisters to
become enemies! How greatly we could prevent that if we
learned instead to be rejoicing in each other's blessings!

Other lessons of Romans 12:15 unfold for us if medi-
tating on this verse brings Jesus' words to mind. In the
Beatitudes he promises, "Blessed are those who mourn, for
they shall be comforted" (Matt. 5:4). Two principles in his
words — their setting and their promise — bring new insights for understanding Paul's exhortation more clearly.

First of all, the location of that beatitude within the
other beatitudes that Jesus pronounces reminds us that
mourning is one of the attributes of a life fixed on God's
purposes. The life-style also includes hungering and thirsting after righteousness, being meek, suffering persecution,
and so forth. All these character traits were modeled for us
by Jesus himself, who mourned openly in many situations.
He grieved over the misunderstanding of the Jews at
Lazarus' tomb; he wept over Jerusalem; he was constantly

239

moved with deep compassion for suffering persons. His announcement that those who mourn are blessed invites us into his heart, to share his grief over the pain of a sick world.

Many of our Christian communities seem severely to lack this blessedness. Are our hearts broken by the things that break the heart of God? This doesn't mean that we should go around moping all the time about everything. But we do need to be shaken out of our complacency, to grow in our care for the hurting.

Once on an evangelistic mission to canvass for a congregation in Canada, I wound up spending most of my time with a Native American couple who were both pitifully drunk. The lady kept saying, "I don't want to be like this." When I naively insisted that she could change things, she'd respond, "No, it's too late. I'll be sick tomorrow because I've already drunk too much."

After leaving their apartment, I couldn't stop crying for a long time. I had just experienced more personally than ever before in my sheltered life the woes of persons trapped in life-styles they don't really want. When Laurie's pain made me so sad, I caught just a glimpse of how much our tender Father must suffer as he watches his creatures violating his perfect designs and destroying themselves. Great changes came in that mourning — a deepened commitment, a greater love for others, a larger thankfulness for God's presence in my life, a heightened level of energy for serving God. To share the Father's grieving heart even in the small ways that we are capable of helps us to experience more clearly the genuine Hilarity of his infinite love for us and for the world.

Second, Jesus explicitly promises this blessing for those who mourn: "they shall be comforted." This is not an empty promise, though sometimes we seem to be too deep in blackness ever to see light again. Yet God has an infinite number of ways to comfort us. His promise is steadfast; it has never yet been broken, and it is sure to be fulfilled no matter what the cause of our mourning.

We cannot see God's light alone. We need the Christian community to incarnate it for us. Similarly, our Joys are too great to hold within ourselves. The old saying that shared griefs are halved and shared Joys are doubled certainly is true within the Hilarity of the Christian community.

Our Christian communities especially need to spend adequate time contemplating questions such as those listed below so that we can get in touch with the ways in which God's comfort has come and does come to us. Then we will be encouraged to reach out to others with means for comfort, to share in their Joys without jealousy, and to give them the gift of our healing presence in their grief and gladness.

Therefore:

1. What aspects of our personal and corporate lives cause us to rejoice?

2. What dimensions of our lives are cause for mourning?

3. Who needs us to be with them in rejoicing or mourning at this time?

4. How have we failed to be with someone in rejoicing or mourning in the past, and what can we learn from those mistakes?

5. Why is it necessary to share on both the static and the dynamic levels in our Christian communities?

6. In what ways does God comfort us in our mourning? How does the Hilarity of God's love in our pain enable us to bring such comfort to others?

7. In what ways has the true Hilarity of rejoicing with others deepened our relationships with them and prevented envy or jealousy?

26. Living in Harmony

Live in harmony with one another; do not be haughty, but associate with the lowly [or, give yourselves to humble tasks]; never be conceited.

— ROMANS 12:16, RSV

WHEN WE WERE KIDS, my brother and I often sang together while we did the dishes. I'd make up a melody, and Glen would either harmonize or imitate me in a fugue. Because his gifts are so extraordinary, I thoroughly enjoyed our times of song — except when Glen would choose to be obnoxious.

Sometimes just for fun he would purposely sing every note about a half step sharp. I'd beg him to stop that painful grating on my ears, but he would just sing with more dissonance. We'd wind up howling with laughter — unless I was so aggravated that I couldn't forgive him. (To this day, Glen's humor necessitates an occasional off-key song just to keep us all on edge.)

My brother's harmonization illustrates several aspects of Paul's exhortation in Romans 12:16 about our attitudes toward one another. First, we must remember that the Hilarity of true harmony doesn't just happen; community must be intended. To work together as God's people requires a common commitment.

For music to be pleasing to the ear, our care for our individual pitches influences our intonation together. Similarly, everyone in the community suffers if anyone becomes sloppy about his or her participation. (Sometimes one wonders if individuals intentionally choose to bring disharmony to the Church!)

This takes us back to the body imagery of Romans 12:4-5; we are indeed all members of one another. In similar language, Ephesians stresses that when the various parts of the body are fitted together properly "by that which every joint supplies," and when each part is functioning correctly, then the whole body grows and builds itself up in love (Eph. 4:15-16).

The original Greek verbs in Romans 12:16 are participles, so the first phrase invites us into the continuing action of "minding the same thing" with each other. Furthermore, Paul chooses a verb that accentuates careful planning and purposes resulting from deliberate pondering. (In Chapter 8 we encountered the same verb in four different forms in Rom. 12:3.) That points to the strong intentionality of working toward the same goals in the Christian community. We won't necessarily think alike on every matter, but our basic orientation in purpose is the same — to be God's people, followers of Jesus Christ, having his mind (as Paul stresses with the same verb in Phil. 2:5).

The members of the board of Christians Equipped for Ministry have learned the necessity of careful pondering together throughout its twelve-year history because the policy of the CEM Board since its inception has been to make all decisions by total consensus. Sometimes we have to wrestle a long while before we come to the same perspective. Occasionally we have needed several meetings in a row with prayer time in between in order to discover what God would have us do about a particular matter. Sometimes our patience with each other wears thin when we want to arrive at unity of mind faster, but that only drives us more deeply into prayer. Much effort is needed to be minding the same thing, but when consensus is made a top priority in the Christian community we will indubitably increase our Hilarity because we will experience the resultant gladness in finding unanimity rather than mere majority in our decisions.

However, good intentions are not enough. Glen is good at harmonizing because of a great musical gift. Once again (as so frequently in our study of Romans 12) we are pulled back into dependence upon God's grace-gifting for our harmony. The truest unity is that which he creates. Remember these words from Jesus' high-priestly prayer for us just before his death:

> I pray not only for these [disciples],
>> but for those also
>> who through their words will believe in me.
> May they all be one.
> Father, may they be one in us,
>> as you are in me and I am in you,
>> so that the whole world may believe it was you
>>> who sent me.
> I have given them the glory you gave to me,
>> that they may be one as we are one.
> With me in them and you in me,
>> may they be so completely one
>> that the world will realize that it was you
>>> who sent me,
>> and that I have loved them as much
>>> as you loved me.
>
> (John 17:20-23, JB)

The Jerusalem Bible's printing of this prayer in poetic form is especially helpful for us to notice the structure. We can understand then that the repetition of various phrases is not empty wordiness but a deliberate piling up of significant ideas to build to this climax: the effect of the unity of the Christian Church on the world. What a tragedy that we do not display such unity — and thus that the world does not know the message we were given!

God intends such unity — and creates it by his grace. We obstruct his plan when we do not enter into the community he has designed, when we fail to celebrate each other's gifts and to live as persons who belong to each other.

Thus, to be like-minded requires intentionality, but it is first of all based on the gifts of God's love. That again demonstrates the paradoxical combination in the Christian life of activity and passivity. We depend on God's love for everything, but he calls us to radical discipleship in the total involvement of living out the reality of our faith.

That leads to another dimension of like-mindedness that my brother's harmonizing illustrates well. Besides being very gifted musically, he was so good at adapting to my melodies because we sang together often — while we did the dishes, when we traveled on the train home from college, or in Dad's choir. Similarly, the unity of the community of faith requires practice.

That practice might involve some confrontation, but that, too, is an important lesson about the unity of the Church that we must learn. Too often we think that unity is achieved by backing down on certain things in order to keep the peace. If peace in a congregation is achieved by some people giving up their principles or being overly nice so that everyone can agree, then the community might as well not exist. It will have lost the Hilarity of truth.

Healthy unity is achieved by wrestling together until we come to agreement. God's Spirit is at work in us to make us into the community of Christ, but the sandpaper of our relationships grinds down the rough spots. As the CEM

Board deliberates over decisions, for example, each person's input leads to clearer understanding and greater unity. We refocus our priorities, remember our purposes, choose our goals afresh, and discover new Hilarity together.

The next phrase in Romans 12:16 — literally, "not the high things minding" — almost identically repeats the phrase in 11:20 in which Paul commands the Gentiles not to be proud that they are saved, but to be afraid, for the fact that the Jews became broken off from God's plan reminds us that we, too, would not be spared except by God's grace. The use of the same phrase here causes us to connect chapter 12's discourse about the meaning of community more closely with chapter 11's emphasis on God's special love for the Jews. Both sections remind us that unity is broken when any group considers itself better than others in the community. Hilarity is destroyed by arrogance.

In Paul's time the haughtiness in the house churches in Rome must have concerned the relations between Jews and Gentiles. In the twentieth century we might apply his rebuke to relations between denominations or to factions in congregational arguments — those for or against an organ or building expansion project, the social action advocates versus the evangelizers, the doctrinal liberals against the conservatives. The divisions are very real and must be worked at carefully; haughtiness only exacerbates the tensions.

Each of us must face up to ways in which sneaky pride pushes in its ugly head. Remembering the emphasis of this whole chapter of Romans, we recall that all our abilities are grace-gifts in the first place so they cannot be a source of pride to us. On the other hand, we don't want to be so afraid of pride that we cannot receive the affirmation of others and understand our worth as members of the Body. (In Chapter 8 we discussed the necessity of having a balanced, sane assessment of our own worth.) The Hilarity of our community is hindered by condescension or self-debasement in our relationships. God has gifted us and uses us for his purposes, and we need not be afraid or ashamed of that.

In the next phrase in verse 16, Paul gives the other side of the "high things." Literally the text reads, "but associating with the lowly." Two possible interpretations for the phrase depend upon whether "lowly" signifies tasks or persons. Paul might be urging us to share in doing what is humble or to be involved with humble people.

Communities cannot function unless some are willing to do the lowly jobs. Other exhortations in Romans 12 have pointed out the necessity of recognizing and using gifts of service (v. 7), of "slaving in the Lord" (v. 11). This third phrase of verse 16 might complement those earlier emphases, then, by urging us to discover the glad Hilarity and elegant spirit of engaging in menial tasks. We are reminded of the hymn in Philippians 2:5-11, which describes Christ emptying himself to take the form of a servant and humbling himself all the way to death, even the most despicable of deaths.

This does not suggest a fawning subservience that makes Christians into doormats. To think in lowly terms or to have true humility of mind requires courage and wisdom and strength of character — as those qualities are demonstrated in the attitudes of Christ. His was never the humility of wishy-washiness; rather, he chose to lay down his life for others. The complete control that is so often stressed in the Gospel of John (see, for example, 10:17-18) underscores his total willingness to sacrifice himself for our sake. Undoubtedly we need this humble mind of Christ in our contemporary communities.

To choose to associate with humble things might also imply a rejection of the materialism in our world gone crazy over luxury and self-indulgence. To accommodate ourselves to humble ways flies in the face of the upward mobility of our culture, and it certainly sets the Christian community apart as an alternative society following the downward pattern demonstrated by Christ.

Paul's motivation might compel us to live in less pretentious houses or perhaps in Christian communities, to forego luxuries that others find necessary, to spend our money more for others than for ourselves, to choose to eat and dress more simply, and so forth. My husband and I wrestle constantly to reconcile living simply with having what we need to serve well. We must constantly search for a godly balance to share freely with others and yet enjoy the gifts of God's creation without being too luxurious. The balance for all of us requires sensitivity to God's unique guidance in our lives. The input of other members of the Christian community will help us find a godly perspective on what we *need* to possess to fulfill our calling and use our gifts.

The second possible interpretation of Paul's exhortation — to associate with humble people — has led to some profound experiences of growth in my faith. During college I spent one complacency-shattering weekend in the inner city of Chicago. We stayed in broken-windowed rooms crammed with bunk beds and infested with bugs and rats. I could not sleep. The situation heightened my awareness of our broken-windowed world. Moreover, the rich experience of being with — and being loved by — the people who lived there all the time taught me a lot of things about myself that I didn't like.

Several persons who were broken and poor stayed at our EPHESUS Community when we were offering a crisis ministry. One of the guests rightly blasted me one day for my insensitivity to the feelings of those coming out of a different life-style from my own. Too easily those of us with well-paying jobs and emotional security are judgmental of those fighting to find themselves and to preserve their dignity when they are reduced to the point of begging.

We can't associate with "humble folk" without first purging from ourselves any sort of sense of superiority. The fact that others have external needs is, to a great extent, our fault. What are we doing to change a society that is so unjust, in which true equality of opportunity does not exist?

The early Church was characterized by a radical mixing of social levels, a great contrast to the class distinctions of Roman society. The contemporary Church, on the other hand, suffers in most local communities from a severe stratification. Our parishes don't often easily mix blue-collar workers and academicians or professionals — to the great loss of all of us. The church-growth emphasis on homogeneity seems to me to contradict the inclusiveness of the gospel and its invitation to demonstrate to the world the unity of all kinds of persons in the Christian community.

We all — rich or poor, laborers with muscle or mind, athletically fit or physically challenged — have wonderful things to teach each other. Paul's exhortation to associate with the humble people invites us all to care about each other without pretensions, to become more involved with all those who can help us become more like Christ. We would all benefit if our communities were more directly associated with rescue missions, shelters for the homeless, ministries to the lowly and the outcasts of our society.

Inappropriately, some Christian groups interpret the phrases "Do not be haughty in mind, but associate with the lowly" to be a criticism of high culture or the arts. Several of my friends who are concert musicians or artists have been criticized for not being more overtly "Christian" in their work. Such a misinterpretation should be vigorously resisted in our communities, for such things as classical music and paintings and ballet can be great sources of inspiration and enlightenment, of refreshment and relaxation for us. The enjoyment of cultural gifts can certainly become elitist, but it would be wonderful if the Church could instead be at the forefront in supporting the arts so that they can become more accessible to all levels of society. Certainly, the arts foster greater sensitivity (in contrast to the pervasive violence of our world) and are a means for us to grow in Hilarity as we appreciate more thoroughly the wonder and beauty of God's gifts of creativity.

The final phrase in verse 16 says literally, "Do not be wise according to yourselves." That phrase, too, gives two significant directions for our consideration and obedience.

First, the phrase warns us against any sort of conceit. If we are struggling against ungodly ambition, to be associated with the lowly minded will enable us to recognize the limitations of our abilities. Our crisis house guest's criticism of a superior attitude on my part forced me to realize how rarely I should trust my own abilities and how little I understood the situations of persons trying to escape drugs and alcohol, poverty and despair.

We must constantly be on our guard against becoming opinionated, hard-hearted, or stiff-necked (three terms that Martin Luther uses in his comments upon this verse).[1] As John Murray notes, the opinionated person "is intractable and impervious to any advice but his own."[2] We want instead that our character would be open for God to change us through the wisdom of others. This phrase really indicts the Church for dogmatism in our teaching and for opinionated mind-sets that fracture the community and its Hilarity.

Second, besides admonishing us for our self-elevation, this final phrase of verse 16 also invites us to recognize that wisdom cannot come to us individually but must instead develop in community. Though none of our English transla-

1. Luther, *Lectures on Romans,* trans. and ed. Wilhelm Pauck (Philadelphia: Westminster Press, 1961), p. 353.

2. Murray, *The Epistle to the Romans,* 2 vols., The New International Commentary on the New Testament (Grand Rapids: William B. Eerdmans, 1965), 2:137.

tions renders the verse in this way, such an interpretation is in keeping with the cotext of the Greek phrase and the emphasis on community in the whole discourse. As we have seen, throughout Romans 12 Paul has been urging the people of God to be growing together as a community, rather than as a bunch of individuals or house churches operating independently, not cognizant of the unity of Jews and Gentiles. All of us are invited to gather our gifts together for the benefit of one another. Thus, this final phrase in verse 16 culminates that emphasis on community before Paul moves on in verse 17 to ideas of vengeance and overcoming evil with good. His concluding remark on the subject is this exhortation to find our wisdom in community rather than for ourselves.

In CEM we have learned the wisdom of the group. When I don't know how to proceed with different dimensions of the ministry, I can throw my ideas out to the board and trust that they will pray about those matters. Discussing them together, we will, with the Spirit's direction, find the best ways to proceed.

Often in the Church we copy the "rugged individualism" of our culture and think that plans can be made faster and more effectively if certain people just do things alone. Nevertheless, to act this way is to forget that God has given gifts to each member of the community and that, when all those gifts are working together in harmony, a much richer manifestation of God's love can be experienced and demonstrated to the world. The attaining of wisdom cannot be a solo effort. Always the insights of another will modify our own and draw us both more closely to the center of truth.

Another warning inherent in this phrase, then, is an admonition against ambition for personal aggrandizement. Solo efforts are terribly destructive to our functioning together as a community. Gifts are given to each person for stewardship to build up the Hilarity of the whole Church (1 Pet. 4:10).

Once again two sides in tension force us to look for a biblical balance. Godly ambition has stirred those who attempt great things for God, and the result has been powerful ministry. On the other hand, too easily we who think we are serving God might really be attempting great things for ourselves.

The Christian community is a society in which we can be asking each other critical questions all the time. Are we engaging in certain activities as genuine service or for the sake of our personal reputations? How easily our motives can become impure. We constantly need the admonition and encouragement of other believers to push us back to a balance, to fight the temptation to mix up our work and God's grace-gifts, to find again the Hilarity of using our gifts with freedom and godly ambition within the unity of the whole community.

Therefore:

1. How much do the members of our community intend to be minding the same things? What are the major issues that divide us? How do our divisions destroy our Hilarity?

2. How could we become more intentional about our life together as a community, our ministry to each other, and our outreach to the world?

3. How have we found and not found balance in our life concerning our willingness to do the menial tasks and to be associated with people of lowly position? Are we involved in ministries that cross the lines of social classes? Does our congregation include all kinds of people?

4. In what ways do conceit and pride obstruct our ministry?

5. How godly are our ambitions — personally and corporately?

6. Is our humility balanced? Are we able to avoid servileness

but still be lowly, according to the pattern of the mind of Christ? How does true humility deepen our Hilarity? How does Hilarity set us free for humility?

7. How have we experienced the greater wisdom that can be developed only within the community? What procedures could we use in our Christian community so that the group as a whole listens more carefully to the way in which the Holy Spirit uses each member of the community to reveal God's will?

27. *Not Evil, but the Good*

To no one repaying evil for evil; giving attention to
doing what is good before all persons.

— ROMANS 12:17

FIVE CHRISTIAN MISSIONARIES were murdered by the
Auca Indians. Their wives and children continued trying
to serve them and to establish relationships with them. The
Indians were impressed and wanted to know more about
the message these strange people had come to proclaim.

Before *glasnost,* oftentimes Communists persecuted
Christians. Nevertheless, when party members were ill or
dying, not their comrades but Christians were often the ones
to care for them. Even official government reports from Si-
beria carried stories of the concern Christians had shown.
Many asked why.

Increasingly, priests and other religious leaders and
volunteers are becoming more willing to get involved in the
lives of the poor of the Third World. Many of these dedicated
believers have lost their lives in the Central American countries they serve. The world cannot help but notice.

Similar stories can be found all around the world and

throughout the ages of history. One of the most impressive ways in which Christians command a hearing for their message is when they manifest their Hilarity by repaying with good those who have inflicted evil upon them. Romans 12:17 introduces to us a powerful means for demonstrating the love of God in our times.

As we have seen elsewhere in this book, every phrase of Paul's writing is significant. In verse 17 it is especially the case; one little preposition speaks volumes against what would be our natural human reaction for responding to evil. The order of the words in the sentence is also significantly emphatic in this verse.

Literally, the first phrase says, "To no one evil against evil recompensing." Paul uses the same verb in Romans 2:6 to remind us that God will justly recompense each person for what he or she has done. Because God will requite, we won't (a point to be stressed in v. 19, as we shall see in Chapter 29). Furthermore, Paul's placement of "to no one" at the beginning of the phrase underscores his point that in our relations *with no one* should we ever resort to repaying evil for evil.

Our human nature immediately stiffens against such an injunction. Sometimes we protest, "But she deserves to be treated terribly; look what she did to me!" or "See how he's messing up everything; don't you recognize how rotten a person he is?" Now, of course, some people *are* rotten and deserve to be treated with evil. Indeed, that *some* includes you and me. Whoops.

Paul's instruction is all-inclusive, as if to say, "to absolutely no one without exception should you be giving back whatever evil that person gives you." The pronoun, placed at the beginning of the phrase for emphasis, gives us no leeway.

The preposition in this first phrase is the stickler. It commands us to recompense to no one evil *in exchange for* evil. We would have preferred it if Paul had written, "Be careful that your just retribution does not escalate." To be totally forbidden even an equal response is much harder to take.

Jewish laws were unusually just for the historical period in which the Israelite nation developed to its peak. The Hebrew Scriptures demand this equality of response: "But if there is serious injury, you are to take life for life, eye for eye, tooth for tooth, hand for hand, foot for foot, burn for burn, wound for wound, bruise for bruise" (Exod. 21:23-25, NIV). That law prevented the terrible avenging which characterized Semitic societies. God was requiring that punishment of offenders could only be equal to the crime. His command was eminently fair (and helpfully difficult to put into practice).

But then Jesus came along and took God's work of creating a people of peace one step further. Remember that he said this:

"You have heard that it was said, 'Eye for eye, and tooth for tooth.' But I tell you, Do not resist an evil person. If someone strikes you on the right cheek, turn to him the other also. And if someone wants to sue you and take your tunic, let him have your cloak as well. If someone forces you to go one mile, go with him two miles. Give to the one who asks you, and do not turn away from the one who wants to borrow from you.

"You have heard that it was said, 'Love your neighbor and hate your enemy.' But I tell you: Love your enemies and pray for those who persecute you, that you may be sons of your Father in heaven. He causes his sun to rise on the evil and the good, and sends rain on the righteous and the unrighteous.

"For if you love only those who love you, what credit is that to you? Even tax-collectors do that! And if you exchange greetings only with your own circle, are you doing anything exceptional? Even the pagans do that much. No, you will be perfect as your Heavenly Father is perfect." (Matt. 5:38-45, NIV, and 46-48, JBP)

Not profoundly enough do we recognize how radical Jesus was. In that set of instructions to his disciples he completely overthrew all sense of human justice in favor of loving care. Not only are we not to allow aggravation to escalate, but we are to choose a positive response instead, serving the needs of our oppressor. Rather than equivalence in the Christian life, we are to be characterized by love and a gracious response to whatever pain others inflict.

The form of the final Greek verb in Matthew 5 is a simple future. Rather than holding a club over our heads by translating this passage as the command "you must be perfect" (TEV and RSV), J. B. Phillips more fittingly translates it as "you will be perfect." Even as our heavenly Father is always characterized by the perfect love exemplified in his gift of sun and rain to everyone, so we are invited to become non-violent, non-retributive, willing to bear the cost by our own suffering.

If we recompense to no one even evil to match the evil we've received, then the question of what a person deserves does not at all enter the picture any longer. In the same terse style that has marked this whole chapter in Romans, Paul here uses only a simple continuing participial form of the verb. Together with the opening negative pronoun, the verb emphatically reminds us that to no one in any circumstance are we to be characterized by giving back evil to match that person's evil.

Following that enormously strong prohibition, Paul tells us what should characterize us instead. The second participial phrase of our text says literally, "taking care to do right things before all persons."

The verb emphasizes thinking prior to something so that one can respond appropriately. In contrast to his use of the same verb in Romans 13:14, where Paul warns his readers to "stop planning ahead so as to satisfy the desires of your sinful nature," in 12:17 he encourages us to consider with the utmost care beforehand how our behavior will affect those who observe us.

When we stop to consider the results of our repaying evil for evil, especially in light of the words of Jesus, we will realize the destructiveness of such an action. Everything will hinge, necessarily, on how we choose to respond and the character that we want to manifest.

Paul chooses the word *kalos* for the style of life we want to exhibit before all other persons, and that word's rhyming with *kakos*, the word for evil used in the beginning phrase of this verse, highlights their contrast in Greek. *Kalos* in the Scriptures carries a whole range of meanings, and Paul probably uses it here quite comprehensively. Fundamentally it means beauty or quality, in the sense of accordance with the purpose of something. From this basic meaning of good and useful, it stresses appropriateness with such concepts as moral goodness and noble praiseworthiness.

Various translations of verse 17 demonstrate this diversity. The RSV urges us to "take thought for what is noble in the sight of all," while the JB invites us to "let everyone see that you are interested only in the highest ideals." J. B. Phillips' paraphrase urges us to "See that your public behaviour is above criticism."

Such injunctions are again too large for us; trapped in our sinful human nature we find the challenge impossible. We know we don't always act nobly; we can't always live above criticism. Consequently, this verse drives us once again to the forgiveness and empowerment of God's love. Only the Hilarity of knowing that God works through us gives us the courage to choose the character of Jesus for our life-style, to plan beforehand morally upright behavior.

The hard part is responding nobly in all circumstances, before all persons. Throughout Romans 12 Paul has been teaching us how to live with one another in the Christian community — how to be supportive of each other's gifts and to belong to one another. Now he widens our relationships and urges us to live with all persons as we live among Christians. That is especially difficult when we know that some people beyond our fellowship denigrate our choice of the life-style of Jesus, of nonpower and active reconciliation.

Several years ago some newspaper reporters didn't like Billy Graham's style of ministry, so they set out to find ways to knock down his credibility. They observed him closely and interviewed him and many of his colleagues, they scrutinized his records, and finally they came to this lovely conclusion: he was so godly that they had changed their minds about him! They had discovered that he consistently models the virtuous life that Romans 12:17b advocates.

The responsibility for living so nobly in public is made much easier by the realization that if we live together in the Christian community as the rest of Romans 12 has exhorted, then the Spirit-empowered outpouring of such caring into the wider sphere of the world will surely be honorable. The attitudes and actions of love, service, and humility that we have already discussed will be seen by the wider world as good, praiseworthy, and morally upright.

In other words, we won't put on another kind of behavior when we go before the world. In fact, to do so would be destructive in its phoniness.

We will not treat unbelievers in any way different from the way we treat our close Christian friends in the community. Usually the former will respond to such treatment with delightful surprise. Persons who don't know God as we do usually are pleased to be wrapped in the Hilarity of his love and grace.

Only by demonstrating God's character in tangible ways do we gain credibility for our message about his love. Rebecca Manley Pippert's wonderful book *Out of the Salt-*

shaker and Into the World advocates such a life-style of evangelism.[1] We won't have to worry about witnessing consciously, although plenty of opportunities will arise for us to speak directly about our faith. Rather, when we demonstrate to the world the Hilarity of the community in the life-style of the gospel, when we manifest God's love publicly under the Lordship of Christ, others will ask us to account for our hope (1 Pet. 3:15-16).

Sharing our faith happens not only because of what we won't do — that is, to recompense evil for evil — but also because of what we will choose to do instead — to aim for the highest ideals in manifesting the meaning of the gospel. God is mightily at work through our lives; what he wants is to fill us with Hilarity to share as we actively pursue his purposes.

Therefore:

1. To whom might we owe an apology because we have recompensed to them evil for evil?

2. How can we find the courage not to want to get even when we are hurt by others? How does the Hilarity of the community help us?

3. In what ways can we take better care to aim for the highest ideals before all persons?

4. How can we prevent such "taking care" from being a command over us that we resist, rather than a freely chosen discipline?

5. Are there ways in which our public behavior is different from our behavior within the Christian community? How can we prevent such phoniness before others?

1. Rebecca Manley Pippert, *Out of the Saltshaker and Into the World: Evangelism as a Way of Life* (Downers Grove, IL: InterVarsity Press, 1979).

6. How have we had opportunities to tell others about God's love because of our life-style, because of the freedom and Hilarity that grace gives to us?

7. What persons model for us consistent praiseworthy behavior — both in the Christian community and in the world?

28. Striving for Peace

If it is possible, as far as it depends on you, live at peace
with everyone.

— ROMANS 12:18, NIV

I TRIED AS MUCH as I could, but the person with whom I
worked just did not like my style. Not wanting to become
bitter and resentful, I confessed to him my bad feelings about
the situation. I asked for forgiveness, but he dismissed my
request with a wave of the hand. Reconciliation was impossible.

Romans 12:18 speaks directly to such situations. Paul
begins realistically: "If it is possible." Those words set us
free from self-incrimination because they enable us to accept
the fact that sometimes we cannot be reconciled with everyone. The phrase is especially deeply comforting to persons
who have been rejected or deserted, to those who are saying,
"But I didn't want a divorce." Sometimes things just cannot
be restored. Then what?

We bear no guilt if we have done the best that we can
to restore broken relationships. If another party is not willing

to relate, then we need the courage to move on in life without carrying around vestiges of that pain.

Paul knew indeed what he was saying. His relationship with Barnabas, his missionary companion, had been disrupted by the issue of John Mark's accompaniment (see Acts 15:36-41). Undoubtedly that was extraordinarily grievous to him after all they'd been through together and after all Barnabas had done for him. Paul knew that painful disruption is a fact of life in a human world.

The challenge to try again, however, predominates in Paul's exhortation. The second phrase, "as far as it depends upon you," emphasizes that efforts to restore relationships should be continued, continued some more, and still continued even more until we are thoroughly convinced that reconciliation is not achievable. Then, if we finally have to give up, the phrase "If it is possible" acknowledges the reality of human barriers that we cannot break.

A key principle in communication skills is deciding whose problem a situation is. We need to discern, whatever the circumstances, for what we are accountable. To make a clear distinction frees us from false guilt and helps us know when to take responsibility to do more to try to remedy a situation.

As followers of Jesus, furthermore, we are enabled to go beyond what is humanly reasonable in attempting to create peace. As Paul writes to the Corinthians, "The very spring of our actions is the love of Christ" (2 Cor. 5:14a, JBP). Our human motivations don't create sufficient potential for peace, but we are not operating under those principles any longer. Our faith gives us trampoline springs under all of our actions. Our ability to seek peace and pursue it has all the resources of God's love and grace at its disposal.

Furthermore, we remember that Jesus said, "If someone wants to sue you and take your tunic, let him have your cloak as well. If someone forces you to go one mile, go with him two miles" (Matt. 5:40-41, NIV). These words carry us beyond mere interpersonal relations and into the political realm. The Jews in Jesus' day were required to carry the packs of the Roman soldiers for one mile upon demand; Christ was encouraging the oppressed Jews to be willing to carry the soldiers' packs twice as far as required. Jesus invites us to surprise our enemies by responding with more than they demand.

Similarly, in Romans 12:17 Paul began widening his instructions to the Christian community to include "all persons," and here that widening out into the world is repeated. Paul encourages us to be cultivating peace with everyone. His use again of a present continuing participle stresses the unceasing action, the unwavering vigilance that is necessary for peacebuilding. We want the description *peacemaking* to characterize the people of God. We want the world to notice that our Hilarity causes members of the community to try constantly, as much as possible within the framework of our responsibilities, to create, keep, and live the peace which God himself bestows.

How can God's people cultivate peace in a world of gross injustice, a world in which there is civil unrest in many nations and religious wars that have raged for many years? The task is just too great! The issues of violence and poverty are so huge that most persons feel helpless to do anything about them. Yet somehow we must encourage individuals and Christian communities to believe that they can be effective peacemakers. The Hilarity of God's peace within us enables us.

A Lutheran theologian writing in East Germany before the fall of the Berlin Wall provides a wonderful tool for helping people make peace. In his contribution to an excellent collection of essays, Gerhard Liedke writes about "The Christian Understanding of Peace."[1] He emphasizes that

---

1. Gerhard Liedke, "Das Christliche Verständnis von Frieden," in *Christen im Streit um den Frieden: Beiträge zu einer neuen Friedensethik* [Chris-

peace is a *process* and a way rather than a position or a state of being. Because peace is often understood *negatively* as the absence of war or of large-scale violence, during the Cold War East-West deterrence was considered effective in maintaining peace. The difficulty of proving that claim shows the weakness of this negative definition of peace.

On the other hand, a *positive* definition of peace as the rule of social justice seems much too demanding or utopian to most people. That is why Liedke insists that peace for the world must be grounded in the peace of God. The Old Testament legacy of *Shalom* provides a foundation for the apostle Paul's declaration to the Romans that the kingdom of God stands in justice, peace, and Joy in the Holy Spirit. Thus, when we pray "Thy kingdom come," we must see the kingdom of God as the final goal in the process of peace-building.

To build peace, Liedke says we must minimize violence, need, bondage, and anxiety. Jesus conquered these powers in his life, death, and resurrection, and God will ultimately bring about their complete elimination. Meanwhile, we are God's agents ("thy will be done" in and through our lives) in the work of minimizing these four dimensions.

Liedke emphasizes that such minimizing can be concretely undertaken at all levels — in the world, in religion, in society, in large or small groups, and with individuals. Modifying his list slightly, we can construct a chart to show people how they can contribute significantly to the process of peace.

---

tians in the debate about peace: Contributions toward a new peace ethic], ed. Wolfgang Brinkel, Burkhardt Scheffler, and Martin Wächter (Freiburg: Dreisam-Verlag, 1982), pp. 29-35. To my knowledge, this superb piece has not yet been translated into English; the next several paragraphs are a condensed report of Liedke's urgently needed ideas.

	Violence	Minimization of Need	Bondage	Anxiety
with individuals				
in small groups				
in large groups				
in the local church				
in the local community				
in the state				
in the nation				
in the global Church				
in the world				

This chart shows clearly why deterrence is ineffective as a peacebuilding tool. Although it might minimize violence on the national or world level, it increases need and anxiety on several levels. The world spends as much on military equipment in one day as it would take to feed, clothe, and house the entire world for a year! The overall process of peace must minimize all four dimensions (violence, need, bondage, and anxiety) on all levels. Consequently, in order to contribute to world peace an effort at any level must not shift the burden by increasing another dimension.

Furthermore, so long as we don't merely shift the burden, we can make progress toward peace by making a net reduction in any dimension at any level. How hopeful and empowering it is to see that each of us, as members of the Christian community, can contribute to peace in significant ways!

Liedke outlines a strategy for peacebuilding by stressing that we must not merely displace conflict, but must instead work to minimize violence on all the levels. We must reduce war between and within nations and also reduce brutality in families and communities. Furthermore, our world cannot minimize need anymore by intensifying growth, but must choose instead a more just distribution of available goods. We can reduce bondage through democratizing and encouraging participation at all levels.

Particularly, Liedke suggests that our special Christian strategy will include suffering, renunciation, representation, and unconditional acceptance of others. Finally, he concludes that this is not an unreasonable demand, since Jesus has gone beyond the world's strategies ("you have heard it said") by adding, "but I say to you, love your enemies."

The chart above suggests all kinds of possibilities and inspires great motivation and hope. The Christian community can be a significant force in building peace in the world! Because of our Hilarity in knowing God's grace and peace, EVERY CHRISTIAN can reduce violence, need, bondage, and anxiety.

To respond to a hateful remark with a gentle answer minimizes *violence* between individuals. A person can be an agent of small group reconciliation on the job or in congregational arguments. Some people will become mediators to decrease violence on a worldwide scale, but such large contributions ought not to eclipse the fact that every individual effort to minimize any sort of violence on any level contributes to the calming of the world as a whole.

An example of this can be seen in the small groups at work in Israel to bring together Jews and Palestinians in the search for a peaceful solution to the problem of their common need for a homeland. That points to another dimension that must be minimized at all levels, for the issue of *violence* in Israel is inextricably connected to the fact that each side in the struggle has a legitimate *need* for a home.

Our Christian communities significantly minimize *need* when we work in soup kitchens, bring groceries to food banks, shelter the homeless or help to build them a home, contribute to agencies that bring medical aid to the poor, vote for legislation to combat poverty, question the use of government funds for disproportionate military spending, or "live more simply so that others may simply live." The World Vision poster mentioned in Chapter 23 proclaims the effectiveness of every person's contribution when it stresses that the way to feed all the hungry in the world continues to be "one at a time."

The people of God can participate in minimizing *bondage*, for that evil takes many forms in our world. Not only do we want to free the political prisoners of various totalitarian states, but we also want to deliver our friends and neighbors and enemies from the bondages of fear or loneliness, the slavery of ideological delusions, the prisons of despair and meaninglessness.

Similarly, the followers of Jesus can deliver others from a multitude of *anxieties* on various levels of society. Simple notes to those under stress to remind them of our concern, a kind word to someone in a difficult leadership position, the fervent prayers of the Church on behalf of world rulers — these are just a few ways in which Christians can serve to minimize anxiety and thereby build peace. Madeleine L'Engle tells a wonderful story in *A Stone for a Pillow* about Jerome Hines' ministry to Khrushchev (and consequent minimizing of world anxieties) through his unusual operatic performance of *Boris Gudonov*'s triumph in tragedy, his prayers for the Soviet leader, and his words to him — "God bless you, sir" — just before the Cuban missile crisis.[2]

The Christian community can seek, as far as possible, to cultivate peace in the world by pointing out to others the interrelations of violence, need, bondage, and anxiety.[3] We

2. Madeleine L'Engle, *A Stone for a Pillow* (Wheaton, IL: Harold Shaw, 1986).

3. The Hebrew prophets continually warned the Israelites about the connection between their economic injustice and their own bondage. (See, for example, Amos 5:11-24.) Throughout the Scriptures we see this inex-

cannot reconcile the massive stockpiling of military weap-
onry in the world with the fact that 40,000 persons are dying
every day of starvation and malnutrition and related illnesses.

The politics of Jesus might seem simplistic, but what
would happen if we really tried them? What would happen
in Third-World countries, for example, if instead of selling
militants more arms or putting embargoes on their trade we
worked to bring about economic justice? What would happen if we put food on their tables, taught them skills that
gave them dignity, and freed them from their fears by caring
about them without violence? If the Christian community
were providing for the needs of the poor, they might more
gladly receive our words about God's love as a credible
message of hope.

Each day we are each given many opportunities to
check the squares in the chart above, to contribute to reducing violence, need, bondage, and anxiety on various levels
of our world. Because we know that God himself always is
at work (ultimately successfully) to bring the world to
Shalom, to wholeness, we can have hope as we pursue our
own unique part of the whole — even when it seems that
our efforts are not effective.

The forms our actions will take will vary. We can write
to members of Congress to ask them to channel funds toward
education, help for the handicapped, and food for the hungry
instead of military escalation. Perhaps we can run for political
office ourselves and join those working for peace on the local
or national level. Some of us will march in protest against the
building and deployment of nuclear weapons. Others might
refuse to pay the taxes that contribute to military spending.

---

tricable connection between oppression of the poor and defeat by enemies.
Those who perpetrate injustice cannot survive; ultimately, God's justice
will prevail. When Israel failed to listen to her prophets, she was taken
into captivity.

All of us can be more generous in minimizing the needs and anxieties of the hungry and homeless.

Furthermore, because we know that every Christian in the community can find places on the chart to be involved in the process, we can each encourage others around us to become more active in the ministry of peacebuilding. We will experience heightened Hilarity as together we who are followers of Jesus cultivate peace with everyone.

Finally, because Christians around the world are contributing to reducing violence, need, bondage, and anxiety at many levels, we can continue to envision the significance and power of the whole. God is at work through each of us — and all of us together — to build peace! In the Hilarity of God's *Shalom*, the Christian community can expend every possible effort to bring wholeness to all persons in the world.

Therefore:

1. What are we doing to strive after peace and wholeness for our neighbors?

2. What are we doing to strive for peace in the world?

3. What is our congregation doing to bring wholeness to our community?

4. What is our church denomination doing to contribute to peace in the world?

5. What do we think Jesus would do if he were physically here today? How does the Hilarity in which his love enfolds us set us free to follow his example?

6. Do our values and our actions regarding peacebuilding correspond? Could we be living in ways that are more faithful to our ideals?

7. What connections have we observed between the oppression of the poor, bondage, anxiety, and violence in the Scriptures? in the modern world?

29. Giving Place to God's Wrath

Never take your own revenge, beloved, but leave room for the wrath of God, for it is written, "Vengeance is mine, I will repay," says the Lord.

— ROMANS 12:19, NASV

WHY ARE WE SO presumptuous that we dare to take matters into our own hands? Why do we human beings have such a need to vindicate ourselves?

Romans 12:19 stopped me cold for a long time. The text certainly leads (with its cotext of vv. 17-21) into the Romans 13 injunctions concerning Christians' relations with governing authorities; in these bridging verses the exhortations begin at relationships within the Christian community and then widen out to the world. However, the message of this text seemed so obvious, and my study and meditation didn't create any insights worth putting on paper.

Suddenly now I know why. I couldn't dig into the text because I wasn't submitting myself to it. I am too guilty of wanting to take revenge.

In a particular situation that hurt me deeply, I have wished that somehow the persons who betrayed me would

271

feel some sort of pain, too. I could rationalize very subtly and insist that I don't actually want to inflict any harm on them myself, but why do I want so much for the other persons to be repentant and to feel remorse? When I look at my motives under the glaring light of truth, I recognize a sinister desire for retribution that kills my Hilarity.

It is difficult to be so real in print. Will you still trust my theology if I confess the truth about my struggle to write this chapter? Yet we must admit those shadows and face up to the ugly self in each of us. It is critically important in the Christian community that we help each other struggle in stark confrontations with our dark sides. God's love enfolds us in forgiveness and frees us to be changed, so we can face the truth of his Word. This text profoundly indicts me, and now I must explore what God wants to teach me in it. My responsibility to you as fellow members of the Christian community and as partners in studying this text helps me be more ready to listen.

Paul continues his terse style and writes literally, "Not yourselves avenging." The compound Greek verb, used here as a participle according to the pattern of this whole section of Romans, means "to repay harm with harm, on the assumption that the initial harm was unjustified and that retribution is therefore called for." The first word of the phrase is *not*, and the ones we are not to be avenging are ourselves. That hits the nail right on the head of my problem. I have been thinking I was right to pursue justice, but Paul specifically tells us that the Christian life-style is not to be characterized by such attitudes and resultant actions. The present participle urges us continually to refrain from seeking the punishment of those who have hurt us.

Of course, Paul realizes the difficulty of resisting our human impulses to seek revenge. We are comforted by his insertion at this point of a term of affection for his readers — a matter of style which is infrequent in this letter. Not closely associated with the Roman church, as we noted earlier, Paul uses terms of deep relationship rarely in this letter. Yet here he suddenly addresses his readers as "beloved ones."

The term is the same one that Paul applies to his dear friends at Philippi in his deeply intimate letter to them from prison (Phil. 4:1). Moreover, he uses it frequently to describe how Christian believers are beloved of God (see, for example, Rom. 1:7) — and that belovedness is the source of our Hilarity!

Paul evidently intends this word of affection at this point as extra encouragement for the Roman Christians in the difficult task of giving up their rights to justice. Holy anger against injustice has its place, and the Scriptures — especially the Hebrew prophets — exhort us to work for the rights of others. However, in cases concerning ourselves we are urged not to seek retribution. That injunction is terribly hard to follow. I know; I'm struggling right now to give up my desire that those who hurt me would suffer as much as I have.

Paul's next phrase doubles the difficulty. Choosing the stronger of two Greek conjunctions for *but*, he tells us "greatly to the contrary" what should characterize us instead of avenging. Paul's point is accentuated by the fact that here he puts the verb in the imperative, a rare form in Romans 12. Previously almost all the phrases since verse 6 have used participles (or the two present infinitives of verse 15), strung together like beads on a chain, describing the various qualities that compose the life-style of the Christian community. The only exceptions were the similar imperatives in verse 14, which also gives commands involving goodness to enemies. Now, all of a sudden, Paul uses an aorist imperative, which signifies a decisive once-for-all action that we should undertake.

What we should do, he writes literally, is "give place in the wrath." J. B. Phillips' paraphrase underlines this

273

point: "Never take vengeance into your own hands, my dear friends; stand back and let God punish if he will."

We are to give place, once and for all. That means to give the outworking of wrath over to another, to give up with finality our desire to inflict punishment on one who has wronged us, and to NEVER GO BACK!

Then, to convince us further, Paul adds a quotation from Deuteronomy. He introduces that quotation with the standard formula "for it stands written." This formula carries great weight when it is used throughout the New Testament because the verb translated "having been written" is in the perfect tense and thereby stresses that at some decisive point in time the Scriptures were recorded and therefore continue to be in effect thereafter. Thus, the formula asserts that whatever God has caused to be written in the Scriptures will continue always to apply and can be counted on as an authority for our lives.

That phrase is very encouraging and a source of security. When all else passes away, we can know that God's Word abides forever.[1]

Precisely what "has been written" in this instance is the fact that vengeance belongs to the Lord; he himself will do the recompensing.

That quotation's context in the Hebrew Scriptures is surprising. Moses' final speeches to the Israelites, recorded in Deuteronomy, warn them to be faithful to their covenant God, who had revealed himself to them in a special way at Mt. Sinai and who had carried them safely through many years of wandering in the wilderness. The songs encourage the children of Israel to hang on tightly to their relationship with Yahweh as they enter the Promised Land so that they won't be led astray by the false gods of the people they must

---

1. See my comments about the abiding of God's Word in chapter 6 of *To Walk and Not Faint* (Chappaqua, NY: Christian Herald Books, 1980).

conquer in order to establish themselves as a nation. Deuteronomy 32 contains Moses' final song and God's command to Moses to ascend Mt. Nebo, where he will die. In this concluding admonition Moses counsels the people to pay especially close attention to his words: "Take to heart all the words I have solemnly declared to you this day, so that you may command your children to obey carefully all the words of this law. They are not just idle words for you — they are your life. By them you will live long in the land you are crossing the Jordan to possess" (vv. 46-47, NIV).

The middle of the final song in chapter 32 declares how the children of Israel will be rejected by God because of their disobedience and failure to be faithful to him. The nation is collectively denounced for having "abandoned the God who made [them] and rejected the Rock [their] Savior" (v. 15b). Indeed, the people "made him jealous with their foreign gods and angered him with their detestable idols" (v. 16). Therefore, "The LORD saw this and rejected them because he was angered by his sons and daughters" (v. 19). Consequently, God declares,

"They made me jealous by what is no god
    and angered me with their worthless idols.
I will make them envious by those who are
        not a people;
    I will make them angry by a nation that has
        no understanding.
For a fire has been kindled by my wrath . . .

They are a nation without sense,
    there is no discernment in them.
If only they were wise and would understand this
    and discern what their end will be! . . .

"Have I not kept this in reserve
    and sealed it in my vaults?

275

It is mine to avenge; I will repay.
  In due time their foot will slip;
their day of disaster is near
  and their doom rushes upon them."

The LORD will judge his people
  and have compassion on his servants
when he sees their strength is gone
  and no one is left, slave or free.
He will say: "Now where are their gods,
  the rock they took refuge in . . .

"See now that I myself am He!
  There is no god besides me.
I put to death and I bring to life,
  I have wounded and I will heal,
  and no one can deliver from my hand.
I lift my hand to heaven and declare:
  As surely as I live forever,
when I sharpen my flashing sword
  and my hand grasps it in judgment,
I will take vengeance on my adversaries
  and repay those who hate me. . . ."

Rejoice, O nations, with his people,
  for he will avenge the blood of his servants;
he will take vengeance on his enemies
  and make atonement for his land and people.

(vv. 21-22a, 28-29,
34-37, 39-41, 43, NIV)[2]

---

2. I have added italics to indicate Paul's quotation. However, in this particular instance the form of Paul's quotation corresponds neither to the Hebrew manuscripts nor to the Septuagint version of the text, but to the Aramaic Targums on the Pentateuch. See F. F. Bruce, *The Canon of Scripture* (Downers Grove, IL: InterVarsity Press, 1988), p. 53.

This song helped the Israelites to understand later in their history that persistence in unfaithful and rebellious behavior had caused God to execute his wrath upon them by means of the Babylonian Captivity. However, he would take vengeance on their enemies; after all, he had particularly called Israel to be his people and had continuously provided for them. Why did they persist in idolatry and thus continue to deserve his anger? And did they not perceive that God would not let the enemy go too far in their punishment? Ultimately, his justice would prevail.

This cotext of Deuteronomy and its context in the history of the people of Israel make the quotation in Romans 12 a more deeply effective warning. Every time we take for ourselves the task of vengeance we run the danger of becoming rebellious like the Israelites and risking the execution of God's wrath upon us. After all, how can we be so presumptuous as to think that we have a monopoly on justice? Those who have been unjust to us make only as many mistakes as we. And, like Israel, we each specialize in our own idolatry.

Keeping in mind the purpose of the quotation because of its context, we can now grasp more accurately what the quotation specifically says. Actually, as can be observed above, the text that Paul quotes occurs at two places in the Hebrew song. Verse 35 literally begins, "To me vengeance and retribution," with "to me" placed emphatically forward to remind us that only the God of justice has the right and the authority to execute judgment. Verse 41b says literally, "When I sharpen lightning [which is] my sword and my hand lays hold on judgment, I will render vengeance to my adversaries and to my haters will I repay."

Paul emphasizes these phrases by adding extra pronouns. Thus, his quotation from Deuteronomy stresses, "To me vengeance; I myself will requite."

Because vengeance belongs to him and him alone,

Yahweh declares that rightly and surely he himself will do the recompensing. We can trust his wisdom to know how, when, why, and to what extent punishment should be inflicted.

That forces us to face our own presumptuousness. What makes us think that we can properly seek justice against someone else? Why do we fail to see that our own idolatries deserve God's avenging? God, who alone holds the total plan of everything, knows in what way a person can most effectively be chastised. Furthermore, we know that truly he will ultimately deal justly.

Therefore, if in my particular situation I am bothered because the ones who have hurt me seem to feel no remorse or pain, I am both presumptuously ignoring my own sinfulness and faithlessly failing to acknowledge that God alone has the right to execute justice. God, who knows every bit of pain that anyone has ever experienced, is the proper one to judge whether or not my afflicters should be allowed to suffer some affliction to call them back to true spirituality.

In the final phrase of Romans 12:19, recognizing our persistent difficulty in giving up our vengeance, Paul once again seals the assurance that the matter will be dealt with properly. He adds another formula statement: "says the Lord." This phrase was always used by the prophets of Israel to confirm the source of their messages, and in the Hebrew Scriptures the phrase carries all the weight of God's reliability behind it.[3] God's words are never lightly given. What he says, he will accomplish. Therefore, we can confidently leave all matters of vengeance in his hands and trust that whatever is appropriate will happen.

The text has convinced me. My work on it ends with a fervent prayer that God's love will empower all of us in the Christian community to set aside with finality the desire

3. See my comments in chapter 1 of *To Walk and Not Faint*.

to be avenged — in our relationships with each other and with the world. Not to have to struggle any longer with what to do in a particular situation gives release. The matter can be closed because God will decide on the avenging.

Your partnership with me in facing this text has enabled me decisively to set aside my desire for retribution. The Hilarity of the Christian community sets me free to get back to pursuing peace.

Therefore:

1. Do we still have a desire for vengeance against anyone?
2. How have we experienced in our lives the fact that vengeance is never helpful to us, that it steals away our Hilarity?
3. How have we experienced the Hilarious release of giving place in wrath?
4. How does it encourage us to know that once written the Scriptures remain written — and therefore authoritative for our lives?
5. Do we really believe that everything the Lord says can be trusted?
6. What does it mean to us that vengeance belongs to God?
7. How do we react when God doesn't seem to be repaying, when justice doesn't seem to prevail? How can we learn to wait and give up our own feelings of revenge? How can the Hilarity of the community help us?

30. Heaping Coals of Fire

"But if your enemy is hungry, feed him, and if he is
thirsty, give him a drink; for in so doing you will heap
burning coals upon his head."

— ROMANS 12:20, NASV

I HEARD THIRD-HAND that one of the leading women of
the congregation I was serving was angry with me. Somehow we always hear the whispered rumor: so-and-so is
really upset with the way you did such-and-such. Why can't
those who have criticisms of us tell us directly?

Nevertheless, her disgruntlement was real, so what
could I do? I was having a hard enough time trying to
encourage the women of the congregation to get involved
in deeper Bible study. Her frustration with me didn't help
at all, especially when her reason, from my perspective,
wasn't worth the hassle.

The more I prayed about the situation, however, the
more I realized that this woman's bitterness came out of a
much deeper source than my particular action in one situation. I began to notice the many contributions she was
making to the congregation for which she received no grati-

tude. Consequently, I decided that I would do my best to be more affirming and grateful to her.

The results were delightful. Not only did her opinion about me change, but she became one of the staunchest supporters of my work and a true friend.

Every time I take Romans 12:20 seriously in a specific situation, following the biblical principle leads to growth in my relationships. Some enemies don't respond and become great friends, but obeying this principle helps me at least to feel that I have done my best to seek peace and pursue it.[1]

Again we need to overcome this book's chapter divisions and recognize the close connection between this verse and the preceding three. Showering our enemies with love and kindness is one way to put the right behavior before others rather than to recompense evil for evil (v. 17), one way to do all that we can to cultivate peace (v. 18), and one way to avoid seeking revenge (v. 19). Paul offers excellent directions for fulfilling the previous three exhortations by quoting from Proverbs 25.

The stronger of the Greek conjunctions for "but" begins the injunction, stressing "greatly to the contrary." Rather than resorting to vengeance and so that we might give place to God in wrath, this is a much better way to react.

Any quotation from Proverbs is difficult to assess since the book is such an odd collection of epigrammatic statements coming out of the Wisdom movement beginning with Solomon in Israel and bearing influences from other cultures. Since other Scriptural and apocryphal uses of "burning coals" (Gen. 19:24, Lev. 10:2, Ps. 11:6, Ezek. 21:31, and

1. A lovely collection of stories for children about overcoming evil with good is Elizabeth Hershberger Bauman's *Coals of Fire* (Scottdale, PA: Herald Press, 1954 and 1982). In some of these true stories about early Christians and modern Mennonites, Brethren, and Quakers, love wins over the enemy, but in others the Christians' nonresistant love leads to suffering and death.

2 Esd. 16:53) indicate judgment, which contradicts the primary thrust of Romans 12, some commentators have utilized the metaphor of "burning with shame" to explain Paul's use of the quotation.

I have always been suspicious, however, of interpretations that stress the shame of the enemies because actions of heaping coals with that purpose in mind could easily slip into vengeance. If we are extraordinarily good to them purposely to make them feel bad, then our action violates the principle of peacemaking. Instead, in keeping with the thrust of Romans 12, Paul must have used a quotation that would have shown to his first readers how to respond to evil positively with deep kindness. Though the metaphor he chose has been lost to modern readers, we know that it must entail a surprise which motivates a change of attitude and behavior on the part of the enemies.

Ray Stedman proposed long ago that the image refers to the way fires were lit in past times and to the fact that in Semitic cultures things were carried in baskets on the top of one's head. Thus the image in Proverbs 25 could suggest this great act of kindness: when enemies are in trouble because their fires have gone out, we treat them with special love by giving them a heaping basket of coals to carry home (on their heads) to start their fires again.[2]

Peter Cotterell and Max Turner offer a much better explanation of this difficult passage. They urge us to read Proverbs 25:21-22 with its cotext of verse 23 for a more fruitful approach to its meaning:

If your enemy is hungry, give him bread to eat;
  and if he is thirsty, give him water to drink;
for you will heap coals of fire on his head,
  and the LORD will reward you.

2. Ray C. Stedman, *From Guilt to Glory*, vol. 2: *Reveling in God's Salvation* (Portland, OR: Multnomah Press, 1978).

The north wind brings forth rain;
and a backbiting tongue, angry looks. (RSV)

Verse 23 first perplexed commentators because the north wind in Palestine doesn't bring rain; but in Egypt the north wind does bring rain, and this fact led William Klassen to look to that culture for the origin of the metaphor in the previous verses. As Cotterell and Turner summarize the research,

> Klassen points for an explanation to an Egyptian text first published by F. L. Griffith, *Stories of the High Priests of Memphis*, from which it appears that a penitent would go to the individual he had wronged, bearing on his head a clay dish containing burning coals. The meaning of the metaphor as it is used in Proverbs then becomes clear: if a man acts generously towards his enemy he may bring him to repentance. And if this is the sense of the metaphor as Paul understood it, then he is telling us that if a Christian has an enemy, and instead of threatening him forgives him, then he is likely to bring his enemy to the point of repentance; metaphorically the Christian is himself putting the clay bowl of burning coals on the man's head and starting him on his way to repentance.[3]

The usual interpretation that to heap kindness on the enemy forces him to be embarrassed, to have a sense of shame, has a retributive tinge to it and contradicts Hilarity. If instead the metaphor is understood as Klassen suggests, the Christian frees the enemy for repentance — an interpretation that makes more sense of the movement in Romans 12 between verses 17 and 21.

3. Peter Cotterell and Max Turner, *Linguistics and Biblical Interpretation* (Downers Grove, IL: InterVarsity Press, 1989), p. 304. This book gives an excellent overview of approaches to the text and a more detailed explanation of Klassen's argument on pp. 302-5.

Paul's quotation gives us two specific instances of need on the part of our enemies. If he is hungry, if she is thirsty, we can respond tangibly. When we put this figure into our modern experience, we realize that these instructions apply very practically on a global scale. What would happen in the world if we strengthened the economies of Third-World nations instead of threatening them militarily? The wise man's instructions to minister to our enemies in practical ways requires a good job of assessing their needs. For each enemy we can surely find certain needs about which we might do something.

The commands in the Hebrew text of Proverbs 25 are in a form that means "to cause another person" to eat or to drink. Our response to our enemies' hunger or thirst, therefore, is to satisfy it. Maybe we do that by giving them emergency food supplies. Perhaps we do that by releasing them from an enormous debt that drowns their economy in interest payments. Perhaps we help them to develop new methods of farming or new strains of bug-resistant crops. The point is that our actions are specific and intentional and directed.

Of course, this instruction takes us back to all our previous considerations of such things as genuine love and the diligence with which we are to seek peace. The Hebrew-Christian faith is eminently practical in its application.

When Paul puts these instructions from Proverbs into his Greek text, he uses present continuing imperatives to match the present continuing subjunctives in which the enemies' needs are described. The thrust of the phrase, then, is that as long as our enemies keep hungering or are in a state of thirsting, we are to continue supplying them with whatever they need.

Furthermore, from the cotext of the metaphor in Proverbs we can add one other insight. Proverbs 25:22 ends, "and Yahweh will reward you." The Hebrew verb in that clause

is related to the Hebrew noun *Shalom* (which we have discussed previously in Chapters 14 and 28). The basic verb
means "to be entire" or "to be safe and sound," but in
Proverbs 25:22 it is used in an intensive form that includes
in its meaning "to preserve or keep uninjured," "to complete
or finish," "to restore or make good," "to requite or recompense."

The whole metaphor in Proverbs, therefore, promises
that when we react to our enemies by caring for them,
Yahweh will make us more whole. That summarizes well
what we have learned in Romans 12:19-20. To be vindictive
does not lead to wholeness for ourselves or for our community. Rather, to give up our desires for revenge and to work
instead toward meeting the needs of our enemies is a means
by which Yahweh can bring us back to *Shalom*.

The incredible Hilarity of that was wonderfully apparent to me the day I first wrote this chapter. The preceding
night, after writing the rough draft of Chapter 29, "Giving
Place to God's Wrath," I struggled through a time of hard
crying and praying to give up my claims for justice in the
situation mentioned in the beginning of that chapter. Then
I composed a letter wishing the best to the ones who had
wronged me. The next morning I awoke with a delicious
sense of peace about it all. God had indeed brought greater
wholeness. How grateful I am now, several years later, that
the process of writing this book helped me work through
that situation and set me free from its agony. Whether or not
God avenges the wrong has become irrelevant. Having
found peace in the situation, I no longer need retribution.

That this twentieth verse urges such positive action in
response to our enemies is in keeping with the whole emphasis on love in Romans 12. How delightful that not only
our relationships within the community but also our relationships with our enemies can lead to a deepening of our
wholeness! And as the community is extended to include

even those who once opposed us, our gift of Hilarity to them will increase the Hilarity of all.

Therefore:

1. What opportunities have we had to heap coals of fire on the heads of our enemies — to get them started on their way to repentance?

2. In what situations could we have responded to enemies with love, but didn't? What were the results?

3. In what situations of our present experience could the freedom of our Hilarity enable us to choose to respond to enemies with love and care?

4. How has a lack of vindication led to wholeness for us?

5. How does an emphasis on loving action lead to wholeness?

6. What is the relation of verse 18 to verse 20 in Romans 12?

7. How can the Hilarity of the community give us the courage to keep on feeding and giving drink to our enemies if they keep on being enemies?

31. Hilarious Overcoming

> Do not be [constantly] being conquered by evil, but,
> greatly to the contrary, be conquering [by means of or]
> in the good the evil.
> — ROMANS 12:21

THE MALFUNCTIONS of my body push me into many spiritual lessons. Often simple exercise or household tasks give me ample time to study overcoming.

My body's metabolism can't handle sudden big pushes. Consequently, most times when I want to do anything strenuous I have to battle not only an energy problem, but also my attitudes. I get so exasperated and discouraged and long for heaven, where I'm finally going to have a perfect body that works right.

Today I had the choice either to let myself be overcome by the problems of my body or to overcome them by patient endurance and constant toil. The key is my attitude — whether I am willing to hang in there until the metabolism begins to function or whether I will give up and let myself be defeated.

Similarly, our attitudes are the key factor in fulfilling

this final verse in Romans 12. Either the evil that we must constantly face in a world governed by darkness will seem too large for us and we will give in to despair, or we will remember that Christ has already conquered the principalities and powers and that he shares his triumph with us. To choose the latter will give us the motivation and the power and the Hilarity to overcome evil with good. We especially need each other in the Christian community for reminders of Christ's victory and for encouragement to keep fighting faithfully against the powers of evil that we encounter in our daily lives and work.

The words for good and evil in this verse are the same that we encountered in verse 17 (see Chapter 27), but a few significant grammatical changes in this text make it more than just a summary. Carefully noting those differences will help us grasp the larger purposes of this verse.

First of all, the movement of the verb forms in Romans 12 is highly significant. Beginning with verse 6, Paul used participles. He did not write complete sentences but instead used simple and terse phrases to outline the characteristics of the people of God. Then in two key places he poignantly switched to powerful imperative verbs: in verse 14 he used a plural continuing verb that commanded us together as a community to keep on caring for our enemies, and in verse 19 he used a plural decisive verb that commanded us (together again) once and for all to give place to wrath. Then, in his second quotation from the Hebrew Scriptures (v. 20), his imperative and future verbs copied Proverbs 25:21-22 and switched to singular. Now, however, when Paul no longer quotes the Hebrew Scriptures, he does not return to the plural imperatives. Both of the verbs in this last verse are singular, emphasizing that each of us as individuals must do our own overcoming of evil, or else we as particular persons will be overcome.

This final emphasis on the singular is not meant to take us out of the community and set us off by ourselves. We especially notice that it prepares us for the message of chapter 13 (which is falsely set off by our biblical chapter divisions). Rather, in the framework and with the support of the whole Body of Christ, we are encouraged for the battles that we have to fight alone; but ultimately each of us must deal with our own particular attitudes.

Many friends who understand my body's malfunctions stand by me with support and patient encouragement. Nevertheless, the handicaps are mine to deal with. I'm the one who has to grit my teeth and hang in there when I want desperately to quit. The Hilarity of the community, however, equips us with courage and persistence. I wouldn't have been able to finish a two-mile run several years ago except that all the participants in the retreat I was leading — who had urged me to join the run in the first place — kept cheering me on.

Paul's injunction is straight talk: literally, "do not be being conquered by the evil." The present continuing imperative verb reminds us that we must always be on our guard lest we be overcome. Also, significantly, the noun for evil is preceded by an article that means, specifically, *the* evil. Evil doesn't just hit us generally. It comes to each of us in particular temptations, specific trials, individual difficulties and persons and things. We are not to be conquered by any of those unique forms of the evil.

Immediately, Paul gives the other side. I enjoy this about the apostle: he always follows his negative statements with what to do positively. Here again he introduces the other side with the stronger Greek word for "but" to conclude, "greatly to the contrary, be conquering in the good the evil."

The final word in the sentence, *evil*, leads us immediately into the particular manifestation of the principalities in the governing authorities. Romans 13:1-7 has, throughout the history of the Church, been interpreted to mean that

Christians should at all times submit to their rulers, and verse 1 specifically has been thought to signify that governments are necessarily good because they are ordained of God.

Such an interpretation does not take into consideration the more complete message of the Scriptures that earthly governments are part of the principalities and powers — created by God (Col. 1:16), but fallen (Rom. 8:19-22); overcome by Christ at the cross (Col. 2:15), but still to be battled (Eph. 6:10-20). Romans 13:1-7 deals with a specific situation encountered by the Roman Christians — most likely a severe and unfair taxation[1] — for which Paul gives corrective advice. The text must be interpreted not as normative, but as corrective — dealing not with a universal principle that must always be applied, but with a specific solution to a particular problem in Christian history.[2]

After his specific injunctions about the situation at Rome, Paul continues to urge the Christians there to care about one another, whether weak or strong. All the rest of the book nurtures specific behavior for the upbuilding of the entire community, so this small section with singular verbs (12:20–13:5) must be understood within its place in the whole.

All of Romans 12 has been about conquering. Offering our bodies as holy and living sacrifices acceptable to God, withstanding the tendency of our culture to conform, being

1. Johannes Friedrich, Wolfgang Pöhlmann, and Peter Stuhlmacher, "Zur historischen Situation und Intention von Röm 13,1-7," *Zeitschrift für Theologie und Kirche* 73, 2 (June 1976): 131-66.

2. The whole subject of Romans 13 is much too large a topic to consider adequately here — it needs a separate book. However, it is important for us not to take Romans 12 in isolation. Rather, we recognize the connections of this whole section on the Christian community (Rom. 12) with a particular application to a situation facing the Roman Christians (Rom. 13:1-7). Romans 13:8 returns again to discussing the general nature of Christian love.

transformed by the renewing of our minds, recognizing our place in the community, stewarding our particular grace-gifts for the upbuilding of the community, learning to love with genuine love, abhorring the evil and clinging to that which is good, being tenderly affectionate and honorable, not flagging in diligence, retaining a boiling fervency of the spirit, slaving constantly in the Lord, hoping with Hilarity, remaining under tribulations, persevering in prayer, ministering to the needs of the saints, practicing hospitality toward those not part of the community, being kind to the ones persecuting us, sharing together in the emotions of other members of the community, not being haughty but being humble, not taking revenge, pursuing peace as much as possible, heaping coals of fire and love on our enemies' heads — by all these aspects of our Hilarity we are continually overcoming the evil.

The fact of life is that evil exists. But we don't have to be overcome by it; instead, we have the power to overcome. The verb *nikaō*, which we translate "to overcome" or "to conquer," is used twenty-eight times in the New Testament, and seventeen of these instances are in the Book of Revelation. In the assurance of the final overcoming of evil at the end of time we discover true hope (remember Chapter 21). We know that at the cross Christ defeated all the powers of evil and death arrayed against him, and someday all the forces of evil will be ultimately overcome. Moreover, the eschatology of the Christian community (our understanding of the last times) emphasizes that this victory of God's new age is also available to us in this life. We cannot perfectly master the forces of evil at all times (in fact, to think that we can do so is destructive), but the assurance of that ultimate victory gives us the courage to keep battling. In the face of (humanly) insurmountable odds, the Christian community can display an unusual gladness in the struggle. Our Hilarity provides a realistic alternative to both the world's despair and its blind optimism.

We can hang in for the long haul because we know the ultimate outcome of our faith. Just as I keep trying gradually to get past my body's weakness and dizziness because I know that eventually my metabolism will kick in, so we who uphold the good can be sure that ultimately justice will triumph. However, if I don't keep exercising, my body will lose its strength and endurance and will not be able to overcome its problems. Similarly, it is essential that God's people continue to struggle against the evils of this world and to offer the alternative of its Hilarity to the despair and hopelessness of our times.

In the Christian community we need to encourage each other with reminders that we can actually overcome evil with good. For example, World Vision International began working in Cambodia in 1970 and built a children's hospital there in 1975, only to have to flee from the Pol Pot regime just as the hospital building was completed. During that regime's terrible tyranny the building was used as a place of torture. However, several years later World Vision was allowed to return and to re-establish the hospital, which began immediately to serve hundreds of children each day on an outpatient basis.

The good of this Christian organization offers a magnificent illustration of our text. World Vision overcame the evils of the terrorists' reign by treating the children who were injured and maimed and suffering from malnutrition. God's love was superbly demonstrated in their Hilarious seizing of the opportunity.

Martin Luther's explication of Romans 12:21 offers several profound and currently relevant insights into the power of such overcoming as follows:

> This means: see to it that he who hurts you does not cause you to become like him, namely, a wicked person, nor let his wickedness defeat your goodness. For a man

who changes another man by causing him to become like him, while he himself remains unchanged, is a victor over that man. No, by doing good to him, you must make him into a good person who resembles you. Thus your goodness will overcome his wickedness and change him into you.

Now, to be sure, men commonly regard as the victor the one who has the last word and can deal the last blow, whereas, as a matter of fact, he who is the last to inflict pain is the one who is worse off, for the evil remains with him while the other is done with it.

. . . For if you answer folly with folly, you will never cause the fool to see himself as he is, but your reply in kind will only make him still more of a fool.

. . . For as long as folly sees something like itself, it does not become dissatisfied with itself, but it becomes dissatisfied with itself only if it sees something that has no resemblance to it at all.[3]

Many persons in our culture are seeking alternatives to the values that don't satisfy, to the violence that continues to escalate, to the meaninglessness that overcomes. The Christian community offers alternatives of hope and Hilarity — which do not resemble at all our society's superficial hype and happiness.

The verbs of Romans 12:21 are singular. In the specific circumstances of your life and mine we must proceed, but in the community as a whole we will find resources for the struggles, support and advice for the decisions, wisdom for

3. Luther, *Lectures on Romans,* trans. and ed. Wilhelm Pauck (Philadelphia: Westminster Press, 1961), pp. 356-57. Obviously, Luther's writing and this translation took place before people became conscious of the need for inclusive language. Necessary changes would have been too cumbersome, so I apologize for the inconsistency of this text with my own efforts to include the whole Christian community in every description.

the methods. We each go away from this section of Romans into the situations of our jobs, our families, our neighborhoods, the world of the twentieth century — but we go enfolded in the Hilarity of the community that enables us to continue constantly in the process of overcoming the evil.

The chapter ends with the phrase "the evil." That is the challenge before us. Our basis for fighting it is the *therefore* with which we began this book. With our eyes wide open to the mercies of God, we can live as a community of God's people amid the challenges of the evil of the world that surrounds us. By the Hilarity of his love we shall continue to overcome.

Previously in Romans 8:37 Paul combined the verb *to conquer* with the Greek preposition which means "more than" to emphasize that in all things — whatever evil we might encounter — we who are God's people can be "completely and overwhelmingly victorious" through the one who loved us. That magnificent verse — the only place this compound verb appears in the New Testament — provides the backdrop for the challenge here in Romans 12:21 to continue overcoming. Indeed, this is part of the foundation on which we have been building all the exhortations of Romans 12. How good to know before we start that we shall ultimately be victorious. The reason is described in these next two verses from Romans 8:

> For I am convinced that neither death, nor life, nor angels, nor principalities, nor things present, nor things to come, nor powers, nor height, nor depth, nor any other created thing, shall be able to separate us from the love of God, which is in Christ Jesus our Lord. (Rom. 8:38-39)

Knowing the assurance of God's love, from which we will never be separated, we can drink deeply of the Hilarity of God's promises about overcoming. (See, for example, Rev.

2:7, 11, 17, and 26; 3:5, 12, and 21; and 21:6-7.) This is part of the *therefore* on which all that we are and do as a community is based.

I finished writing the first draft of this book on the day before Easter almost ten years ago, but I still remember my delight in the timing of that day. On Easter we celebrate God's seal on the fact that the overcoming is accomplished. I pray that whenever you read this, you, too, will experience the assurance of the empty tomb. In the Hilarity of God's promise and by the strengthening of the community's support, together we will be overcomers.

Therefore:

1. How have we seen evil overcome by good?
2. What dimensions of our lives need a healthy dose of good to overcome things that are evil?
3. How does the framework of the Hilarious community enable us as individuals to meet the challenges of evil that we encounter personally?
4. How does the Hilarity of the community help us maintain the stamina necessary to be continually overcoming evil with good?
5. How has our community life changed since we began reading this book?
6. What goals do we have for deeper study of the Scriptures together?
7. What changes do we want to be working on in our congregation in order that we can together be the community of Christ more effectively, more lovingly, and more Hilariously?

Bibliography

Resources on Romans

Bruce, F. F. *The Canon of Scripture*. Downers Grove, IL: InterVarsity Press, 1988.

———. *The Letter of Paul to the Romans*. Rev. ed. Tyndale New Testament Commentaries. Leon Morris, gen. ed. Grand Rapids: William B. Eerdmans, 1989.

———. *Paul: Apostle of the Heart Set Free*. Grand Rapids: William B. Eerdmans, 1977.

Childs, Brevard S. "Romans." Chap. 12 in *The New Testament as Canon: An Introduction*. Philadelphia: Fortress Press, 1984.

Donfried, Karl P., ed. *The Romans Debate*. Minneapolis: Augsburg, 1977.

Friedrich, Johannes, Wolfgang Pöhlmann, and Peter Stuhlmacher. "Zur historischen Situation und Intention von Röm 13,1-7." *Zeitschrift für Theologie und Kirche* 73, 2 (June 1976): 131-66.

Holmberg, Bengt. *Paul and Power: The Structure of Authority in the Primitive Church as Reflected in the Pauline Epistles*. Philadelphia: Fortress Press, 1978.

Käsemann, Ernst. *Commentary on Romans*. Trans. and ed. Geoffrey W. Bromiley. Grand Rapids: William B. Eerdmans, 1980.

Lenski, R. C. H. *The Interpretation of St. Paul's Epistle to the Romans.* Minneapolis: Augsburg, 1936.

Luther, Martin. *Commentary on Romans.* Trans. J. Theodore Mueller. Grand Rapids: Kregel Publications, 1975.

————. *Lectures on Romans.* Trans. and ed. Wilhelm Pauck. Philadelphia: Westminster Press, 1961.

Morris, Leon. *The Epistle to the Romans.* Grand Rapids: William B. Eerdmans, 1988.

Murray, John. *The Epistle to the Romans.* The New International Commentary on the New Testament. F. F. Bruce, gen. ed. Grand Rapids: William B. Eerdmans, 1965.

Ridenour, Fritz, ed. *How to Be a Christian without Being Religious.* Glendale, CA: G/L Regal Books, 1967.

Sanders, E. P. *Paul and Palestinian Judaism.* Philadelphia: Fortress Press, 1977.

Scroggs, Robin. *Paul for a New Day.* Philadelphia: Fortress Press, 1977.

Stedman, Ray C. *From Guilt to Glory.* Vol. 2: *Reveling in God's Salvation.* Portland, OR: Multnomah Press, 1978.

Stendahl, Krister. *Paul Among Jews and Gentiles.* Philadelphia: Fortress Press, 1976.

Resources on Prayer

Baillie, John. *A Diary of Private Prayer.* New York: Charles Scribner's Sons, 1949.

Bewes, Richard. *Talking About Prayer.* Downers Grove, IL: InterVarsity Press, 1979.

Brother Lawrence. *The Practice of the Presence of God.* London: Samuel Bagster and Sons, n.d.

Eastman, Dick. *The Hour that Changes the World.* Grand Rapids: Baker Book House, 1978.

Foster, Richard J. *Celebration of Discipline: The Path to Spiritual Growth.* San Francisco: Harper & Row, 1978.

Houston, James. *The Transforming Friendship*. Oxford: Lion Publishing, 1989.

Huggett, Joyce. *The Joy of Listening to God*. Downers Grove, IL: InterVarsity Press, 1986.

Hunter, W. Bingham. *The God Who Hears*. Downers Grove, IL: InterVarsity Press, 1986.

Hybels, Bill. *Too Busy Not to Pray: Slowing Down to Be with God*. Downers Grove, IL: InterVarsity Press, 1988.

Keller, W. Phillip. *A Layman Looks at the Lord's Prayer*. Chicago: Moody Press, 1967.

Murray, Andrew. *The Believer's School of Prayer*. Minneapolis: Bethany House Publishers, 1982. (Previous title, *With Christ in the School of Prayer*.)

Ogilvie, Lloyd John. *You Can Pray with Power*. Ventura, CA: G/L Regal Books, 1983 and 1988.

Peterson, Eugene H. *Answering God: The Psalms as Tools for Prayer*. San Francisco: HarperCollins, 1989.

Pratt, Richard L., Jr. *Pray with Your Eyes Open*. Phillipsburg, NJ: Presbyterian and Reformed Publishing Company, 1987.

Rinker, Rosalind. *Communicating Love Through Prayer*. Grand Rapids: Zondervan, 1966.

Stedman, Ray C. *Jesus Teaches on Prayer*. Waco, TX: Word Books, 1975.

Resources on Peacemaking and Justice Building

Aldridge, Robert C. *The Counterforce Syndrome: A Guide to U.S. Nuclear Weapons and Strategic Doctrine*. Washington, DC: Transnational Institute, 1978.

Aukerman, Dale. *Darkening Valley: A Biblical Perspective on Nuclear War*. New York: Seabury Press, 1981.

Bainton, Roland H. *Christian Attitudes toward War and Peace: A Historical Survey and Critical Re-evaluation*. New York: Abingdon Press, 1960.

Bauman, Elizabeth Hershberger. *Coals of Fire.* Scottdale, PA: Herald Press, 1954 and 1982.

Colson, Charles. *Kingdoms in Conflict.* Grand Rapids: Zondervan, 1987.

Friesen, Duane K. *Christian Peacemaking and International Conflict.* Scottdale, PA: Herald Press, 1986.

Gibson, William E., and the Eco-Justice Task Force. *A Covenant Group for Lifestyle Assessment.* New York: United Presbyterian Program Agency, 1981.

Hauerwas, Stanley. *The Peaceable Kingdom: A Primer in Christian Ethics.* Notre Dame: University of Notre Dame Press, 1983.

Kownacki, Mary Lou, OSB. *Peace Is Our Calling: Contemporary Monasticism and the Peace Movement.* Erie, PA: Benet Press, 1981.

Kreider, Alan. *Journey Towards Holiness.* Scottdale, PA: Herald Press, 1987.

Liedke, Gerhard. "Das Christliche Verständnis von Frieden." In *Christen im Streit um den Frieden: Beiträge zu einer neuen Friedensethik,* ed. Wolfgang Brinkel, Burkhardt Scheffler, and Martin Wächter, 29-35. Freiburg: Dreisam-Verlag, 1982.

Lutz, Charles P., and Jerry L. Folk, et al. *Peace-Ways.* Minneapolis: Augsburg, 1983.

Merton, Thomas, ed. *Breakthrough to Peace: Twelve Views on the Threat of Thermonuclear Extermination.* New York: New Directions, 1962.

Shenk, Calvin E. *When Kingdoms Clash: The Christian and Ideologies.* Scottdale, PA: Herald Press, 1988.

Sider, Ronald J. *Rich Christians in an Age of Hunger.* Downers Grove, IL: InterVarsity Press, 1984.

————, ed. *Cry Justice: The Bible Speaks on Hunger and Poverty.* Downers Grove, IL: InterVarsity Press, 1980.

Sider, Ronald J., and Richard K. Taylor. *Nuclear Holocaust and Christian Hope: A Book for Christian Peacemakers.* Downers Grove, IL: InterVarsity Press, 1982.

Wallis, Jim. *Call to Conversion.* New York: Harper & Row, 1981.
Yoder, John Howard. *When War Is Unjust: Being Honest in Just-War Thinking.* Minneapolis: Augsburg, 1984.

Resources on Community

Barker, Steve, et al. *Good Things Come in Small Groups.* Downers Grove, IL: InterVarsity Press, 1985.

Ellison, Craig W. *Loneliness: The Search for Intimacy.* Chappaqua, NY: Christian Herald Books, 1980.

Evans, Louis H., Jr. *Creative Love.* Old Tappan, NJ: Fleming H. Revell, 1977.

Hauerwas, Stanley. *A Community of Character: Toward a Constructive Christian Social Ethic.* Notre Dame: University of Notre Dame Press, 1981.

Hinkle, James, and Tim Woodroof. *Among Friends: You Can Help Make Your Church a Warmer Place.* Colorado Springs: NavPress, 1989.

Mains, Karen Burton. *Open Heart — Open Home.* Elgin, IL: David C. Cook, 1976.

Nouwen, Henri J. M. *Reaching Out: The Three Movements of the Spiritual Life.* Garden City, NY: Doubleday, 1975.

O'Connor, Elizabeth. *The New Community.* New York: Harper & Row, 1976.

Snyder, Howard A. *The Community of the King.* Downers Grove, IL: InterVarsity Press, 1977.

————. *Liberating the Church: The Ecology of Church and Kingdom.* Downers Grove, IL: InterVarsity Press, 1983.

————. *The Problem of Wine Skins.* Downers Grove, IL: InterVarsity Press, 1975.

Vanier, Jean. *Community and Growth: Our Pilgrimage Together.* New York: Paulist Press, 1979.

Watson, David. *Called and Committed: World-Changing Discipleship.* Wheaton, IL: Harold Shaw, 1982.

Welter, Paul. *How to Help a Friend.* Wheaton, IL: Tyndale House, 1978.

Other Resources Cited

Barna, George. *The Frog in the Kettle: What Christians Need to Know about Life in the Year 2000.* Ventura, CA: Gospel Light, 1990.

Cotterell, Peter, and Max Turner. *Linguistics and Biblical Interpretation.* Downers Grove, IL: InterVarsity Press, 1989.

Dawn, Marva J. *I'm Lonely, LORD — How Long? The Psalms for Today.* San Francisco: Harper & Row, 1983.

————. *Keeping the Sabbath Wholly: Ceasing, Resting, Embracing, Feasting.* Grand Rapids: William B. Eerdmans, 1989.

————. "An Introduction to the Work of Jacques Ellul." *Word and World* 9, 4 (Fall 1989): 386-93.

————. *To Walk and Not Faint: God's Comfort from Isaiah 40.* Chappaqua, NY: Christian Herald Books, 1980.

————. *To Walk in the Kingdom: God's Call to Discipleship from Luke 12.* Chappaqua, NY: Christian Herald Books, 1981.

Ellul, Jacques. *The Ethics of Freedom.* Trans. Geoffrey W. Bromiley. Grand Rapids: William B. Eerdmans, 1976.

————. *The Humiliation of the Word.* Trans. Joyce Main Hanks. Grand Rapids: William B. Eerdmans, 1985.

————. *Jesus and Marx: From Gospel to Ideology.* Trans. Joyce Main Hanks. Grand Rapids: William B. Eerdmans, 1988.

————. *The Meaning of the City.* Trans. Dennis Pardee. Grand Rapids: William B. Eerdmans, 1970.

————. *Money and Power.* Trans. LaVonne Neff. Downers Grove, IL: InterVarsity Press, 1984.

————. *The New Demons.* Trans. C. Edward Hopkin. New York: Seabury Press, 1975.

————. *Propaganda: The Formation of Men's Attitudes.* Trans. Konrad Kellen and Jean Lerner. New York: Alfred A. Knopf, 1965.

————. *Reason for Being: A Meditation on Ecclesiastes.* Trans. Joyce Main Hanks. Grand Rapids: William B. Eerdmans, 1990.

————. *The Subversion of Christianity.* Trans. Geoffrey W. Bromiley. Grand Rapids: William B. Eerdmans, 1986.

————. *The Technological Bluff.* Trans. Geoffrey W. Bromiley. Grand Rapids: William B. Eerdmans, 1990.

————. *The Technological Society.* Trans. John Wilkinson. New York: Vintage Books, 1964.

————. *The Technological System.* Trans. Joachim Neugroschel. New York: Continuum, 1980.

————. *Violence: Reflections from a Christian Perspective.* Trans. Cecelia Gaul Kings. New York: Seabury Press, 1969.

Fischer, John, and Liz Fuller O'Neil. *A Single Person's Identity.* Palo Alto, CA: Discovery Papers, 1973.

Fowler, Robert Booth. *Unconventional Partners: Religion and Liberal Culture in the United States.* Grand Rapids: William B. Eerdmans, 1989.

Friesen, Garry, with J. Robin Maxson. *Decision Making and the Will of God: A Biblical Alternative to the Traditional View.* Portland, OR: Multnomah Press, 1980.

Greenberg, David. *The Construction of Homosexuality.* Chicago: University of Chicago Press, 1989.

"How to Beat Drugs." *U.S. News and World Report* 107, 10 (Sept. 1989): 69-86.

L'Engle, Madeleine. *A Stone for a Pillow.* Wheaton, IL: Harold Shaw, 1986.

Louw, Johannes P., and Eugene A. Nida, eds. *Greek-English Lexicon of the New Testament Based on Semantic Domains.* Vol. 1: *Introduction and Domains.* Vol. 2: *Indices.* New York: United Bible Societies, 1988.

Miller, Arthur F., and Ralph T. Mattson. *The Truth About You: Discovering What You Should Be Doing With Your Life.* Old Tappan, NJ: Fleming H. Revell, 1977.

Pippert, Rebecca Manley. *Out of the Saltshaker and Into the World:*

Evangelism as a Way of Life. Downers Grove, IL: InterVarsity Press, 1979.

Richards, Lawrence O. *69 Ways to Start a Study Group and Keep It Growing*. Grand Rapids: Zondervan, 1973.

Schaeffer, Francis. *The Mark of the Christian*. Downers Grove, IL: InterVarsity Press, 1970.

Smith, M. Blaine. *Knowing God's Will: Biblical Principles of Guidance*. Downers Grove, IL: InterVarsity Press, 1979.

Yancey, Philip. *Guidance*. Portland, OR: Multnomah Press, 1983.